THE MIND-BODY STAGE

THE MIND-BODY STAGE

Passion and Interaction in the Cartesian Theater

R. Darren Gobert

STANFORD UNIVERSITY PRESS

STANFORD, CALIFORNIA

Stanford University Press
Stanford, California

© 2013 by the Board of Trustees of the Leland Stanford Junior University.
All rights reserved.

The author and publisher would like to thank the Faculty of Liberal Arts &
Professional Studies, York University (Toronto) for the financial support it
provided to this work.

Printed in the United States of America on acid-free, archival-quality paper

Library of Congress Cataloging-in-Publication Data

Gobert, R. Darren, author.
    The mind-body stage : passion and interaction in the Cartesian theatre /
R. Darren Gobert.
    pages cm
    Includes bibliographical references and index.
    ISBN 978-0-8047-8638-6 (cloth : alk. paper)
    1. Theater and philosophy—Europe—History—17th century. 2. Theater and
philosophy—Europe—History—18th century. 3. Descartes, René, 1596–1650—
Influence. I. Title.
PN2039.G585 2013
792.01—dc23

                                                                    2013010526

ISBN 978-0-8047-8826-7 (electronic)

For Martin Meisel

Contents

List of Illustrations   *ix*

Acknowledgments   *xi*

A Note About Translations   *xv*

Prologue: Another Cartesian Theater   1

1 Mind-Body Union; or, The Cartesian Ballet   17

2 Cartesian Plots, Dramatic Theory, and Emotional Wonder   48

3 Cartesian Acting; or, Interiors   84

4 Cartesian Design; or, Anatomies of the Theater   121

Epilogue: *Cætera desunt*   163

Notes   171

Index   239

Illustrations

1.1 The process of visual perception, from René Descartes,
La dioptrique   23

1.2 The eye in perception, from René Descartes, *La dioptrique*   25

1.3 Floor plan of the Tuileries *salle des machines,* circa 1662   25

1.4 Nonperspectival staging, from Balthasar de Beaujoyeulx,
Balet comique de la Royne   37

1.5 Frontispiece to Jean Desmarets de Saint-Sorlin, *Mirame*   38

1.6 Floor plan for Antonio Brunati's *salle de ballet*
in Stockholm's royal palace, circa 1649   40

2.1 Charles Perrault's *La poésie*   49

2.2 Frontispiece to Pierre Corneille, *Nicomède*   65

2.3 Frontispiece to Pierre Corneille, *Cinna, ou La clémence
d'Auguste*   67

3.1 Charles Le Brun's drawing of passion "H" (*l'amour simple*)   90

3.2 Charles Le Brun's drawing of the subject in love   91

4.1 Pierre-Narcisse Guérin, *Phèdre and Hippolyte*   123

4.2 Floor plan for Paris's Hôtel de Bourgogne theater following
its 1647 renovations   127

4.3 Raymond Poisson, *Le zig-zag*   128

4.4 Jean-François Blondel's gravure of François d'Orbay's *salle
de la Comédie-Française*   139

4.5 Frontispiece to Edmé Boursault, *Les fables d'Ésope*   143

4.6 Reconstruction of the original Queen's Theatre
in the Haymarket, circa 1707   148

4.7 Claude Nicolas Ledoux's theater at Besançon   150

Acknowledgments

Descartes initiated a model of the subject that can declare itself the fully independent author of its thoughts and the words written in its name. But he set this idea in tension with another: that none of us is self-sufficient, each of us the unique product of interaction with others. I feel this tension acutely as I write the acknowledgments to this book. On one hand, it represents my own reading of Cartesianism and its relationship to dramatic literature and theater history—written in a process that was, as for most writers, solitary. On the other hand, neither the book nor its ideas would exist without those whose questions, disagreements, help, and (another key word in this project) dialogue made the writing possible. Acknowledgments can never adequately represent or sufficiently thank such people, all of whom I will always associate with this book.

My research was conducted in London, New York, Paris, and Stockholm, and I first must recognize friends in those cities who made my stays so congenial. I acknowledge, too, the guidance of librarians at the Bibliothèque nationale de France, the British Library, Columbia University Libraries, and New York Public Library, as well as the Thomas Fisher Rare Book Library in Toronto. Sources pertaining to court ballets in Sweden were dispersed, and I am grateful to experts at Kungliga Biblioteket, the Museum Tre Kronor, and Musik- och teaterbiblioteket in Stockholm, as well as Carolina Rediviva in Uppsala. Jeff Papineau of the Bruce Peel Special Collections Library at the University of Alberta helped me procure an elusive image with noteworthy speed and good humor. The journal *Early Music* granted permission to reprint a rendering of the Queen's Theatre in the Haymarket. Joanna Ebenstein took the cover photo of a seventeenth-century anatomical mannequin. And in addition to helping me generally in all matters .tiff, my dear friend Anna Szczepaniak generated floor plans of Paris's Hôtel de Bourgogne in 1647 and the theater at Stockholm's royal palace in 1649, based on research by me and my theater-historian predecessors. I thank her and them.

I am obliged to the research assistants who have supported this project: Romilly Belcourt, Meryl Borato, Thom Bryce, Jane Dunlop, Alex Ferrone, Christina Galego, Belinda Karsen, Bernice Neal, and Sherri Wise. Anonymous readers for Stanford University Press expertly directed the book's final shape; my editor, Emily-Jane Cohen, and her assistant, Emma Harper, made completing it a pleasure; and Joe Abbott and Amanda Paxton provided exemplary copyediting and indexing, respectively. Julia Creet and Art Redding were always supportive of this work when they chaired my home department. I owe a debt, too, to my former dean, Robert Drummond, for making York University a good place to build a career, and my research officer, Janet Friskney, for helping me find resources to nurture it. York's erstwhile Faculty of Arts released me from teaching to make possible a year in Paris. Its successor, the Faculty of Liberal Arts and Professional Studies, provided support in multiple ways, including funding a trip to Sweden when—as happened with Descartes—my search took me there. They have my gratitude.

Friends and colleagues read parts of the manuscript or answered queries as they arose: Luke Arnason, Ross Arthur, Ian Balfour, Sheila Ghose, Matt Klaassen, Marie-Christine Leps, Thomas Loebel, Judith Milhous, Martin Puchner, Deanne Williams, Sarah Wilson, and Hersh Zeifman. Sheila also offered assistance with Swedish while I was conducting research for the first chapter. Ross, polyglot, also scrutinized my translations and provided invaluable help with Latin. Martin also suggested my title, and he edited and published the article that engendered the larger project. (It appears in *Theatre Survey* 49, no. 1, and, for permission to adapt this work, I acknowledge that journal.) Other friends and colleagues sustained me with their support: Alan Ackerman, Marcia Blumberg, Matthew Buckley, Elin Diamond, Stanton B. Garner Jr., Lori Harrison-Kahan, Lora Hutchison, Laura Levin, Julie Stone Peters, Janelle Reinelt, and Marlis Schweitzer. Julie is also always on call during a crisis, and her mentorship means everything. Descartes dedicated his *Principles of Philosophy* to one of his primary interlocutors, Princess Elisabeth of Bohemia, without whom some of his key ideas would not have been generated and who testifies that the story of the solitary, independent thinker—a story told in the *Discourse on Method*—is a myth. I dedicate this book to another great teacher, Martin Meisel. His encouragement and tutelage have shaped me more than he knows.

Finally, my sister, Janice Gobert, and my partner, Ross Gascho, remind me daily of the passionate interactions that sustain us. I owe particular thanks to Ross, who is mostly uncomplaining when research takes me away for months at a time and always glad to see me when I get home.

A Note About Translations

I have engaged with all foreign primary sources in their original languages: French and, to a lesser extent, Latin and Swedish. All quotations appear in English in the body of the text, but the original is provided in the notes. Unless otherwise indicated, translations are my own. In some cases I benefited from consulting published translations (for example, Lisa Shapiro's elegant English edition of Descartes's correspondence with Princess Elisabeth of Bohemia) even if I ultimately preferred—as was necessary for my purposes—literal, technical, and historically bound connotations over fluid prose. This necessity was particularly pressing when translating dialogue by Corneille, Molière, and Racine, where published translations rightly sacrifice technical or historical meanings to aesthetic considerations; I hope that readers find compensations for my inadequate renderings of these writers' celebrated work. In other cases I have cited published translations (for example, Stephen H. Voss's rendition of Descartes's *Les passions de l'âme*) but clearly indicated any modifications I have made. Apart from works by Plato and Aristotle, all secondary critical sources have likewise been scrutinized in their original languages. In these cases I quote from English translations but draw attention in the endnotes to any linguistic play—for example, Martin Heidegger's imposition of a hyphen into the word *Vorstellen*—that may be germane or just of interest to the curious.

Prologue: Another Cartesian Theater

René Descartes's articulation of subjectivity forever changed the way dramatic characters would be written and read, performed by actors and received by audiences. His coordinate system for geometry radically reshaped how theatrical space would be conceived and built. His theory of the passions revolutionized our understanding of the emotional exchange between spectacle and spectators—an emotional exchange whose elusive workings have anchored dramatic theory since Aristotle's *Poetics* and antitheatrical discourse since Plato's *Republic*. Yet theater scholars have not seen Descartes's transformational impact on theater history. Neither have philosophers looked to this history in order to watch Descartes's theories in action or to understand his reception and cultural impact, despite plenty of rich evidence on display.[1] After Descartes, playwrights self-consciously put Cartesian characters on the stage and thematized their rational workings. Actors adapted their performance styles to account for new models of subjectivity and physiology. Critics theorized the theater's emotional and ethical benefits to spectators in Cartesian terms. Architects sought to intensify these benefits by altering their designs.

Such critical oversights are not difficult to understand in light of the relationship between philosophy and theater, whose uneasiness goes back, of course, to Plato. On one hand, philosophy has looked to the theater for some of its most potent images, as Plato himself did when he imagined humankind in a theater-like chamber, sitting in the dark and apprehending the shadows before them that were understood, for a time at least, to be real. On the other hand, the use to which philosophy sometimes puts these images may make the theater scholar bristle. When his cave-spectators are "cured of their delusions," Plato holds up philosophy as truer than the fallible theatrical display he likens to puppetry.[2] Theater, we see, is coercive (his spectators are chained); the dramatic poet, we know, is banned from the *Republic*. Elsewhere when it appears in philosophy, the essentially physical work of theater remains sublimated to metaphor. For example, in the first book of his *A Treatise of Human Nature*, David Hume wrote that the "mind is a kind of theatre, where several perceptions successively make their appearance; pass, re-pass, glide away, and mingle in an infinite variety of postures and situations."[3] Hume was hardly the first to describe the immaterial characters and plots whose dramaturgical effects we call consciousness; mental activity has been likened to theatrical spectacle since antiquity, and by philosophers and theorists of quite different persuasions. Descartes himself may have given the metaphor particular traction when he envisioned a performance space in the pineal gland, where, as on opening night, "it all comes together." I borrow the phrase from philosopher Daniel C. Dennett, whose immodestly titled *Consciousness Explained* derides this pervasive understanding as "The Cartesian Theater"—an ersatz image with appeal to "crowds . . . transfixed by an illusion," not unlike Plato's enslaved spectators.[4] Dennett speaks of audiences; Hume, of postures being struck; Plato, of sight lines.[5] But the strenuous labor and pleasing tactility of the theatrical endeavor remain unrecognized.

There is another Cartesian theater. In it Descartes revolutionized stage practices, and playwrights, actors, designers, and even audiences made manifest his ideas. But the disciplinary barriers of the modern academy replicate the quarrel that Plato describes and shield this other Cartesian theater from view. Philosophers exaggerate Descartes's monologic mode: that of a man for whom the theater could never be anything but metaphoric, spending as he does "the whole day shut up alone in a room heated by a stove" with "complete leisure to talk to [himself] about [his] thoughts."[6] Emphasizing Descartes's metaphysics, these philosophers ignore the rich matter that theater history—an embodied history of ideas—offers to our understanding of a thinker who authored a rich scientific corpus on space, motion, physiology, and other matters vital to stage practice. Meanwhile, theater historians tack in the opposite direction. They might be particularly attuned to the dialogic mode that we see in some of Descartes's other writings, his insistence on the metaphysical benefits of a passionate interaction between actors onstage and off. But if philosophers have retreated to their thoughts as Descartes does at the beginning of *Discourse on Method*, theater historians have steered clear of philosophical questions and focused on the material research concerns— props and playhouses, production costs and box-office receipts, actors' and audiences' respective kinesiologies—that have helped to define the disciplinary contours of theater studies and to delimit its sometimes vulnerable position in the humanities. Those in the theater may fret that their work is easy metaphoric grist for colleagues in the loftier recesses of the academy, in other words. But their focus on material evidence obscures this other Cartesian theater and the explanatory potential of its philosophical insights.

A savvy reader will recognize the figures I have conjured: philosophy favoring the mental; theater clinging to its material; the two in perennial discord, like Punch and Judy in the fairground booth of the academy. In this tableau the boundary between disciplines is made to impersonate the old slash in mind/body, whose much-discussed problem, we have been told, Descartes caused in the first place. But if my caricature ignores the nuances of much work in philosophy and theater studies, it does its dramaturgical work: for the problem of dualism does undergird the relationship between theater and philosophy as academic disciplines, and it does complicate each discipline's view of another Cartesian theater. The solution, Descartes knew, is interaction: the replacement of a bifurcating slash with a hyphen or *trait d'union*, in its telling French name. Presented with a philosopher's immaterial metaphor, a theater scholar could respond with a few bars from Stephen Sondheim:

A vision's just a vision
If it's only in your head.
If no one gets to see it,
It's as good as dead.
. . . .

Bit by bit,
Putting it together.
Piece by piece—
Only way to make a work of art.
Every moment makes a contribution,
Every little detail plays a part.
Having just the vision's no solution,
Everything depends on execution.[7]

Listen to Sondheim. He betrays a dualism in his central terms as Descartes did, but like Descartes he reconciles them. In the next line of this song, from 1984's *Sunday in the Park with George*, the play's main character offers the song's signal advice: "Putting it together, / That's what counts."[8] The song finds its dramatic power in its clear metatheatricality, as Sondheim foregounded when he rewrote the song for the 1992 revue *Putting It Together*, in which George's painting process was transformed into the process of putting on a show: "Working for a tiny compensation, / Hoping for a thunderous ovation," etc.[9] Every contributing little detail supplied by actors, directors, designers, and any number of theater personnel has an immaterial dimension—a vision in the head—but finds gloriously material expression in its execution, which the audience gets to watch while the actor playing George sings and moves, breathes and sweats. Sondheim teaches us that the conceptual, the immaterial, the mental are *experienced* in material form not only by the theater artists who put it together but also by the conscious spectator who apprehends by getting goose bumps or (a lot depends on George) yawning. Sondheim thus provides a pithy précis of Descartes's doctrine of mind-body union, and he thus suggests a new perspective on the relationship between philosophy and the theater history that serves to embody it. It is this doctrine, and this relationship, I explore in *The Mind-Body Stage*.

The philosopher is purported to have authored the mind vs. body, thinking vs. extension split that has so bedeviled the philosophy of mind and to have suggested the ontological distinction between costumes and consciousness that sometimes makes the practitioner suspect the theorist, or theater suspect philosophy. But while there is no denying the dualistic physics that inform Descartes's understanding of human beings, careful readings of his work suggest a different emphasis. Twenty years ago, a foundation for such readings was laid by Daniel Garber, whose book *Descartes' Metaphysical Physics* argued for the inextricability of Descartes's scientific interests—his preoccupations with bodies, with motion, with geometry—and his philosophical concerns with everything metaphysical. The picture that Garber presents in this work, succinctly captured in the title of his later collection *Descartes Embodied*, inaugurated a wholesale reenvisioning of Cartesian physiology and psychology and of Cartesian aesthetics and ethics. Subsequently, a body of scholarly work—by Lilli Alanen, Paul Hoffman, Amy Morgan Schmitter, and Lisa Shapiro, to name a few—has illuminated Descartes's doctrine of mind-body union. The effect has been to turn critical attention away from Cartesian dualism and toward what Deborah J. Brown, another revisionist reader of Descartes, has audaciously described as "phenomenological monism," "an *experience* of being one unified and embodied substance."[10]

As Brown diagnoses, a failure to see mind and body as united works in tandem with a reductive view of the Cartesian passions.[11] Descartes is often inaccurately said to have constructed the emotion/reason opposition that Antonio Damasio's best-selling book bluntly denominates *Descartes' Error.* As a result one encounters claims that hastily map one binary on top of another and soon take them as fully synonymous. (One example, from Nancy Tuana: "in rejecting the body as a source of knowledge, emotion is also excluded from the realm of the rational, and rather is seen as a source of error.")[12] These critics see Descartes in Platonic terms, wrongly imagining him to value mind over its rigorously separate counterpart, body, and to oppose reason to emotion. In fact, Descartes defines the emotions as bodily perceptions and thus precisely as a source of knowledge.[13] His explanation of how emotion informs reason relies on the connection he finds between body and soul, since through our bodies we register (and retain) the experience that grounds understanding. Failing to understand the workings of mind-body union, critics such as Damasio and Tuana therefore not only misread Descartes's concept of mind but also miss the crucial role that the passions play in the process of reason. As Schmitter puts it, emotions "have an indispensable role to play in promoting the ends of our *theoretical* reasoning, i.e., good reasoning, and the attaining of truth and the avoidance of error."[14] The theater—surely the most passionate and embodied of arts—enacts this insight with particular urgency and power.

My precise reading of Cartesian mind-body union differs in its details from those of Alanen, Brown, Hoffman, Schmitter, and Shapiro, just as their readings differ in details from one another. But like these philosophers I focus on Descartes's later texts, particularly his six-year correspondence with Princess Elisabeth of Bohemia and *The Passions of the Soul*, which he wrote at her request during the winter of 1645–46.[15] In these texts, which represent the fullest and most nuanced versions of his thinking, Descartes teaches us that the passions unite mind and body and that, whatever his commitment to substance dualism, the material and immaterial are inextricable. It is precisely this inextricability to which I hope to do justice in my discussion of the Cartesian theater, not only in my considerations of mind and body but also more generally as I discuss both the archive and the repertory, both literary texts like plays and embodied performance texts like choreography.[16] Analyzing key shifts in theater practice in the one hundred years after Descartes's death, I demonstrate how these shifts—in dramatic theory and plot construction, in acting theory and technique, and in theater architecture—reflect and are implicated in the cultural shift that Descartes engendered. I scrutinize artifacts that include religious jeremiads, aesthetic treatises, and curtain-raisers, treating them not only as archival texts to be analyzed but also as traces of performances to be imagined with the help of other historical artifacts: firsthand accounts, letters, frontispieces, architectural plans, ballet libretti. In other words I balance a study of permanent materials with a study of evanesced practice, mindful that the latter provides a valuable way of knowing even in a context—Cartesian philosophy—that might initially seem surprising. At the same time, I recognize that the process by which philosophical principles are performed by a culture and expressed in (and promulgated by) its artifacts is complicated, and, as in any process of translation, dissonances arise. By paying attention to these dissonances, manifested as they are in theater history, we can better understand how misapprehensions about Descartes arose in the first place. "The history of the theater is a history of ideas," in Joseph Roach's formulation.[17] Here, I attend to how the history of Cartesian ideas has expressed itself in the history of theater and to how performance has helped to physicalize and promote these ideas. In considering the stage after Descartes, I track how Descartes's thought came to be distorted into the received wisdom of

"Cartesianism" and how both this thought and its distortions were performed, sometimes self-consciously and sometimes unwittingly, in theater after his death in 1650. In each chapter I begin my analysis in late seventeenth-century France but move outward to show how key theoretical concepts and material practices resonated elsewhere, especially in England after the restoration of Elisabeth of Bohemia's cousin, Charles II.

In today's academy, and especially in light of the discord between philosophy and theater, the arguments here are necessarily considered interdisciplinary. But we must recall that, however old the quarrel between theater and philosophy, boundaries between academic disciplines are of recent vintage. Punch and Judy have always been part of the same show. Descartes himself wrote on any number of topics from mathematics to music and, as Garber has shown, considered his inquiries into metaphysics and physics to be part of the same knowledge-seeking endeavor. Indeed, he also tried his hand at various kinds of dramatic writing, including *The Search for Truth by Means of the Natural Light*, a philosophical dialogue for three characters, and an untitled four-act play, left unfinished.[18] Many of the key figures considered here—Charles Perrault and Charles Le Brun in France, John Dryden and John Vanbrugh in England—likewise worked across fields in ways that undo the distinctions between disciplines or métiers. Accordingly, I have not separated this book's philosophical from its theatrical considerations, and my analyses of Descartes's writings and of the rapidly shifting material conditions of the stage after 1650 are braided together.

This means that a philosopher looking for my reading of mind-body union will find it not in one place but rather threaded through considerations of actors' lives, audience behaviors, and a wide range of theatrical and paratheatrical activities including masques and impromptus (for "theater," too, was in an earlier time a more capacious category). This philosopher may find value in the perspective provided by these performances, only some of which explicitly thematize mind-body union but all of which express it. To take an example from my first chapter, Descartes explains in *The Passions of the Soul* that wisdom inheres in the body's physiological receptivity to joy allied with the mind's recognition of what is beneficial to the subject's health. But the treatise's insights can be understood more fully by contemplating the ballet *The Birth of Peace*, in which "eternal wisdom" (*sagesse eternelle* [*sic*]) appears not as disembodied words but as the dancing body of one of the ballet's participants, Queen Christina of Sweden.[19] Similarly, the theater historian looking to understand how a broad range of cultural documents and performances came to express and inculcate the growing Cartesianism of European culture will find these arguments nestled among readings of Descartes's writings. This theater scholar may find that these writings chafe against certain material explanations long accepted as definitive. To take an example from my fourth chapter, Paris's Hôtel de Bourgogne theater switched, in 1689, from individualized set designs to a single, neutral set that could serve any tragedy in the theater's repertory, the so-called *palais à volonté*. Theater history has explained that the new need to run more shows in a given week may have made set changes materially unfeasible. But an understanding of the cultural pressures wrought by Cartesianism suggests another explanation: the universalizing perspective of the *palais à volonté* may have sought to minimize the variability of spectator response, and this variability gained a discomfiting urgency in light of Descartes's articulation of subjective experience.

Readers from both philosophy and theater studies may also encounter methodological maneuvers that strike them as dissonant. Philosophers may be surprised to see first editions cited whenever possible, even in cases when bad early editions are suspected. Leah Marcus has argued that so-called standard editions are often unwittingly shaped by assumptions and ideologies that may cloud the best view of the text, and in my work I have encountered many instances that parallel those she explores in *Unediting the Renaissance*—perhaps especially in Molière's *The Versailles Impromptu*, whose first edition contains marvelously productive ambiguities (as I explore in Chapter 3) that have been tidied by subsequent editors. Therefore, I have heeded Marcus's call for a "temporary abandonment of modern editions" in favor of editions "that have not gathered centuries of editorial accretion around them."[20] Apart from ignoring stylistic typographical ligatures, I have cited text exactly as it appears. Where textual corruptions are suspected, I have alerted the reader. Relying on period sources, I have also sought to avoid the conventional adjectives that editorial scholarship has imposed on the arts of the period. For reasons this book will make plain, theater's "neoclassical" elements sometimes strongly resemble the very elements that philosophy deems "modern." I have therefore tried to use these and other terms (*classical, baroque,* etc.) only as writers of the period used them and to let the arising dissonance tell us something about the conventions that govern our understandings of theater and philosophy's respective histories.

The theater historian will approve these choices but find other surprises. One of the purposes of this book is to clarify the physiology of the passions as this physiology was understood by Descartes and by the culture, steeped in Cartesianism, in the century after his death. As I have written elsewhere, emotions are cultural expressions of particular moments in time and space; a transhistorical understanding of an emotion would be impossible to formulate.[21] At the same time, if Descartes is worth reading not only for historical interest but as philosophy (and thousands of syllabi suggest that he is), there must be something in his formulations that helps us to understand problems from our own time and place—problems that undergird the vogue for cognitive-scientific theater research, to name only one example. Certainly the emotions remain ineluctable; their precise physiological workings, elusive; and we do not have to believe in dubious concepts like the animal spirits or the ensouled pineal gland to find Descartes's writings on the passions philosophically clarifying. Therefore, while my historian's commitment to historical structures of feeling is deeply felt, I have employed the philosopher's habit of occasionally shifting into the present tense to imagine a present-day experience with which to assess Descartes's theory of the passions and its explanatory potential. We can ignore neither the differences that separate us from historically remote writings nor the uncanny endurance of key philosophical questions.[22] My juxtaposition of historical and ahistorical postures, then, is meant to be productive, to put the past and present in dialogue even (and perhaps especially) when tension results.

Several books of the last decade—among them Martin Puchner's *The Drama of Ideas: Platonic Provocations in Theater and Philosophy,* Freddie Rokem's *Philosophers and Thespians: Thinking Performance,* and Paul Woodruff's *The Necessity of Theater: The Art of Watching and Being Watched*—have suggested the exegetical benefits of putting theater and philosophy in dialogue. If we emphasize the monologic mode of the opening gambit of *Discourse on Method*—if we focus on a solipsistic method and the individual "I" that governs the *Meditations*—we may be surprised by the extent to which Descartes dwells, in his last texts, on others, on interaction, even on intersubjectivity. In *The Aesthetic Body* Erec R. Koch reminds us that the Cartesian subject is "passionately shaped by contact with others, by socialization. Interaction with other subject-bodies enters into the play of forces and stimuli that act on the individual and that provoke sensation and passion."[23] Here, I take up the transformative effects of such contact between subjects: onstage and offstage subjects but also the subjects of theater and philosophy. I foreground the perceptions and emotions—both, we will see, are for Descartes representations—that mediate between two parties in an encounter, each an audience to the other's performance. Looking beyond the monologic mode, I identify in late Descartes a performative or dialogic mode and define and enlist its epistemological benefits.

It is no accident that Descartes's ideas matured through his intersubjective exchange with Elisabeth—the person, he said, who understood his philosophy better than anyone else.[24] In dedicating his *Principles of Philosophy* to her, Descartes acknowledged this exchange and even adumbrated the very epistemological distinctions between monologue and dialogue, archive and repertory, that I am deploying here. "The greatest advantage I have received from the writings that I have previously published," he writes, "has been the honor of becoming known to your highness, and of being able to speak with her. It has allowed me to observe in her qualities so rare and so estimable that I believe it does a service to the public to propose them as an example to posterity."[25] Even taking into consideration the rhetorical flourishes of its genre (and those of courtly flattery), the dedication is remarkable. It performs two maneuvers. First, it subordinates the value of his published work to the advantage it has gained him: conversation with Elisabeth. His books have facilitated exchange with her, an exchange he values as "the greatest advantage." And he implicitly recognizes this experience, this intersubjective encounter, as a valuable way of knowing. (The scientific method of late Descartes stresses experiential knowledge; he frequently employs the word *expérience*, which, tellingly, means both "experience" and "experiment.") Some of the epistemological benefits of this encounter, in turn, he hopes to contain for his readers, for "posterity." At the same time, he tacitly acknowledges the difficulty of this containment, suggesting the drawback of a performative episteme. Performance, we know, evanesces. We can never recuperate the experience, or even the content, of Descartes's conversations with Elisabeth, especially their in-person conversations in Holland.[26] However, traces remain. Extant letters provide a written dialogue of considerable hermeneutic significance. The difficulty is in remaining attuned to their performative potential. The letters provide us texts for analysis, to be sure, but they also alert us to new ways of knowing Descartes.

When Elisabeth was asked to publish her letters to Descartes, after his untimely death in 1650, she declined. His letters to her were published in 1657.[27] As a result philosophers were left quite literally with another monologue (one with a confusing dramatic structure, since the ordering of the letters was incorrect),[28] and the conclusion of the mid-nineteenth-century critic Gottschalk Eduard Guhrauer was that philosophy would "forever mourn the absence" of the other voice.[29] Forever lasted just over two hundred years: the discovery of Elisabeth's letters in the 1870s by an antiquarian book dealer led to their publication, in 1879, by Alexandre Foucher de Careil (and to the dates of Descartes's own letters being corrected).[30] This event, in turn, opened a vista into the *Passions*, which the letters had spawned, and led more generally to the reassessment of Cartesian thought that we see, for example, in Brown's *Descartes and the Passionate Mind*. In transforming a monologue back into a dialogue, Elisabeth's letters reorient both Descartes and his readers away from the language of objectivity and generality. She shifts the universal subject—the "I" of the *Meditations*—back to a properly subjective one. Her constant appeals to her own bodily experience remind Descartes that he had set out to displace Scholastic axioms with personal observation, *expérience*; she grounds his sometimes unworldly philosophy in the world and its stimuli, returning him to the notion that knowledge inheres in the (sometimes passive) interaction of the mind with things from outside of it. In turn she alerts us to the epistemological benefits of performance. More particularly, Elisabeth's correspondence with Descartes helps us to understand another Cartesian theater not only because of what the two writers say about it. The letters' dialogic form illuminates a concern with intersubjectivity that is particularly germane in light of the dynamic exchange between actors and spectators.

The poetics of performance that emerges from Descartes's dialogue with Elisabeth is the subject of my first chapter. Elisabeth had suggested the inadequacies of mind-body dualism by pressing him on the question of health, seeing correctly that an ailing body might find its reason impaired. Descartes built on this insight in *The Passions of the Soul*, stressing how good health might be seen as evidence of mind-body union and highlighting the emotions' role in guaranteeing it. These ideas find expression in the ballet *The Birth of Peace*, whose libretto Descartes is said to have written and whose 1649 performance at the court of Queen Christina I imagine with the help of research conducted in Stockholm and Uppsala. The ballet celebrates the end of the Thirty Years' War, in which Descartes had himself served and which profoundly shaped his thinking; its end made possible the new philosophical order that the ballet represents and in many ways inaugurates. Thematizing mind-body union in the embodied form of ballet, *The Birth of Peace* argues for—and, more crucially, demonstrates—the health benefits of joy, perhaps especially for the disabled soldiers it audaciously represents. In May 1641 Descartes had written to Henricus Regius that "I am one of those who deny that man understands with the body," and this letter has been cited in the scholarship hundreds if not thousands of times.[31] But despite the collective force of this reiteration, it overlooks how much of late Descartes speaks precisely to the body's central role in understanding. The ballet, like Descartes's correspondence with Elisabeth, restores the body to a place of prominence by showing also how it serves as the repository of experience and memory. And if experience (especially emotional experience) reshapes the body, as Descartes showed as early as his mechanistic *Treatise on Man*, theater, like ballet, could encourage salutary physical effects by providing joyful experience and building joyful memories.

The book's second section concerns playwriting after Descartes. It demonstrates how the much-discussed problem of dramatic catharsis originates in an incommensurability produced by Cartesianism, since the universal experience of pity and fear theorized by Aristotle cannot be reconciled with an audience of individualized subjects. Pierre Corneille responded to this incommensurability in his play *Nicomède*, whose script I analyze alongside two of its performances: one at the Hôtel de Bourgogne in 1651, the other at the Louvre in 1658. The playwright's diminution of pity and fear and his concomitant elevation of emotional wonder sought to overcome the philosophical difficulties that Descartes presented for tragic playwriting. Previous critics have dwelt on the question of whether Descartes had read Corneille's work or Corneille had read Descartes's, or on the question of whether the two shared a common influence, such as François de Sales.[32] By contrast, Gustave Lanson—who inaugurated this line of scholarly inquiry in 1894 by first connecting the two figures—famously declared that Cartesian philosophy and *grand siècle* French literature developed as "effects of the same causes" and "independent expressions of the same spirit."[33] I have followed the lead of Ernst Cassirer, who took up Lanson's thesis in his book *Descartes: Doctrine—Personality—Influence.* Juxtaposing representative details from philosophy and theater of the period, I trace their consonances, explore the similar cultural work they performed, and thus demonstrate how a new worldview came to be consolidated. Descartes and Descartes-influenced playwrights initiated paradigm shifts in philosophy and tragedy, respectively, and the undeniable harmony of these shifts is made plain in Corneille's deviations from classical form. For Corneille reconfigures tragedy in order to foreground wonder, the precise emotion that Descartes located at the center of his emotional physics and moral philosophy. And thus Corneille wrapped his "ingenious fictions" (as Charles Perrault would have it)[34] around a truth of both nature and morality that had been lately conceived. These Cartesian innovations, theorized in Corneille's copious theoretical writings, were in turn mimicked in English theater and dramatic theory of the period—especially that of John Dryden, whose *Of Dramatick Poesie, an Essay* (1665) and *The Conquest of Granada* (1671) I discuss.

The book's third section concerns acting after Descartes. It considers the Cartesian notion of interiority, whose ramifications for bodily representation can be glimpsed in a series of English rehearsal burlesques of the late seventeenth and eighteenth centuries: George Villiers, Second Duke of Buckingham's *The Rehearsal* (1671), the anonymously written *The Female Wits* (1696), and Samuel Foote's *Diversions of the Morning* (1747). I explore these burlesques' borrowings from Molière's metatheatrical entertainment *The Versailles Impromptu* (1663). Representing the relationship between actors' interiority and their physiological onstage expressions, Molière's entertainment anticipated the terms worked out in Charles Le Brun's treatise on art, *Conference on General and Particular Expression* (1668), famous for inspiring early treatises on "natural" acting in both France and England, such as Foote's own *Treatise on the Passions* (1747). Le Brun deviated from previous work on emotional expression in the arts by depending not on observation but on a reasoned argument derived from Cartesian first principles.[35] But Le Brun's theory was unable to account for the particularities of mind-body union, a deficiency diagnosed already by his contemporary André Félibien, who found Le Brun to miss the *je ne sais quoi*—that "which cannot be properly expressed" and which he analogizes to "the secret knot that joins the two parts of body and spirit [*esprit*]."[36] What supplies this *je ne sais quoi* on the stage is, of course, the actor, whose mind-body union came to be celebrated by the public. It is no coincidence that the period saw the rehabilitation of the actor's reputation.[37] In the century after Descartes's death a picture of actors as inherently more passionate than nonactors—and therefore more dangerous—transforms radically into a picture of actors in greater control of their emotional channels, a control all the more remarkable since these channels are so well-trafficked as a result of the actors' emoting on the stage.

The book's fourth section concerns theater architecture after Descartes. In Cartesian theory the physiology of perception—in which the eye apprehends an external stimulus and relays it to the brain by a process he called representation—is inextricably connected with the physiology of emotion, which represents feeling by means of animal spirits in the blood vessels. Jean Racine's *Phèdre*, I demonstrate, stages this tension between ocular and sanguinary representation, but the play's precise theatrical meanings are determined by the anatomies of the theaters in which it is enacted. I show how several spaces collectively trace the development of a Cartesian theater architecture. First, I anatomize the Hôtel de Bourgogne, site of *Phèdre's* debut. The space retained the memory of an earlier kind of theatergoing, with its intermingling actors and spectators (allowed not only to sit on the stage but also to wander backstage if the mood struck); it thus encouraged its inhabitants to perform the same seepages—between self and other, inner and outer, individual and collective—that the play's characters understand as passionate, bloody contamination. Racine disavowed such seepage and protested that the play was meant only to "visually present" the passions, "to show all the disorder they create."[38] Such a presentation was better facilitated by new theater designs of the period, with their ocular spaces and corneal proscenium arches. I consider the Comédie-Française (designed by François d'Orbay), which Racine's play inaugurated in 1689, and London's Queen's Theatre in the Haymarket (designed by John Vanbrugh), home to *Phèdre*'s English premiere in 1707 in an adaptation by Edmund Smith. One of Phaedra's messages, we will see, is that she always exceeds the boundaries of her self, no matter how desperately they are policed. It is meant to be rhetorically productive, then, that the play spills out of its chapter and into the epilogue, in which I consider the contemporary Cineplex. There, Helen Mirren's performance as Phaedra (in a production directed by Nicholas Hytner) was given a "live re-broadcast" to audiences in 2010 while Mirren shot a film in Hungary, her corporal integrity intact even as close-ups severed her head from her body.

Each of these four spaces offers wildly divergent experiences to the-atergoers, and this bodily experience, Descartes teaches, shapes our way of seeing and constitutes our own corporal memory. Experience has taught me that my endeavor in this book requires some justification, perhaps because of the villainous role that Descartes has been made to play in critical theory in recent decades. An age of representation, the seventeenth century understood experience as subjective, and this understanding for-ever changed how theatrical representation and reception would operate. Descartes was a key player in this new understanding, and he therefore warrants a place in our theater histories; some of the most ostensibly clas-sical elements of these histories appear rather different when examined in the light of Cartesian philosophy. These histories leave Descartes out precisely because of their reliance on the archive; after all, he wrote little about the theater. As theater scholars have apprehended the lessons of per-formance studies, however, they have moved beyond written records and physical monuments and understood a much broader range of mnemonic materials as constituting the history of the practice. And by turning to this broader range of materials—to speech, to images, to gestures[39]—we see more clearly the contribution of Descartes (along with his frequent interlocutor, Elisabeth of Bohemia) to some of the most vexing theoreti-cal debates and puzzling material changes in theater history. The book's structure reflects this focus: I analyze a series of performance events with dates ranging from 1649 to 2010. So I turn to December 9, 1649, when Antoine Beaulieu's dancers slipped into their masks for *The Birth of Peace*, but Descartes demurred. I turn to October 14, 1663, when Molière directed his actor Marquise-Thérèse de Gorla in the *salle de la comédie* at Versailles and gave her a perplexing note about her acting: "sometimes violence to ourselves is necessary."[40] I turn to April 18, 1689, when the stage decorators at the Comédie-Française's first permanent home readied a set for Racine's *Phèdre* that was markedly different from that used in the play's 1677 premiere, and to later that day, when spectators took their seats by a markedly different path through the theater. Each of these moments, we will see, can be illuminated by "reread[ing] Descartes a little," as Luce Irigaray has advised us to do in a landmark essay.[41] So, too, can we illuminate other moments, farther afield and less long ago, as I demonstrate when the book makes excursions away from Paris, to Stockholm, to Toronto, and especially to London.

These moments, I show, can illuminate Descartes too. They can help us in our rereading.

We are told by Sophie of Hanover, heiress to the English throne and the mother of George I, that her sister Elisabeth of Bohemia once acted in Corneille's *Médée* in a private performance.[42] But Elisabeth's interest in the theater, at least one of her biographers notes, was displaced by an interest in philosophy once she had met Descartes.[43] I believe that theater and philosophy need not be mutually exclusive interests or endeavors. In *The Mind-Body Stage* I harvest the insights into performance offered by Elisabeth's dialogue with Descartes; I nudge an important and under-recognized philosopher back into performance with her favorite scene partner. Elisabeth's insights enriched Descartes's thought, and they help us to recognize the debt that theater history and practice owe him. I also ask him to make good on a debt to theater historians and practitioners. It is a commitment made in one of his earliest texts, from 1619. Let it serve as a cue: "So far, I have been a spectator in this theater which is the world, but I am now about to mount the stage."[44]

1

Mind-Body Union; or, The Cartesian Ballet

La naissance de la paix, Kungliga Slottet,
December 9, 1649

The scene is the royal palace in Stockholm, Sweden, December 9,
1649.[1] In one of a series of events celebrating the end of the Thirty Years'
War, and in honor of her twenty-third birthday, Queen Christina of Sweden has organized a court ballet entitled *La naissance de la paix* (*The Birth
of Peace*).[2] Largely as a result of the war, Christina now keeps one of the
most opulent courts in Europe, so no expense has been spared. Elaborate
sets have been built in the new perspective style—which guides spectation toward an upstage vanishing point—that take full advantage of the
technical capabilities of Christina's *salle de ballet,* designed by the talented
Italian architect Antonio Brunati and inaugurated less than eight months
before, in April. The set design represents the spectacularly contrasting
milieux of the ballet's interdependent dances, or entrées: for instance, a
military camp cedes to "heaven"—every baroque set designer's dream—
where Justice will dance with Mercury, Apollo, and, indeed, "all the gods"
(*tous les Dieux*).[3] Their choreography, as well as that of Earth, Fame, and
the nine Muses, along with various crippled soldiers and ruined peasants,
has been devised by the French ballet master Antoine de Beaulieu, already
resident at the Swedish court for more than a decade; Beaulieu, in his grotesque mask and his costume of velvet and black lace, is to dance the key
character of Panic Terror himself.[4] Andreas Düben, the queen's German

master of music, has composed music for the vocal solos that introduce each of the three acts; these solos are encomia to Peace, and indirectly to the queen whose ability to quell decades-long war the ballet celebrates. She will dance the role of Pallas Athena. A verse summary of the ballet's plot has been prepared in French and handsomely published and distributed alongside versions in German (by the court librarian, Johann Freinsheim) and in Swedish (by the celebrated poet Georg Stiernhielm).[5] Alternatively written in alexandrines and octosyllabic meter and totaling 344 lines, the verse narrative *The Birth of Peace*, although unattributed in this original printing, is popularly agreed to have been written by Christina's tutor, René Descartes, who had taken up his position as a court philosopher ten weeks before, on October 1, 1649.[6]

Descartes's early biographer Adrien Baillet notes that Descartes composed the verses while successfully resisting Christina's desire that he dance in the ballet himself alongside her, Beaulieu, and the other dancers.[7] One wonders what role Christina imagined for the fifty-three-year-old philosopher, then just two months from his death. Was it one of the cavaliers praising Pallas—and, of course, the queen herself—at the end of the second act? Was it the double-faced Janus, who celebrates the peace that the queen has brokered while reflecting on the remembered horrors of decades of war? After all, and no doubt unusually among Christina's courtiers, Descartes had himself served as a soldier in the Thirty Years' War. Was it one of the infantry who are commanded to dance for Pallas?

The performance of *The Birth of Peace* at the Swedish court that December represents a concatenation of the theoretical ideas and material conditions that this book explores. In its portrayal of soldiers and civilians emotionally devastated by war, the ballet stages the relationships among mind, body, and emotion in a way inconceivable before Descartes. But, more important, the ballet also refocuses our perspective on Descartes and serves as a corrective to much criticism of his philosophy. It does so in three ways. In its plot the ballet highlights the role of memory in human emotions and reason, an underemphasized aspect of Descartes's thought. In its complicated gender politics—by situating a woman as the embodiment of the good reason that manages to end the war—it undermines critical clichés about the gendering of reason in Descartes; as I will argue, while cultural forces since Descartes have feminized the emotions and masculinized reason, Descartes himself did not. Finally, in its form as a ballet it portrays the human subject as both conscious *and* embodied, thus physicalizing a key Cartesian concept that is often overlooked. Moreover, that the ballet celebrates the end of the Thirty Years' War is particularly apt, for this conflict shaped Descartes's thinking, and, as Timothy J. Reiss has persuasively argued, its end made possible a new philosophical order.[8] The relationship between this new philosophical order and a new theatrical order is the subject of this book, whose title, *The Mind-Body Stage*, aims to encompass both.

By wonderful coincidence, Descartes's *The Birth of Peace* premiered during the same month that *Les passions de l'âme* (*The Passions of the Soul*) appeared in print. After the first Düben-scored solo, whose lyrics implore us to revere Athena and to recognize Peace as the "greatest of her benefits" (*le plusgrand de ses bienfaits*), the ballet begins with the first of its twenty dances, the entrée of Mars.[9] Beaulieu's choreography precedes the first dance notation systems, so we can have no idea what it looked like. But we know its thematic content. The verse summary conveys the intentions of Mars to wreak havoc, a havoc that the audience would have recognized from the previous decades of war. Mars declares:

I intend to make every corner of the Earth tremble
And to show all mortals that no other god
Ever had as much power in this place as I do.
Not even he [i.e., Jupiter] who unleashes thunder.

His lightning and fire cause only a little fear,
Whereas my cannons and other machines,
My mortars, my petards, my fire-bombs and my landmines
Bring death along with terror everywhere.[10]

These verses foreground the ballet's thematization of war and the emotions. Note the central distinction that Mars makes between himself and Jupiter: one manages a little fear (*un peu de peur*), the other terror. It is a critical commonplace that Descartes, whatever his claims to have begun a new method deracinated from the classical tradition, used Scholastic concepts as needed.[11] Here, as would have been expected according to the style of the day and as would have been dictated by Christina, the classical gods appear. But they are finally subordinated to the ballet's interest in the passions and to its central personifications: the titular Peace and her antagonist, who is not Mars or even War but Panic Terror. Mars takes credit for unleashing terror, but it is revealing that once Terror arrives, she does not acknowledge this lineage.[12] As we sometimes experience in our day-to-day lives, emotions have a life of their own, quite divorced from their precipitating causes.

Introduced in the key third entrée, Panic Terror echoes Mars by noting that she makes not the earth but its people tremble (*trembler*). She boasts:

It is wrong that Pallas and Mars
Brag that among hazards
Their power is incomparable,
Mine is much more formidable.
It takes them much work
It takes them much equipment:
Powder, horses and arms
And men to call to arms [*vont aux alarmes*]
To submit for a single fight

. . . .

When I intend to bring terror
To a million warriors,
And trample all their laurels,
I need only a chimera,
A dream, a faint shadow
That I send into their brains.
And they tremble like calves
They flee, they turn pale
And often they throw themselves
Into evils they should fear more
Than those they try to avoid.[13]

The passage is particularly Cartesian, as captured in the wonderfully ambiguous phrase "vont aux alarmes." The term is military, of course, and Panic Terror refers to the men who would answer alarm calls and submit to battle.[14] But as early as the late sixteenth century, the word *alarme* had come to connote worry and fear, and to answer an alarm meant to submit to these emotions' perturbations. (For example, Racine, whose *Phèdre* illustrates the effects of such submission, uses the word *alarme* in this psychological sense twice.)[15] As the libretto makes clear, terror rattles the brain, disordering the body and impelling it to subsequent action, to throwing it into "evils." In *The Passions of the Soul* Descartes describes precisely this process: how an emotion can cause physical perturbation in the body (and particularly in the brain, a physical organ) before the mind, which is immaterial, even begins to apprehend the emotion, to identify it and possibly to allay its effects. That is, the physical changes in the body—disordered brain, trembling calves, blanching faces—affect the mind, or, put another way, the mind submits to a body perturbed by emotional stimulation.

Descartes emphasizes this much-misunderstood causality when he asserts that the passions of the soul are just the actions of the body understood from a different perspective: "the Action and the Passion never fail to be the same thing, which has these two names because of the two different subjects to which we can relate it."[16] That these actions and passions are "the same thing" testifies precisely to the union of mind and body; we cannot conceive of the soul's passions independently of their corporal effects.[17] Thus, in the summary of Deborah J. Brown, "the relationship between actions and passions is an expression of the experience of unity each of us has with our bodies."[18] It is the role of the mind to assess the passion being experienced by the soul and, depending on the context, to counteract or augment the actions of the body with an action of the will: when I am scared by a mouse, my mind stills my jitters; when I am scared by a car careening into my path, my mind hastens my legs' flight.

Of course, to say that terror is caused by a "chimera," as *The Birth of Peace* does, seems to overlook the genuine terror presented by certain stimuli, especially in war. But the ballet means to emphasize the role of Panic Terror over the role of Mars, to highlight (as in Descartes's theoretical writings) the central role played by images in the brain during the disturbance of the body. The brain's role in the emotions is complicated, and an analysis of how it unfolds according to Descartes repays careful attention. He writes in Article 35 of *The Passions of the Soul*:

If we see some animal coming toward us, the light reflected from its body casts two images of it, one in each of our eyes, and by the mediation of the optic nerves these two images form two other [images] of it on the inner surface of the brain, facing its hollows. Then, by the mediation of the spirits with which its cavities are filled, these images radiate from there toward the little gland which these spirits surround, in such a way that the motion that composes each point of one of the images approaches the same point of the gland which that motion approaches that forms the point of the other image representing the same part of this animal. By this means the two images in the brain compose only a single [image] of it on the gland, which, acting immediately on the soul, makes it see the animal's shape.[19]

Descartes here describes visual perception in the same terms he had worked out years earlier in the *Dioptrique* (*Dioptrics*), to which he makes explicit reference in Article 13.[20] (Descartes's diagram of this process is provided as Figure 1.1.) Two retinal images are transmitted by the animal spirits—his term for the smallest parts of matter, "very fine air or wind" and "very fine parts of the blood," that produce muscular movement[21]— in such a way that the image is apprehended by the soul, which he situates in the pineal gland. The proximate cause of a perception is therefore not the seen object itself but its image as transmitted by the animal spirits, an image finally as chimerical as a thought. But the animal spirits do more than facilitate visual perception. They also facilitate passionate perception by causing whatever physical perturbations they are accustomed to causing. (For Descartes, all emotional responses are conditioned by past experience, hence the importance of memory, which resides partly in the body insofar as the animal spirits respond without the mediation of the mind.) As Descartes writes, during the state of fear the animal spirits proceed "toward the nerves that move the legs to flee," but they also "cause another movement in the same [pineal] gland by means of which the soul feels and perceives this flight—which can in this way be excited in the body merely by the disposition of the organs without the soul contributing to it."[22]

Distinguishing mind from body, Descartes distinguishes his model of the soul from the Scholastics', asserting that there is only one rational soul with no diversity of parts.[23] Aristotle assigned the soul nonrational activities such as the vegetative activity of sustaining life or the locomotive activity of sustaining movement, and Plato opposed the agencies of reason and desire within the soul in his tripartite model with its appetitive, spirited, and rational parts.[24] While Plato's *Republic* could therefore imagine a poet calling forth the worst elements of the soul and nourishing them, Descartes insists on a vision of the soul that does not allow for

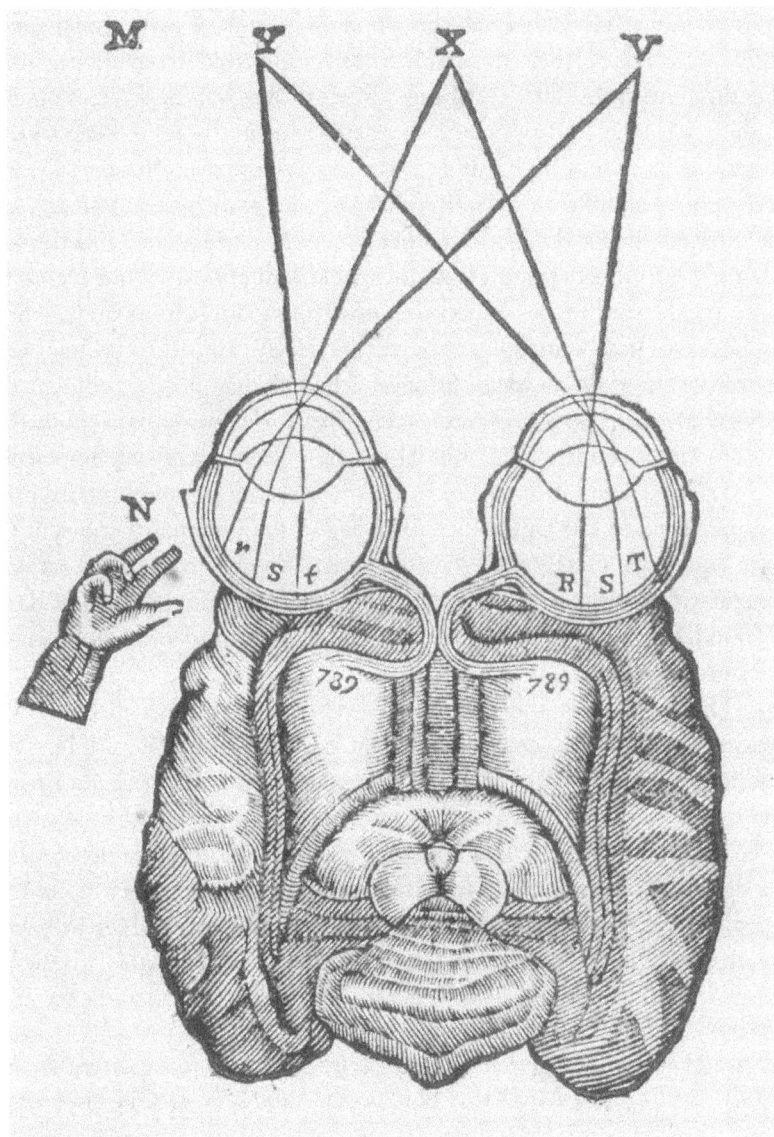

FIGURE 1.1. The process of visual perception, from René Descartes, *La dioptrique*, 49, in *Discours de la méthode pour bien conduire sa raison, & chercher la verité dans les sciences, plus la Dioptrique, les Météores et la Géométrie qui sont des essais de cette méthode* (Leiden: Jan Maire, 1637). Courtesy Rare Books and Special Collections, McGill University.

contradictions. He elaborates this point by means of a theatrical meta-phor: he castigates "the error that has been committed in having [the soul] play different characters."[25] All impediments to reason he situates outside of the soul. The soul does not do battle with itself, as in Plato's view; rather, the body may do battle with the soul, whose seat Descartes located in the pineal gland after reflecting that all other parts of the brain are, like the external organs, doubled. In other words the pineal gland, like the soul it houses, is uniquely singular and incapable of duplicity.[26] Thus Descartes contrasts the soul to the sometimes unwittingly duplicitous body, whose doubled eyes (for example) can sometimes deceive and whose animal spir-its convey multiple messages at once. Passions may pose a problem not because they oppose reason but because they are expressed as actions that are sometimes counter to reason. This difference is not trivial. Something frightful is seen and its image recorded on the retinas; something frightful is experienced by the legs, which have begun to flee. These actions of the body equate to a passion of the soul: fear. Whether this fear is rational depends only on the fearfulness of the stimulus according to the standards of good judgment, the difference between a mouse and a careening car as emotional stimuli.

Descartes calls the process by which the animal spirits convey these messages "representation."[27] That is, both visual perceptions and emotions are signs—and insofar as they are fabricated in the brain, we might call them chimerical—that are transmitted between the soul and objects in the world. As I discuss in later chapters, this characterization has important consequences for how Cartesian ideas are taken up in the-atrical practice, since emotional representations share critical features with the theatrical representations—for example, actors' gestures, theatrical designs, dramatic poetry—that mediate between stage and audience. The

FIGURE 1.2 (opposite page, left). The eye in perception, from Descartes, *La di-optrique*, 82. Courtesy Rare Books and Special Collections, McGill University.

FIGURE 1.3 (opposite page, right). Floor plan of the Tuileries *salle des machines*, inaugurated in 1662. Note the newly rounded amphitheater and corneal prosce-nium arch. The image is a detail of the "Plan des Tuilleries du costé de la Cour achevé sous Louys le Grand" (as listed in the "Table des planches") from Daniel Marot and Jean Marot, *Architecture française* (Paris: P.-J. Mariette, n.d. [1670?]), n.p. [174]. Courtesy Bibliothèque nationale de France.

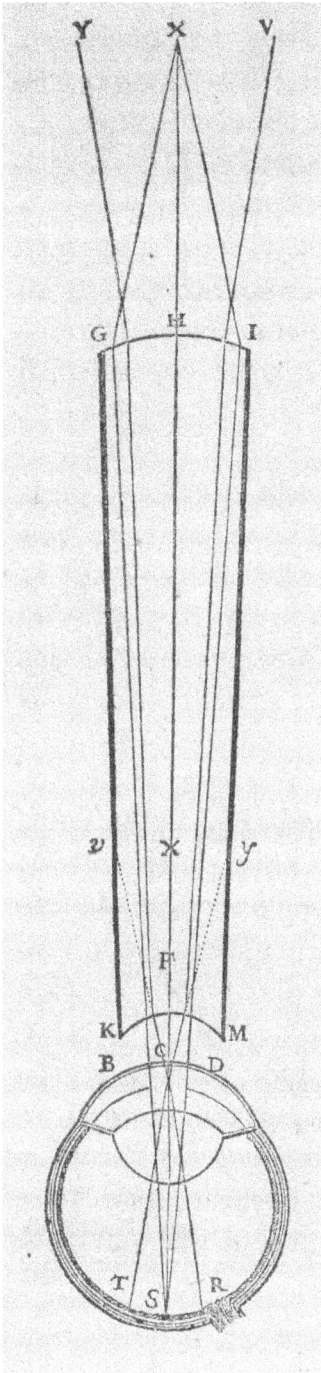

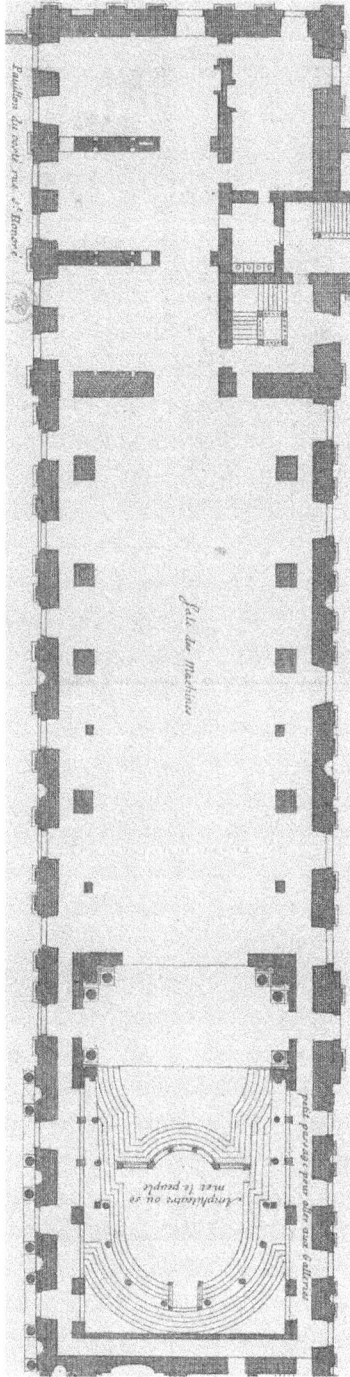

Pavillon du côté rue s'Honoré

Salle des Machines

petit passage pour aller au théâtre

Amphitheatre ou se met le peuple

proscenium arch, ascendant in the mid-seventeenth century, becomes an aperture that works like an eye's lens; it initiates the translation through which the object becomes a representation. (Think, for example, of the resemblance between Descartes's diagrams of visual perception and the-ater plans of the late century, after the previously rectangular spaces of the *jeu de paume* theaters developed proscenium arches and rounded amphi-theaters. See Figures 1.2 and 1.3.)[28] Descartes had aligned the process of visual perception with the process of thinking in the *Dioptrics* of 1637, in which he explained how visual perception involves the conveyance of images to the mind by the animal spirits. In the *Meditationes de prima philosophia* (*Meditations on First Philosophy*) of 1641, too, he had articulated how thoughts are "images of things" (*rerum imagines*)[29] transmitted from the mind to the body. (For this reason, dreams, such as those Descartes describes at the beginning of that book, can unsettle us, as can our own terrible imaginings—for example, when we contemplate the death of a loved one.) Eight years later, in *The Passions of the Soul*, Descartes built on this picture. And while explaining the similar representational processes that constitute the emotions, the book makes apparent how utterly perva-sive these representations are. The picture it completes is one in which our visual perceptions, our thoughts, and our emotional responses coexist in a cocktail of mental representations with which we are literally suffused, as the animal spirits convey them through our brains and bodies. As Susan James puts it in her book *Passion and Action*, we experience not only our bodies but the entire world as part of an "ever-changing kaleidoscope" of representations.[30]

With this conception Descartes inaugurates a new paradigm. In it one's perception of the world no longer directly concerns the external objects themselves but rather the signs that stand for them. (Michel Fou-cault understood the Cartesian era of representation, in which what signs convey need not conform to the objective reality of the things conveyed, in opposition to the Renaissance model of "resemblance.")[31] In Chapter 2, I explore the implications of this conception for theatrical spectators, who must ocularly and emotionally apprehend—and represent to themselves— the theatrical performances they witness; and in Chapter 3, I explore the implications for stage performers, whose subjective experiences of onstage emotion, one kind of representation, need to be intelligibly conveyed to audiences in another kind of representation. As we will see, both kinds of representation are governed by previous experience and conventions, which is to say that they are constructed. For now, it will suffice to note two things. First, we note that perception, thought, and emotion are all essentially performative: they are scripted either by the mind's will or by objects in the world and enacted by the animal spirits in the theater of the body. Second, we note that the emotions are not an "irrational" part of our being but, mingled as they are with thoughts and perceptions, integral to reason. Indeed, Descartes defines the passions explicitly as a form of knowledge (*connoissances*), noting that our soul learns from the passions that represent objects to it.[32] While mind and body are understood by Cartesian philosophy as having distinct natures, he conceives of the human being as a union of the two. The performative operations of being bind this union. This idea, implied even in early texts such as the *Discours de la méthode* (*Discourse on Method*, 1637), comes into sharper focus in his later work.[33]

In the seventh entrée of *The Birth of Peace*, a group of war-wounded soldiers dance. The libretto addresses the ballet's spectators, noting in blunt trimeters—my translation does not capture the meter—that

> He who sees what's been done to us
> And thinks that war is beautiful
> Or thinks it is greater than Peace
> Is crippled in the brain.[34]

This contrast between bodily injury and brain injury adumbrates the ballet's preoccupation with disturbed bodies, disturbed minds, and their interrelationship. One wonders how Beaulieu's dancers performed the handicaps of the crippled soldiers (*soldats estropiez*),[35] content that would seem audacious and atypical for a court ballet; the only Swedish precedent I have seen is in the twentieth entrée of 1645's *Le monde réjoui* (The delighted world), in which a crippled soldier (*soldat estropie*) briefly appears, carried on the shoulders of another dancer, and testifies that Christina "loves all soldiers, as her father had."[36] What is clear is that the performance of *The Birth of Peace* would have contrasted the handicapped soldiers' bodies with another set of physically disordered bodies: the army fugitives who dance the fourth entrée. (The poem identifies them as "some fugitives whom Panic Terror has caused to flee the

Army before combat.")[37] While they are physically uninjured, their bodies would reflect Panic Terror, whose dance they immediately follow and whose capacity to cause corporal derangement is described in the libretto. In other words Beaulieu would have needed to distinguish those whose bodies have been compromised by war from those whose bodies have been compromised by disordering emotion. For whatever their physical afflictions, the crippled soldiers in the seventh dance are mentally sound, as evidenced by their wisdom about war. The fugitive bodies in the fourth dance, however, reflect a mental abdication. It is explicitly marked by their emotional confusion, which one of the poem's many puns manifests. Playing on the word *cœur*, the fugitives defend themselves against the audience's presumption that they are cowardly; they protest that, despite their desertion, they were not lacking courage (*manquions de cœur*).[38] But they immediately deploy "heart" in its romantic sense: "You have ours," they proclaim "to the ladies" in the audience. "Please give us yours."[39] Their terminological slippage renders plain their emotional incontinence, but so, too, does their flirtation more generally. Since the ballet's first act represents the war's devastating effects—physical handicaps, pillage, the ruin of the peasantry—this flirtation is inappropriate in context and wrong in tone. It appears not as comic relief but as a jarring interpolation.

Elisabeth of Bohemia, traveling in Germany in the 1640s, noted the war's devastation on the bodies of its victims,[40] and it was she who pushed Descartes to recognize that the state of the body could compromise the capacity of the mind.[41] A strong dualist viewpoint, such as that seemingly taken by Descartes early in his career, would hold that the mind's clear thinking should be unimpeded by the condition of the body, since this body is only a machine whose workings physical laws can explain. This supposition would be repeatedly challenged by Elisabeth's own experience, not only of the war (which exiled her family to Holland) but also of her own sometimes frail physical health. In only her second letter to Descartes she promptly took up this theme, writing that "it is nevertheless very difficult to understand that a soul, as you have described it, having had the faculty and custom of reasoning well, can lose all this because of some vapors and that, being able to subsist without the body and having nothing in common with it, it [the soul] is still so governed by the body."[42] Her insight is essential to understanding Descartes's shift in thinking in the late 1640s, a shift reflected in bolder statements about mind-body union in late letters and *The Passions of the Soul.* In his response to her complaint, for example, he writes simply that she should feel free to attribute matter and extension to the soul and to conceive of the soul as united with the body.[43] He is disarmingly casual about his own dualism. "To conceive of the union between two things is to conceive of them as one single thing," he writes.[44] Two years later, his thinking about the inseparability of mind and body had shifted so markedly that he could write to her by slyly echoing her earlier letter: "I always note in [your letters] thoughts so distinct and reasoning so firm that it is not possible to persuade myself that a mind capable of conceiving them is lodged in a weak and ill body."[45]

As Elisabeth would have understood, the letter also echoes one of Descartes's recurrent metaphors for the mind-body relationship. In the *Discourse on Method* he had written that "it is not sufficient that [the soul] is lodged in the human body like a pilot in his ship, unless perhaps to move its limbs, but that it is necessary that [the soul] be joined and united more closely with him, in order to have, in addition, sensations and appetites similar to ours and thus comprise a real human."[46] And he elaborated further in the sixth *Meditation,* by noting that "I am present to my body in the way a sailor is present in a ship, but . . . I am most tightly joined and, so to speak, commingled with it, so much so that I and the body constitute one single thing."[47] In light of this union, he writes, we know that we are hungry or thirsty not because of rational knowledge but because of physiological sensations, apprehended by the mind with which the body is united. Thus the culminating *Meditation* argues for the impossibility of mind without a body. *The Birth of Peace* enacts this conception of mind-body interaction beautifully in its second entrée, a dance of infantry and cavalry members. The libretto mobilizes, for its first but not last time, a pun on *corps*; it presents the army as the body animated by Pallas, who is aligned explicitly with the soul. The soldiers proclaim:

> She is in our corps
> The leader without whom it cannot live;
> And we expend all of our efforts
> To have the honor of following her.
> Without her, this divided corps
> Would be despised by all.[48]

It would be a mistake to see this image as representing the mind or soul as somehow transcending the lowly body of the army; rather, the image emphasizes their union. Without the soul, which is "in" the body, it could not live; it would be divided. These lines lay a somewhat different emphasis than does the sixth *Meditation*, in which Descartes had argued that the body was divisible, the mind indivisible.[49] The poem stresses the indivisibility of the entire subject, its union of body and soul. Compare Article 30 of *The Passions of the Soul*: "the soul is truly joined to the whole body, and . . . one cannot properly say that it is in any one of its parts to the exclusion of the others, because [the body] is one, and in a way indivisible."[50] The body is "in a way" indivisible insofar as its cohesion is assured by the soul, to which it is "truly joined." As a performance, a ballet would have made this point potently. After all, in it the physical union of soul and body is neither philosophically contemplated nor deduced by Cartesian logic. It is enacted by embodied subjects: Beaulieu, his dancers, and the rest of the participating court.

What preserves and guarantees this union is the emotions. They knit body to mind as the animal spirits bear representations from one to the other about what the body is doing (its actions, the soul's passions) and about what the mind wills it to do (the soul's volitions). Importantly, these representations convey information about what is beneficial or detrimental to the subject; therefore, they serve the indivisibility manifested in the cavalry corps.[51] Consider the reprisal of the corporal metaphor at the end of the ballet's second act. This act has focused on the glories of Peace, so its emotional register has appropriately shifted. Panic Terror has been banished. Significantly, however, terror is not displaced by an unfeeling reason but rather by a more salutary emotion, joy. And the corporal impediments associated with terror are likewise replaced by joy's boons. The purpose of joy, Descartes writes, is to "incite the soul to consent and contribute to actions which can serve to preserve the body"—his definition of good.[52] He means that the soul becomes aware of things that are good because of joy's salubrious physical effects; thus, joy moves the soul to love objects that induce it. (By the principle of emotional conditioning or habituation, in turn, love "never fails to produce joy.")[53] When the Cavaliers return to dance in honor of Pallas in the nineteenth entrée, they take up again their pun on *corps*:

We live in a body [*corps*]
Of which we are the arms, you the divine flame
That commands all, and which we call the soul.[54]

If we see the ballet as allegorizing the passions—a view that I encouraged in noting how quickly its opening subordinates Mars to Panic Terror—we will read this nineteenth dance as self-reflexive. In their choreography the cavalry joyfully celebrate not the soul per se but their union with it. Recall that the passions of the soul are the actions of the body and that the passions of the body are the actions of the soul. The soul's volition spurs the body on to good, that which is beneficial; and the body preserves the soul with the passions, which bring both benefits and knowledge. In this way "the emotions express and testify to our embodied condition," as Lilli Alanen puts it in her book *Descartes's Concept of Mind*: "Not only do they constitute the main evidence for the close union between the mind and the body, their principal function is to serve and preserve this union."[55]

The nineteenth dance of *The Birth of Peace* precedes and introduces that of Pallas herself, who partakes in "a grand ballet of ladies" (*le grand ballet des dames*) that constitutes the entire third act.[56] Serving as the ballet's summation, this act performs the soul's embodiment even more literally: Christina-as-Pallas, representing the soul, joins the female corps of dancers. Body and soul are shown not only as synchronized but also as coterminous. It may seem curious that the libretto now calls Pallas "eternal wisdom" (*sagesse eternelle*),[57] that the allegorical claims of the ballet slip even by the notoriously loose terms of a court entertainment. However, the proper union of body and mind literally constitutes wisdom; in the Cartesian equation, wisdom equals the body's physiological receptivity to joy plus the mind's recognition of what is beneficial. The ballet has demonstrated this equation in both the negative example of the terrified fugitives and the positive example of the joyful cavalry. Christina-as-Pallas, then, appears as the apotheosis of the ballet's argument. Juxtaposing the cavaliers with Pallas, the final two dances thematize the different natures of body and mind before celebrating their inextricability.

Defining *joy* in *The Passions of the Soul*, Descartes performs a similar maneuver. He at first separates the emotion of joy from the "purely intellectual joy that comes into the soul by the soul's own action."[58] But he finds this division, if theoretically accurate, practically untenable. The subject-position to which joy is represented—its audience, if you will—is not a disembodied soul but the soul as joined to the body, for, by the equation I have explored, an unhealthy, divided subject would be unreceptive to joy.[59] Descartes therefore undoes the division of emotional and intellectual, concluding that "while the soul is joined to the body, this intellectual joy can hardly fail to be accompanied by that which is a passion."[60] An action of the body, this passion of the soul is a representation of the animal spirits and, of course, physiological. Descartes explains:

The pulse is regular and quicker than usual. . . . A pleasant warmth is felt, not only in the chest, but also spreading into all the external parts of the body with the blood we see entering them in abundance. . . . Thus Joy renders the color more vivid and rosy, because in opening the heart's sluices, it makes blood flow more quickly into all the veins, and, as [the blood] becomes warmer and finer, it gently swells all the parts of the face, rendering its demeanor more smiling and cheerful.[61]

He might be describing the dancers as *The Birth of Peace* builds to its conclusion—the poem, too, emphasizes their faces, by stressing what the audience sees "en regardant leurs faces"[62]—with Pallas dancing with Peace, Justice, the Muses, and the Graces. The dancers represent emotions, and these emotions have a primary function, which is in turn to incite emotion in the spectators. Recall the interrelationship between visual perception and emotion, what an audience sees and what it feels, the "kaleidoscope" of representations that constitutes human experience. Here, bodies that feel, animated by their animal spirits, perform; and as they perform, they impel other bodies, similarly animated by their spirits, to see and also to feel.

We see two departures from usual understandings of Descartes: first, that passions (in this case, joy) can be unequivocally good and, second, that the Cartesian subject is changed by its passionate interactions. As Erec R. Koch reminds us in his book *The Aesthetic Body*, the subject is "passionately shaped by contact with others, by socialization. Interaction with other subject-bodies enters into the play of forces and stimuli that act on the individual and that provoke sensation and passion."[63] Descartes describes a model in which emotions in one group cause emotions in the other and in which vectors of movement, caused by animal spirits in one set of bodies, influence the vectors of movement of another set of bodies.

The porous nature of this relationship resonated in a culture that worried about the impiety and influence of actors, and work like Descartes's must have done little to alleviate the anxiety of the theater's opponents, vigorous in the period in France, as well as England. Their fear is captured well in a warning by the bishop Jacques Bénigne Bossuet, whose *Maximes et réflexions sur la comédie* (Maxims and reflections on the theater) describes how the passion generated in the actor's body enslaves him and then colonizes the spectator. Invoking its "unreasonable part," Bossuet betrays a Platonic and decidedly un-Cartesian understanding of the soul; recall that, for Descartes, it is an error to make the soul play different characters. But generally the consonance between Descartes's model and the bishop's Platonic fears is clear:

By imitating something, we became slaves alongside [*avec*] a slave, and filled with vice alongside a vice-filled man; and, above all, to represent passions it was necessary to cultivate those within us whose outward expression we would wish to show. The spectator also entered into the spirit of things: he praised and admired the actor who could incite these emotions. So the entire apparatus of theater works only to make people impassioned and to strengthen our *brutish, unreasonable part*, which is the source of all our weaknesses.[64]

Descartes assiduously avoided the thorny public debates about the theater's social function that were gripping his native country, sufficiently occupied as he was by the philosophical controversies his work generated. As he put it in a letter to a Jesuit priest, "I abstain, as much as I can, from questions of theology."[65] But based on his letters to Elisabeth, it is clear that Descartes found worries like Bossuet's unfounded. From Descartes's perspective, for an actor to represent an emotion, she must *will* the body into the appropriate physiological state, and an actor who could perform such a successful act of volition presumably need not worry about her mental control. (I will return to the implications of Cartesian thought for acting theory in Chapter 3, where I draw parallels between shifts in thinking about the subject to new standards for stage representation.) As for the spectator, Descartes could theoretically conceive of one whose emotional receptivity to the theater was so sensitive that he could be physically undone by it. But such a weak-souled person would presumably be rare, and in his suggestibility he would be terribly compromised before ever entering the theater. Descartes does concede that some people cannot test the strength of their souls because they are, as he puts it, too carried away (*continuellement emporter*) by the passions.[66] Employing the same metaphor that Bossuet would use some years later, Descartes declares that such a person, in following his passions, renders his soul enslaved (*esclave*).[67] But, generally, Descartes is sanguine, stressing that there is no one so weak that he cannot acquire dominion over the passions.[68]

The theater could play a role in this acquisition, encouraging salutary emotions such as joy. Indeed, in Descartes's view even negative emotions could be useful. Sadness, for example, works as the precise opposite of joy, inducing a bodily aversion and therefore teaching and reinforcing a hatred of those things that cause the subject pain and threaten the subject's mind-body union. As Descartes writes in *The Passions of the Soul*, hatred "repels the things that harm and can destroy."[69] More generally, since all emotional reactions are conditioned—constantly changing according to cumulative experience—an emotional experience could bring benefit insofar as it encouraged helpful emotional associations: Racine's justification for *Phèdre et Hippolyte* (as it was originally called) in his preface to the play.[70] For example, Descartes wrote in an October 6, 1645, letter to Elisabeth that experiencing pity while watching a play is related to being more compassionate outside the theater and that, in general, "the soul is pleased to feel the passions move within it, regardless of their nature, provided that it remains in control."[71] (As the French word for soul, *âme*, is feminine, this final expression takes on gendered connotations: the soul must remain mistress [*demeure maistresse*] of the passions.) But, for some, this proviso was too onerous, and fears of actor-audience intersubjectivity animated Jansenist antitheatrical prejudice in France.[72] A Cartesian philosopher as sophisticated as Nicolas Malebranche—himself a correspondent of Elisabeth of Bohemia—could come to view the movements of performers and audiences as remarkably insidious. In his mammoth *De la recherche de la vérité* (*The Search After Truth*), he would declare that those with vivid imaginations, like actors, were susceptible to their own spirits, which affect their whole bodies "promptly and vigorously":

Since the brain of those with an active imagination receives . . . deep traces of what they imagine, these traces are naturally followed by a great movement of the spirits, which prepares their whole body promptly and vigorously to express their thoughts. In this way, the aspect of their face, the tone of their voice, and their turn of phrase, animating their expressions, will make those who are listening and watching them ready to focus and to receive automatically the trace of the image that is moving them.[73]

Such people would always impose the content of their imaginations on others by a similar physiological mechanism. But note, too, the strange toggling between singular and plural that Malebranche performs, and his ambiguous pronoun-antecedent reference, which leave us finally in doubt about who is being moved and what role, if any, individual agency plays in the passionate process. Such confusions are rhetorically potent given the subject matter that Malebranche addresses. "For after all a man who is stirred by what he says usually stirs others," he concludes.[74]

The theater's response to worries such as those of Malebranche was to temper rather than to intensify the intersubjective experience between actors and audiences. This required more strongly objectifying the actor, rendering him or her an object of contemplation rather than a subject for emotional exchange. As I detail in Chapter 4, the entire material apparatus of theatrical production—especially set design and theater architecture—became reorganized in the late seventeenth century, and the forces driving this reorganization are more complicated than has been recognized. To some it has seemed the triumph of putatively Ancient ideals, of Vitruvian architecture and Aristotelian unities. But this narrative ignores its distinctly modern contours, and especially the impact of the Cartesian coordinate system, which allowed three-dimensional space to be precisely mapped. The well-known argument of Erwin Panofsky's *Die Perspektive als symbolische Form* (*Perspective as Symbolic Form*, 1927)—that the united visual field of perspective can be aligned with Cartesian rationalism—pertains to theater history.[75] The Renaissance interest in Vitruvius[76] had extended his insights and eventually engendered perspectival stagecraft, with its upstage vanishing point (about which Vitruvius may have written nothing),[77] so that by the mid-seventeenth century, set designs had already used perspective for decades. However, the nature of perspectival stagecraft fundamentally changed late in the century when the audience became corralled into an "objective" position vis-à-vis the action. Parterres were first reduced in size and then displaced by seating, which served to anchor spectators' previously unruly bodies. Proscenium arches, at first introduced as liminal markers like triumphal arches, eventually served, along with stage curtains, to reinforce the separation between actors and audience; the arch became an aperture. The ramifications of these changes were strongly felt in countries like France, where medieval-style mansion staging predominated well into the century and where an audience, or at least certain segments of it, was accustomed to traipsing across the stage and interacting directly with the actors. In mansion staging the décor was dispersed: a play's settings were juxtaposed in fixed positions on the stage; there was no convention of stage unity and no attempt to create an enclosed or even spatially coherent space for the action. Indeed, what we think of as spatial coherence onstage derives from a later paradigm. Moreover, given the unstable demarcation between stage and audience, the spatial incoherence of the stage continued out into the parterre and beyond. Perspectival stagecraft, by contrast, not only disciplined audiences into a singular perspective oriented toward a vanishing point (modeled on an ideal vantage usually taken by a ruler) but also separated the theatrical milieu into two distinct ontological spaces, those of the play world and the real world.

At the Swedish court where *The Birth of Peace* was staged, this transformation was already well underway, and the gradual shift there prefigures the disambiguating journey that theatrical production would take throughout Europe. We can discern three distinct steps in Beaulieu's work. At first, his ballets were performed in the state hall or ballroom of the palace, with no décor.[78] He introduced perspective sets and a triumphal arch in 1645 for *The Delighted World*, but presumably without providing an ontologically unified playing space since he did not have a stage; as in the now-iconic *Balet comique de la Royne* (The queen's comic ballet; Figure 1.4), it is likely that the dancers performed in the central area, where they were observed from three sides.[79] (The masques of Inigo Jones provide another analogue. And, indeed, Beaulieu probably borrowed lessons from Jones, whose work he would have seen during his time in England, immediately before coming to Sweden in 1636.)[80] Finally, 1649: in Brunati's theater—with its perspective stage, seventeen meters deep; its proscenium arch; and its white satin stage curtain[81]—Beaulieu would have modified the ballet to one in which the dancers were set off from the audience and observed from a single direction.

Performers and spectators, once literally intermingling, suddenly had their perspectives disciplined and their functions defined more narrowly: performers were to perform, spectators to observe. This narrowing

FIGURE 1.4. Nonperspectival staging, from Balthasar de Beaujoyeulx, *Balet comique de la Royne* (Paris: Adrian Le Roy, Robert Ballard, and Mamert Patisson, 1582), Aiiii^r. Courtesy British Library Board.

FIGURE 1.5. Frontispiece to Jean Desmarets de Saint-Sorlin, *Mirame: Tragico-médie* (Paris: Henry Le Gras, 1641). Courtesy Kungliga Biblioteket, Stockholm.

of functions did not end the emotional interaction between the two groups, of course, but the groups' more emphatic separation would certainly have limited the extent, and changed the character, of this interaction. As at the 1641 premiere of Jean Desmarets de Saint-Sorlin's *Mirame* at Paris's new Palais Cardinal—a space that Beaulieu had likely seen on a Christina-funded trip in that year[82]—a scission has occurred. This scission is wonderfully rendered in that play's frontispiece, which flaunts the theater's new proscenium arch and curtain (Figure 1.5). Once the curtain has lifted (or the page is turned), the audience looks into a space that is not its own. It is not Paris but *Mirame*'s Bithynia. Soon, court scenography could boast of its ability to display an entirely different world convincingly. For example, the title page of the libretto to Beaulieu's *Le Parnasse triumphant* (Parnassus triumphant, 1651) describes its first act thus: "the first opening [of the curtain] was represented by a marvelous perspective onto Parnassus, and the nine muses were painted so naturally and with such art that judgment was deceived by the eye."[83]

This scission resonates strongly with the story of parturition that Susan Bordo tells in her book *The Flight to Objectivity*, in which she seeks to understand the cultural transformations of the mid-seventeenth century. Building on theses such as Panofsky's, Bordo describes the process by which a notion of the self was developed in contradistinction with the world. This self was encouraged by the introduction of perspective to see the world "objectively"[84]—that is, with the precision that the Cartesian coordinate system, for example, could facilitate. "What is clear is that at some point the 'illusionist space' of the perspective painting and the 'theoretic space' of the culture became fully *congruent*," she writes; and the culture therefore developed into a "paradise for analysis, dissection, and 'controlled' experimentation."[85] Paradoxically, the fetishization of objectivity and detachment that Bordo describes was born precisely out of Cartesian subjectivity. This is because an epistemological dilemma would arise from an era of representation, in which mental representations could differ from the thing conveyed, in which one could be deceived, as by the perspective in *Parnassus Triumphant*. As Descartes describes in the third of his *Meditations*, "the principal and most frequent error to be found in judgments consists in the fact that I judge that the ideas which are in me are similar to or in conformity with certain things outside me."[86] Whether in philosophy or in a stagecraft that uses perspective to symbolize an external reality, the pursuit of objectivity responds to this epistemological anxiety, this shadow of doubt cast over the subject's accuracy in perceiving the world. But in seeking shelter from a shadow, one remains shaded. Recall that we cannot verify the accuracy of our visual perceptions; as Descartes notes in the *Meditations*, "whether it is a she-goat or a chimera that I am imagining, it is no less true that I imagine the one than the other."[87] We are returned to Panic Terror, who boasts precisely of the considerable material repercussions occasioned by a chimera in the brain.

Although Bordo restricts her discussion to other arts, the phenomenon that she traces is keenly visible in dance and theater. Choreographing *The Birth of Peace*, Beaulieu would have been armed with all the stage technologies of Brunati's new theater and with the seemingly more objective viewpoint that these technologies granted him. (A floor plan

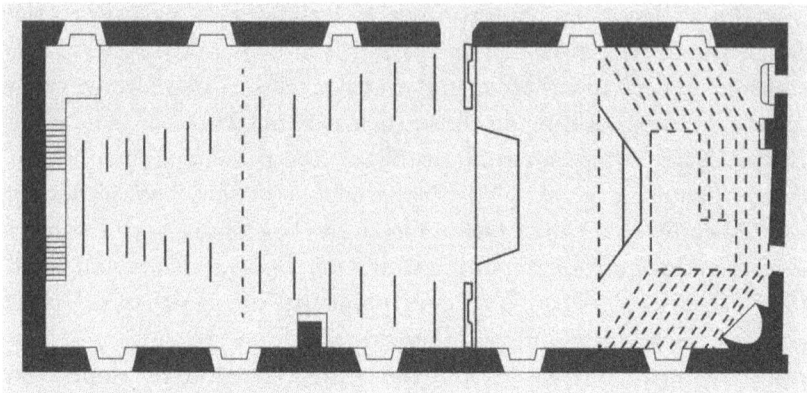

FIGURE 1.6. Floor plan for Antonio Brunati's *salle de ballet* in Stockholm's royal palace circa 1649, as reproduced by Anna Szczepaniak from a detail of a drawing (circa 1660) by Jean de la Vallée, preserved by the Office of the Palace Architect, Kungliga Slottet.

of this theater appears as Figure 1.6.) The new theater had been inaugurated on April 4, 1649, with a ballet entitled *Les passions victorieuses et vaincues* (The victorious and vanquished passions), whose title traces its consonance with *The Birth of Peace*.[88] The vanquishing of certain passions, like the defeat of Panic Terror in the later ballet, is not effected by a disembodied reason but rather accompanied by the victory of other, more beneficial passions. Thus the ballet was intended to fête Christina's accomplishment in regard to her own passions and to celebrate the effective rule guaranteed by this accomplishment. The new stage technologies emerging late in the century would promise that the defeat of certain passions and the victory of others could be effected not only *in* the stage narrative, as in Beaulieu's ballet, but also *by* its performance, first in separating its dancers and spectators and then by moving them farther away from one another than they had previously been. Such an arrangement, we will see, was believed to diminish the possibility that the performers' perturbations could be transferred kinesthetically to those who observed them.

Looking at theater architecture from the late seventeenth century and through the eighteenth, we recognize that the chasm between

performers and audience, once created, widened repeatedly. The ontological divide between the real and play worlds, having been conceived,
became reified. There can be no doubt that antitheatrical concerns about
actor-audience emotional contact encouraged this trend in France, as did
the flight to objectivity (as Bordo calls it) in the culture more generally.
The vogue for analysis and codification in the fine arts further illustrates
this flight. The Académie royale de peinture et de sculpture (discussed in
my third chapter) was founded in 1648, followed by the Académie royale
de danse in 1661, the Académie royale de musique in 1669, and the Académie royale d'architecture in 1671—and each of these academies promoted
a culture of objectivity and detachment no less than the academies that
governed humanities and science research: the Académie des inscriptions
et belles-lettres (1663) and the Académie des sciences (1666). By codifying the arts, the academies hoped to contain an aesthetic and kinesthetic
disorder that they related to the too-great license taken by performers, and
this license was considered a function of the performers' subjectivity, their
personal perturbations. The 1662 letters patent to establish the Académie
royale de danse, for example, notes that the genre has become "disfigured
and corrupted" by "ignoramuses," and it attributes these disfigurements
and this corruption to the "disorders and confusion of the late wars" that
introduced them.[89] As Beaulieu did in his choreography for *The Birth of
Peace* twelve years earlier, the document links the kinesthetic and emotional trauma of civic unrest to the aesthetic derangement of the ballet.
It empowered the academy to "correct the abuses and errors" (*corriger les
abus & defauts*) that had ensued by means of a codified technique and
the introduction of a systematized notation system.[90] One detail tells: a
consequence of the Académie royale de danse was to end all amateur participation in French court ballets.[91]

Sweden followed the French model of disciplining artistic and scientific endeavor, and Descartes had been tasked by Queen Christina with
setting up the Swedish Academy of Arts and Sciences.[92] Generally, however, Descartes's role in this culture of codification and detachment is
more complicated than many have acknowledged, and "Cartesianism" as
it has developed since the late seventeenth century often sits in tension
with the writings of Descartes that theoretically undergird it, as many of
the cultural texts analyzed in this book attest. We see this clearly when

we consider the putative gendering of rationality in Cartesian thought. It is now truistic that Descartes's account of the human subject promoted the separation of "woman" and "reason," an argument put most famously in Genevieve Lloyd's *The Man of Reason: "Male" and "Female" in Western Philosophy*.[93] Descartes's writings everywhere state that the mind has no gender. And his work, precisely because it expounded a philosophical method grounded in observation and logic as opposed to Scholastic learning, was enthusiastically taken up by women—especially those who, unlike Elisabeth, could read neither Latin nor Greek. The sociohistorical cross-pressures on Descartes's writings and reception give rise to a paradox. At the same time that Descartes was tacitly asserting women's equality and his works were explicitly being used to argue for it by writers such as François Poullain de la Barre,[94] the academies that seemed to promote Cartesian principles were fortifying their entrances against women.[95] This paradox will serve as a useful analogue for some of the contradictory impacts of "Cartesianism" in theater history. We must heed the warning of Amy Morgan Schmitter: it is difficult to separate our understanding of Descartes from the cultural processes and practices that have inevitably shaped this understanding, but neither must we claim that Descartes's "texts are themselves somehow responsible for those processes and practices."[96] For while Descartes's legacy might have promoted objectivity and detachment, his writings endorse the sort of salutary intersubjective exchange that theater provides, as performers emotionally and physiologically influence their spectators and, in turn, are influenced by them. In thinking about Descartes, I have therefore been governed by the admonition of one of his most sensitive critics, Luce Irigaray. She warned in 1982, while teaching in Holland, that "we need to reread Descartes a little and remember or learn what's there about movement in the passions."[97]

Contrary to commonplace critical expectations, *The Birth of Peace* specifically genders the mind as female.[98] And the ballet ends precisely by acknowledging the role of movement in the passions, as the female corps dance in the joyful grand ballet. So, too, does the libretto stress the exchange between performers and audience. In an apostrophe to the imagined spectators, it asks:

> People, what do you think seeing so many marvels
> That dazzle your eyes?

One has never seen anything like it on earth.
Imagine your spirit transported to the skies.

. . . .

Will you not judge, seeing their faces,
That all that is beautiful in the heavens is here?[99]

The lines conceive of the dancers as perceptual stimulation. Visually, their marvelous dancing will be transmitted to the spectators, whose eyes it dazzles. Nothing like it has been seen before. And in this visual uniqueness lies the emotional resonance: the spectators marvel. We cannot know exactly how the ballet worked in its performance on December 9, 1649, although a courtier in attendance echoed the libretto in writing that the ballet was "very beautiful to see."[100] But the passion associated with what the spectators see, as described in the text, is quite particular. Indeed, the verses imagine the audience experiencing the very emotion that Descartes theorized at greatest length in *The Passions of the Soul,* and that which Irigaray contemplates. It is "the first of all passions" for Descartes, wonder. As he describes it:

When the first encounter with some object surprises us, and we judge it to be new, or very different from what we knew in the past or what we supposed it was going to be, this makes us wonder and be astonished at it. And since this can happen before we know in the least whether this object is suitable to us or not, it seems to me that Wonder is the first of all the passions. It has no opposite, because if the object presented has nothing in it that surprises us, we are not in the least moved by it and regard it without passion.[101]

The transcendent image in *The Birth of Peace*—of the spirit being transported to the skies—reflects the fact that wonder, uniquely, is constituted by a bodily but not muscular response. Instead, the animal spirits form an indelible impression on the brain "to fortify and preserve" the impression of the object, which is "rare and consequently worthy of being considered."[102] (It is thus unsurprising that both the poem and the treatise emphasize judgment.) As evidenced by its unique failure to produce changes in the heart or the blood, wonder relates physiologically only with the brain.[103] That is, unlike terror, which can distort the body or throw it into evils, wonder's only bodily consequence is knowledge of the marvelous thing seen and felt.[104] And in this difference from other emotions resides the utility of wonder for the spectator and, by extension, the dramatist. The smooth emotional transmission that the poet imagines occurring in the ballet (that is, the dancers, while feeling joy, incite wonder in their spectators) will provide an ideal for Cartesian playwrights, especially tragic playwrights, starting with Pierre Corneille. A passionate interaction of particular benefit can be effected. Descartes's emphasis on wonder is part and parcel of a larger shift in his cultural moment; it is no accident that he extols the benefits of this emotion at the same time that Corneille begins promoting tragic wonder in plays like *Nicomède* (1651). I take up this network of consonances in Chapter 2, arguing that late seventeenth-century wonder is different in kind from its classical forebears and, indeed, the marvelous stage effects in popular entertainments made possible by Giacomo Torelli, the celebrated stage designer and architect, summoned to France in 1645.

To privilege wonder, of course, means to privilege the novel: to show spectators something that they have never seen before. The experience of wonder is one of knowledge *prima facie*, in both its literal Latin and received meanings—at first sight the spectator apprehends something new, and, moved by the passion it stirs, he or she is compelled to judge whether it is beneficial or detrimental. If the stimulus is beneficial, a subsequent encounter will cause joy, and love for the object will be habituated; if the stimulus is detrimental, a subsequent encounter will cause sadness, and an aversion for the object will be habituated. But, having gained knowledge of it, the subject will never experience wonder at the object again. Understood from another angle, wonder provides an experience not only of knowledge refinement and emotional habituation but also of memory building: to see something you have never seen before and experience it as wonderful is to see something that you will never forget. As Descartes puts it in *The Passions of the Soul*, "those who have no natural inclination to this passion are usually very ignorant."[105] This is because "it can be said in particular of Wonder that it is useful in making us learn and retain in our memory the things of which we were previously ignorant."[106]

It remains to consider what it means, for Descartes, to retain things in memory. Descartes distinguishes between "intellectual" memory and "corporal" memory, but again this distinction finally collapses, since the former, too, enlists the body in its working. Intellectual memory is literally a calling-to-mind of the appropriate image, and the mind is accordingly essential to its functioning: when I remember a particularly joyous thing, my mind incites an image of it, a representation. But the form that this image takes—animal spirits conveyed through the brain—reminds us that the body is equally essential. In an era of representation, we recall, objects in the world are subordinated to the signs that effect their visual perception. Similarly, memory is constituted by the patterns of animal spirits that signify it, and for this reason memory requires the body. Descartes first established his theory of memory in the mechanistic *L'homme* (*Treatise on Man*), written in the early 1630s and published posthumously. In it he established that animal spirits leave a trace on the surface of the pineal gland, just as he would later describe in his definition of wonder. In *Treatise on Man*, Descartes likened this trace to the holes left in a cloth after needles have passed through it;[107] in letters to Marin Mersenne, he likened it to the fold that remains in a paper after it has been unfolded, a *pli de mémoire*.[108] When we recollect a thing, the traces help the animal spirits to create an image and convey it, as Descartes describes in *The Passions of the Soul*:

When the soul wills to remember something, this volition makes the gland, inclining successively to different sides, drive the spirits toward different places in the brain, until they come upon the one where the traces [*traces*] are which the object we will to remember has left there. These traces are nothing but this: the pores of the brain through which the spirits have previously made their way because of the presence of this object have thereby acquired a greater facility than the others for being opened again in the same way by spirits approaching them.[109]

Significantly, the pores through which the animal spirits move during the remembrance are widened by their motion. Thus, the memory changes. Bodily matter alters. As the French say, we have a *mémoire du corps*, and this is no less true of intellectual than corporal memory.[110] Of the latter, Descartes explained in a letter to Mersenne that "a lute player has part of his memory in his hands; for the ease of bending and positioning his fingers in various ways, which he has acquired with practice [*habitude*], helps him to remember the passages for which he needs these positions."[111] The more the lute player plays, the better his playing; and this improvement is a function of memory. Such memory acquisition by practice works in the theater as well. The actors' emotional responses, conveyed through their bodies by the animal spirits, habituate them to emotional stimuli, but their memory of these responses strengthens and transforms them. The same holds true for spectators' emotional responses.

If the memories of past performances—not only from rehearsal but also from lived experience—are stamped into a performer's body, they are also indelibly colored by his or her unique emotional habits. As Descartes once wrote to Mersenne, "the same thing that makes some want to dance may make others want to cry."[112] The conception of stage acting that might result from such an understanding of emotion and memory differs markedly from our usual associations of mid-seventeenth-century stage acting, all conventionalized gestures and postures unanchored to a notion of interiority. As I explore in Chapter 3, Cartesian ideas did give rise to a different style of a playing—a *jeu naturel* promoted by Molière—that grounded the actor's performance in his or her own subjective experience of the world. Indeed, the shifting denotations of the word *acteur* are telling: at the beginning of the century the word meant "role," but by the end it had come to signify *comédien* or "actor." The denotative displacement of *comédien* (with its emphasis on the play) by *acteur* (with its emphasis on the player) is resonant, emerging with appropriate simultaneity alongside new theoretical reflections on the art of acting.[113] However, the epistemological anxieties of the Cartesian era, and the antitheatrical anxieties so culturally potent in it, encouraged a countermovement spawned by Charles Le Brun's Cartesian *Conférence sur l'expression générale et particulière* (*Conference on General and Particular Expression*), which sought to recodify and reconventionalize such "natural" acting.[114] In any case the implication of Descartes's lute player remains clear. Performance involves memory, whether we think of an actor remembering lines or a musician remembering notes. But so, too, whether for music, stage acting, or spectatorship, does memory involve performance. Each performance, we might say, contains and revises all the past performances whose physical effects on the body determine it. In *Cities of the Dead* Joseph Roach claims that performances "often carry within them the memory of otherwise forgotten substitutions."[115] Meant figuratively, Roach's account literally describes not only the theoretical structure but also the physiological workings of memory for Descartes. In each reperformed action we animate our traces and surrogate ourselves.

Note that this account rejects an archival model of memory, one that holds it as a past-tense repository of things that have happened. Rather, Descartes's understanding resonates with the repertory. Memory is a present-tense experience animated by the traces of past performances. As a performative act, a recollection of an event unfolds differently each and every time, as the animal spirits that represent and constitute the memory are canalized through the body and the brain. We find, perhaps to our surprise, that for Descartes memory is coterminous with history: a physical aggregate of all that has come before. The eighteenth entrée of *The Birth of Peace*, the dance of Janus, embodies this idea by mobilizing the image of the god's double face. Janus's temple doors were said to be open only in times of war. Here, representing the slim limen between past and future, Janus dances in celebration of the peace that has arrived for the foreseeable time ahead, as signified by the forward-looking face of his mask. But his celebration is necessarily tempered by that which he cannot forget and which he carries with him as he dances, as marked in the backward-looking face. It represents all the strife and turmoil of the ballet's first act: all that has passed (*Toute la vie precedente*) and the memory of what has ceased to be (*le souvenir / Des choses qui ont cessé d'estre*).[116] In this way Janus can be seen to stand for a paradox that Timothy Reiss has identified: while situating himself as the beginning of a new history, Descartes nonetheless carried with him the legacy of three decades of war.[117] We learn that to unite mind with body, for Descartes, is to complicate and enrich a new abstraction—pure thought—with the sometimes terrifying (but sometimes joyful) matter of history, of experience.

As we see clearly in readings of Descartes that perseverate on dualism, too often this evidence of the body is lost when performance disappears: the archival traces that philosophy leaves—treatises, commentary, letters— threaten to privilege thought or mind over the experience that the living body has registered and retained. In what follows I turn to theater history, which can be read as an embodied history of ideas, as a union of mind and body, of conceptual ideas and material expression. Trying to activate the theater's *mémoire du corps*, I scrutinize its corpus and look for the Cartesian traces it has left behind. These *plis de mémoire* may supplement the philosophical record and encourage a different view of Descartes and his legacy; tracing them, we might enliven our understanding of Cartesian mind-body union, of the passionate interactions that bind the mental to the material. These passionate interactions, in turn, animated various paradigm shifts in theater history after Descartes, which, seen in a different light, might testify to his largely forgotten impact on playwriting, acting, and theater design— principal subjects of the next three chapters.

2

Cartesian Plots, Dramatic Theory, and Emotional Wonder

In one of the engravings that illustrate his 1690 *Le cabinet des beaux arts* (The cabinet of fine arts; Figure 2.1), Charles Perrault—the multitasking writer, editor, court administrator, amateur architect, and avid accumulator of Royal Academy posts[1]—represents the figure of Poetry in repose, a smile passing over her lips at the pleasant thought she is about to apprehend (as Perrault's accompanying commentary clarifies).[2] Her laurel crown represents the "glorious Immortality" she confers on deserving verse, and which he subtly associates with heaven, where she directs her gaze; for posterity after death, Perrault claims, will reveal the deserving poets.[3] To her right are three children who represent the three principal genres of poetry—heroic, lyric, pastoral—and to her left sits a fourth, whose eyes address the viewer and who offers a taste of immortal poetry in a collection of plays by Molière, then dead almost two decades; it is the only book whose contents are visible and the only book oriented outward toward us.[4] (Two of the plays listed—*The Ridiculous Young Ladies* and *The Miser*—are in fact written in prose, but Perrault was always among the least pedantic of the academicians.) This smallest child's mask, we are told, represents the "ingenious fictions" with which Poetry dresses the truths—"of nature or of morality"—which she regards as the "finest and noblest part[s] of her creations."[5] As the foregrounding of Molière's book in the tableau attests, Perrault accords a special place to drama, since it

FIGURE 2.1. *La poésie.* The image appears as a plate between pages 15 and 16 of Charles Perrault, *Le cabinet des beaux arts* (Paris: Gérard Edelinck, 1690), whose engravings represent paintings planned for Perrault's own residence—paintings that allegorically celebrated the supremacy of the French (and modern) fine arts. Courtesy Print Collection, Miriam and Ira D. Wallach Division of Art, Prints, and Photographs, New York Public Library, Astor, Lenox, and Tilden Foundations.

has brought Poetry, through the applause that it inspires, "the greatest honor" of all her works.[6] "It is also the genre in which the French most surpass Poets of other nations," he continues, and, indeed, of "all the previous centuries," including classical antiquity.[7] In light of drama's special place, the recessed space at the engraving's upper left corner represents a play that has "always been considered a masterpiece": *Cinna, ou La clémence d'Auguste* by Pierre Corneille, dead since 1684 but, like Molière, already considered immortal.[8] Perrault chooses the "exceedingly recognizable" (*extremement reconnoissable*) scene for which the play (he claims) is best remembered: the fifth-act confrontation between the reluctant assassin Cinna and his target, Auguste, whose remarkable act of clemency gives the play its subtitle and inspired—on the report of Corneille and contemporary critics—its audiences' experiences of catharsis.

Corneille had theorized and repeatedly employed such a catharsis of wonder—the French word is *admiration*—privileging it over an Aristotelian catharsis of pity and fear and thereby risking the rebuke of the Académie française, fixated as it was on classical formulae in the decades before Perrault's groundbreaking defense of "modern" writers. (Perrault's 1690 remarks continued the so-called quarrel of the Ancients and Moderns that he had himself ignited, three years earlier, with his poem "Le siècle de Louis le Grand" [The century of Louis the Great] and its taboo criticism of classical writers.)[9] In his renovation of catharsis, we will see, Corneille brought tragic form in line with Cartesian physiology, which had introduced wonder into the pantheon of emotion—it is absent from classical taxonomies such as those in Aristotle's *Rhetoric* or Plato's *Republic*[10]—and, indeed, privileged it as "the first of all passions."[11] By similarly reconfiguring the emotional experience of tragic spectatorship, Corneille thus sought to reveal a precise truth of nature (and, indeed, morality) by means of the "ingenious fiction" of his plays. And, for this reason, among others, the playwright came to claim the immortal place in history that Perrault's Poetry confers on the "Heroes" whose literary output she inspires.[12]

Although ten years younger than Descartes, Corneille published his work first and made a cultural impact earlier. Almost a decade before the philosopher's first appearance in print, for example, the playwright had shown his flair for comic writing in plays such as *Mélite*, which premiered in Paris in December 1629 or January 1630.[13] He made his debut as a tragedian in 1635 with *Médée*, in which Princess Elisabeth of Bohemia would later act in a private performance to entertain her mother, the exiled Winter Queen of Bohemia.[14] In January 1637 his *Le Cid* secured its place in the histories of theater practice and dramatic theory for reasons beyond its gripping dramatic (and unprecedented commercial) success.[15] For example, the play's debut staging at the Théâtre du Marais inaugurated the fashion for seating spectators onstage, a practice (seen in Perrault's engraving) that conditioned French theatrical history well into the eighteenth century and whose impacts I explore in Chapter 4.[16] Too, the play's mixture of comic and tragic modes, as well as its movement between settings, provoked the ire of the playwright's powerful erstwhile patron, Cardinal Richelieu, leading directly to the imposition of the *règles* or rules—outlined in *Les*

sentiments de l'Académie française sur la tragi-comédie du Cid (The sentiments of the French Academy on the tragicomedy of *Le Cid*)—that would
come to define neoclassicism.[17]

The controversy over *Le Cid* continued for more than a year, generating numerous polemical pamphlets and occasioning Corneille's first hiatus
from playwriting. This period of public chastisement therefore coincided
with the publication of Descartes's gauntlet-throwing debut, *Discourse on
Method*, in which he first articulated Cartesian skepticism, repudiated classical wisdom, and grounded both knowledge and being in the reason of
the subjective "I"—as succinctly captured in the book's most-quoted line:
"I think, therefore I am" (*ie pense, donc ie suis*).[18] The formulation anticipated Corneille's return to the theater, two years later, with *Cinna*, which
climaxes in Auguste's fifth-act declaration, "I am master of myself as of the
universe"—a line that would seem explicitly to declare his, and Corneille's,
Cartesianism.[19] Indeed, the conceptual consonance between Corneille's
post–*Le Cid* plays and the work of his (similarly Jesuit-schooled) contemporary Descartes is by now axiomatic, traced in various ways by various
critics, including, most influentially, Paul Bénichou, Ernst Cassirer, and
Gustave Lanson.[20] Yet *Cinna* inaugurated a series of plays ostensibly written
in deference to Richelieu—among them *Polyeucte* (1642), *Rodogune* (1644),
and *Nicomède* (1651)—all of which abide by the classical unities on which
the academicians perseverated. In this way *Cinna* testifies to the intense
cross-pressures to which Corneille and all French dramatists of the mid-
seventeenth century were subjected. On one hand, they were compelled to
comply with the strictures of classical tragedy in order to be produced; on
the other hand, these strictures suited ill the cultural imperatives—and, in
particular, the emotional imperatives—of their day, so well characterized
and fomented by Descartes's writings.

We see these cross-pressures vividly in Corneille's three discourses
on dramatic poetry, which he published in his three-volume *Le theatre
[sic] de P. Corneille* in 1660 and in which he takes pains to set his dramatic
practice in a classical, Aristotelian frame, as demanded by Richelieu and
the academy in the decades before Perrault's election. For example, in the
second discourse—the "Discours de la tragédie" (Discourse on tragedy)—
the playwright follows the *Poetics* in dutifully explaining the purpose of
tragedy as the catharsis of an audience's collective emotions:

Pity for a misfortune into which we see those similar to us fall brings us to fear the same happening to us; this fear, to a desire to avoid it; and this desire, [brings us] to purge, moderate, rectify, and even uproot in ourselves the emotion, which, before our eyes, plunges persons that we pity into misfortune: for this simple reason, natural and indubitable, for to avoid the effect it is necessary to remove the cause.[21]

Pity and fear, the "Discourse on Tragedy" explains, make for gripping drama, as Corneille cheekily illustrates in a reading of the purportedly unclassical *Le Cid*.[22] But the playwright also reveals his doubt about many aspects of Aristotelian theory, including the idea that the emotional (and dramaturgical) mechanism he describes is possible. "If the purgation of the passions happens in tragedy, I hold that it ought to happen in the manner that I have explained," Corneille claims, "but I doubt that it ever happens, even in those tragedies that meet the conditions demanded by Aristotle."[23] Justifying his doubt after weighing Aristotle's examples—Oedipus and Thyestes—Corneille wonders whether the tragic effect is merely an unrealizable ideal, a beautiful theoretical idea that is never effected in practice,[24] before betraying his own, quintessentially modern skepticism: he summarily declares of Aristotle that he "does not understand his thinking at all."[25] In this inability to understand, Corneille confronts the fundamental dissonance produced by the cross-pressures on his era's dramatic practice: the fact that the classical theory of tragedy conceptually relies on a universally shared experience of pity and fear for its audience, while the nascent, modern understanding of subjectivity fundamentally disavows this possibility because of the individualistic nature of the emotions.

Corneille notes that to facilitate tragic catharsis, a playwright must "choose the characters and the events" which can "excite" the necessary emotions.[26] In this chapter I explore the impact of a new, Cartesian paradigm of emotion on these choices—in other words, on dramatic plotting—by demonstrating one way that late seventeenth-century tragic form, in theory classically derived, was brought into line with a philosophy of emotion that, in practice, rendered the classical ideal untenable. Central to this realignment was the eventual abandonment of pity and fear, the emotional bedrock of Aristotelian theory, in favor of wonder. (The French word, *admiration*, preserves the dual emphasis of the Latin *admiratio* that has receded in present-day English: it denotes both reverence and surprise.) The most successful playwright of his day, Corneille was central to this abandonment, ushering in a fundamentally Cartesian form of tragedy that reconceived the emotional experience of playgoing in order to bridge, as Descartes's late writings had bridged, the gulf between individual and community, between lone spectator and collective audience. At the same time, Corneille disseminated this form to playwrights in other languages and from different national contexts: the plays and dramatic theory of John Dryden, for example, testify to the influence of Corneille's Cartesian inflections in England.

Nicomède, Hôtel de Bourgogne, February 1651

Corneille's *Nicomède* was written for the troupe installed at the Hôtel de Bourgogne, whose architecture I consider in Chapter 4. The play, which concerns twinned crises in the kingdom of Bithynia in the second century BCE—one of succession and the other of public confidence in the king—has been read as a reflection of the Fronde, the series of civil wars that rocked France during the minority of Louis XIV and whose perturbations were particularly acute at the time. Certainly the play's hero bears an uncomfortable resemblance to Louis II of Bourbon, the Prince of Condé, who had been imprisoned in January 1650 by Cardinal Mazarin and the Queen Regent, Anne of Austria, and only released around the time of the play's premiere, in February 1651.[27] But in addition to political disturbances, the play also reflects the cultural disturbances of its time. For example, while seeming to adhere to the classical genre restrictions enforced by the academy, it is animated by a Cartesian skepticism toward precisely this putatively neoclassical tradition. Indeed, the play can be read as thematizing these competing obligations. Enacting them, it ultimately performs their reconciliation just as its hero, the Cartesian prince Nicomède, ultimately finds harmony with his family: his father, King Prusias; his powerful stepmother, Arsinoé; and his younger half-brother, Attale.

It is no accident that Corneille's Arsinoé has had Attale educated in Rome or that this education has left him—in the assessment of Nicomède's fiancée, the like-minded Armenian queen Laodice—a "slave" who superstitiously "trembles to see an eagle."[28] For the play's principal agon opposes the family, associated with classical Rome, to the sui generis prince of the title. In stark contrast to them, Nicomède repeatedly abjures strategic plotting in favor of rational action. For example, considering Attale's claim on the kingdom, Nicomède proposes that an empirical test be used to determine succession:

> I wish to put aside, with the title of first-born,
> The rank of lordship I was to have over you,
> And we will see which lessons make a better man,
> Those of Hannibal or those of Rome.[29]

Refusing his rights, Nicomède shows his typical disregard for the customs and conventions of tradition. These he associates with Rome, whose sway is embodied in Arsinoé's co-plotter, the Roman ambassador Flaminius. The association is resonant. In the play's denouement Bithynia will assert itself as independent from Rome as Nicomède and a thoroughly transformed Attale come to power. Concomitantly, even as Corneille preserves the unities of time, place, and situation, he will end his flirtation with genre conventions, freighted as they are with classical baggage: a tragic conclusion is diverted, and the classical sources are ignored,[30] as Nicomède bestows forgiveness on his family. In both plot and structure, then, and for both its hero and author, the play marries its interest in the Cartesian subject to a repudiation of classical Rome—and, we might say, to a repudiation of the academy's backward-looking ethos. Nicomède concludes the speech in which he forgoes the rights of primogeniture by telling Attale, with clear Cartesian echoes, "Adieu, ponder this well, I leave you to meditate on it."[31]

Corneille thus distinguishes his inward-looking Nicomède as a new kind of tragic hero, as the playwright boasted in his critical writings. "This hero of mine deviates somewhat from the rules of tragedy," he wrote in the prefatory "Au lecteur" in the play's first published edition, adding (in a gesture of Nicomedean understatement) that "it is good to risk slightly and not attach oneself too slavishly to his [i.e., Aristotle's] precepts."[32] Nine years later, in the "Discourse on Tragedy," Corneille would continue this line of defense, describing how he had loosened Aristotle's constraints on the exemplary hero, which he faults for excluding characters outstanding in virtue.[33] Nicomède, by contrast to Aristotle's heroic examples, is a paragon. Faced with Arsinoé's schemes to ruin him, Attale's usurping

moves on both his throne and his beloved, and the vacillations of Prusias (who alternately lauds and imprisons him), Nicomède responds with
understanding, demonstrating the *générosité*—a word that denotes both
emotional magnanimity and rational noble-mindedness—that Descartes
had described two years earlier in *The Passions of the Soul.* In their explora-
tions of Corneille's philosophical consonance with Descartes, critics have
demonstrated that the prince is the embodiment of such *générosité*, a figure drawn with clear if not self-conscious parallels to Descartes's writings.
So axiomatic is this understanding that a text such as V. L. Saulnier's *La
littérature française du siècle classique* can claim that "Corneille brought
Descartes's *généreux* to life."[34]

In his treatise on the passions Descartes had written that *générosité*
inheres

partly in [a subject's] understanding that there is nothing which truly belongs
to him but this free control of his volitions, and no reason why he ought to be
praised or blamed except that he uses [them] well or badly; and partly in his
feeling within himself a firm and constant resolution to use [them] well, that is,
never to lack the volition to undertake and execute all the things he judges to be
best—which is to follow virtue perfectly.[35]

"Esteeming only very little all things that depend on others," the *généreux*
is thus in harmony with the new paradigm of subjectivity described in and
engendered by Descartes's earlier writings, what scholars have considered
the modern subject.[36] Dalia Judovitz, for example, has shown how closely
Descartes's contribution to modern philosophy—his pursuit of truth as
certainty and his disavowal of all received wisdom that "depends on others"—is imbricated with his idea of the empirical subject, the individual
"I" that governs the *Meditations*.[37] As Descartes describes in the second
of these *Meditations*, the existence of the "I" originates in its own essential capacity for thought. In *The Passions of the Soul*, however, Descartes
yokes reason to the emotions and specifically to the emotional magnanimity that governs the generous subject's interactions with others. As
he explains, "because they esteem nothing more highly than doing good
to other men and for this reason scorning their own interest," those who
are generous "are always perfectly courteous, affable, and of service to
everyone."[38] We are thus reminded that, while he claimed to write his
treatise as a scientist and not a moral philosopher, Descartes inextricably

tied the mechanics of emotion to a broader moral vision.[39] This reminder suffuses his correspondence with Elisabeth, with whom the discussion roamed freely from personal anecdotes, as they reported on their lives' events, to the science of emotion, and to discussions of the good—that is, ethical—life. If Descartes's early writings had sundered subject from object, his late writings bridged the gulfs that this and other dualisms had created: between body and mind and between the individual and the community within which his or her actions signify virtue or its absence. Traversing these bridges, Corneille could alleviate the cross-pressures that troubled his cultural moment and reconcile his reading of Aristotle with the nascent Cartesianism of his day. He could conceive of a collective dramatic catharsis as demanded by neoclassicism even from within a modern worldview defined by its radically individualized subjects.

After all, *Nicomède*'s dramatic arc involves not a change in its steadfastly generous hero but a transformation of those around him, especially Attale and Prusias, who eventually find themselves situated between stepson and stepmother, or between "generosity" and "hatred" as Corneille succinctly puts it.[40] When Laodice notes, in the play's opening moments, that the king sees only through Arsinoé's eyes, she recognizes that Prusias mistakes his subjective perception for an objective viewpoint, thus limning the Cartesian connection between vision and perception that I examine in Chapter 4.[41] It is not that Prusias must learn to see *what* Nicomède sees; rather, he must learn to see *how* Nicomède sees. The father must adopt a skepticism about what seems to be. He must ignore the intense pressures—applied, and paralleled, with good rhetoric—of both the queen and Flaminius. In other words Prusias must be taught to forgo convention in favor of reason: to be true to his own natural (and royal) self. In a revealing exchange, the king—weighed down by advice from various quarters, and bemoaning his competing obligations as husband and father—demands existential counsel of Nicomède. "What should I be?" he asks. Cutting his father off, Nicomède ends the alexandrine, fittingly rhyming *moi* with a single blunt syllable: *Roi*.[42] He ties the demands of statehood explicitly to the king as a discrete subject. In this way Nicomède's counsel prefigures the move of Louis XIV, who a decade later would quell political discord in his country precisely with a bold assertion of self: his centralization of power in his own hands, captured in the apocryphal maxim *l'État, c'est moi* (I am the State).

Nicomède himself notes that "wonder [*admiration*] at ideal men / Is no great virtue if one doesn't imitate them."[43] And, appropriately, the "Discourse on Tragedy" stresses his filial role and connection to Prusias.[44] Manifesting the son's positive effects in the behavior of the father, *générosité* bridges the play's heroic subject to its emotional objects, who are themselves recognized as rational agents. Indeed, the play highlights not only their reason but also its potential to harness the passions' benefits. It does so especially in the figure of the young Attale, similarly transformed by his brother's love and example. When Nicomède is imprisoned and Attale's succession secured, the younger brother effects the older brother's liberation in a surprising about-face. "This is no more the ambitious slave of Rome," Nicomède adjudges:

> This is the liberator of a precious blood.
> Brother, with my chains you have broken others,
> Those of the King, of the Queen . . . and your own.[45]

The declaration encapsulates a paradox of Cartesianism central to this book. Nicomède stresses the separation of the play's emotional subjects, who are released from the chains that bind them; he nominates them as discrete individuals whose separateness makes possible their rational actualization—like Descartes himself, alone in his stove-heated room at the beginning of the *Discourse on Method*. But by simultaneously emphasizing Attale's role in this independence, Nicomède (like Corneille) showcases the radiating effects of *générosité*, which serve precisely to connect subjects and to traverse the boundaries between them.

A remarkable epistle to Elisabeth accentuates this underemphasized element of Descartes's thought. On September 30, 1645, the princess wrote to complain that her move from The Hague to Rijswijk had exposed her to more social obligations, which eroded her time for solitary study.[46] Descartes's reply, written a week later, surprises. "If we think only of ourselves," he cautions, "we can enjoy only the benefits that are particular to us; whereas if we consider ourselves as a part of some other body, we also share in the benefits held in common, without being deprived of any that are particular to us."[47] The interconnections of the subject are here represented as literally breaching the boundaries of the body, whose beneficial effects can be shared, he asserts, without being dissipated.

Générosité represents just such emotional plenitude, for it works not only in the generous subject but also on those with whom he or she interacts. It serves to temper the disordering passions of the soul, especially anger, while fomenting the benevolent effects of the body's emotional movements.[48] These effects condition the body to love what is beneficial to it in a kind of emotional exercise that Descartes likened, in another letter to Elisabeth, to physical activity such as "hunting, tennis, and suchlike."[49] And thus *générosité* foregrounds the interconnectedness of passion and reason, for the movements of the former might condition and fortify the latter. This interconnectedness—which Descartes's letters to Elisabeth describe and the ballet *The Birth of Peace* had performed—is neatly allegorized in the startling rapprochement between Nicomède and Arsinoé. The queen had schemed to remove her stepson from his father's favor, paying traitorous soldiers to slander Nicomède and thus evidencing the capacity for hypertheatrical dissemblance with which Corneille signifies her ruthlessness:

> I thought it best
> That he [Nicomède] be lured from his fortress to this region.
> Métrobate brought it about by Panic Terror [*des terreurs Paniques*].
> Pretending to betray to him my tyrannical orders,
> And saying that he had been suborned to murder Nicomède,
> He has (thanks to the gods) brought him here for me.
> He comes to complain to the King, and to demand justice from him,
> And this complaint hurls him to the precipice:
> Without taking any care to justify myself,
> I will know how to strengthen my position.
> As soon as I saw him I acted terrified,
> I changed color, I cried out;
> He thought to surprise me, and he thought that in vain,
> Since his very return is my handiwork.[50]

Nicomède, she wagers, is fooled by her performance since it is in keeping with her emotional nature. Plotting to trick him, however, Arsinoé fails—not because she is outmaneuvered by a superior strategist or rhetorician but precisely because she is mired in old emotional and tragic paradigms.

Thus, she misreads Nicomède's every move, presuming wrongly that she can mobilize Panic Terror (personifying it just as *The Birth of Peace* had done) and presuming wrongly that Nicomède is "driven by his thirst for revenge."[51] The hero cannot be baited, but not because he lacks emotions: indeed, the play accentuates his capacity for emotional engagement in its opening exchange between him and his fiancée, who thus fulfills her primary plot function. (Tellingly, Laodice is the only character Corneille invented from whole cloth.) Rather, Nicomède conforms to Descartes's model of generous subjects who, the philosopher claimed, are "entirely masters of their passions."[52] The prince demonstrates Descartes's theory that, harnessed to a strong soul, the passions work only to the benefit of the subject and those around him.

Thus Arsinoé feels the effects of Nicomède's unexpected magnanimity, as she herself testifies:

> Sir, must you push your victory so far,
> And having in your hands my life and my honor,
> Does the ambition of such a powerful conqueror
> Wish also to triumph in my heart?
> Against so much virtue I cannot defend it;
> It is itself impatient to surrender.[53]

Corneille cleverly deploys Arsinoé's usual rhetoric—of battle, of strategy—but he subverts it, too, for now she knows that her emotional capitulation represents no loss. Rather, she gains the emotional benefit of the stepson standing before her—benefits now held in common, to paraphrase Descartes's letter. The play's ending thus works to demonstrate onstage the very emotional phenomenon that the playwright claims for it offstage, in which an emotional stimulus effects the emotional transformation of those who regard it: catharsis. Another of Richelieu's theoreticians, Jules de La Mesnardière, had written in *La Poëtique* that "tragedy proposes as its aim the tranquility of the soul, since its principal purpose is to calm the passions."[54] In the process of redeeming his theater for Richelieu's academy, Corneille also redeems Aristotle for Descartes—for whom *calm* might be substituted by *refine*. Corneille's "Discourse on Tragedy" describes the nagging deficiencies of pity and fear, but in spite of them catharsis could be rehabilitated thanks to an emotional understanding that (Corneille correctly assesses) Aristotle "could perhaps not have fore-seen."[55] For the crux of *Nicomède*'s novelty, as Corneille identifies it in the 1651 "Au lecteur," is the fact that it "excites only wonder [*admiration*] in the spectator's soul."[56]

Pity and fear, Corneille conceded, could dramatically stir and emo-tionally affect audiences. Descartes and Elisabeth, too, testified to the pleasures of such negative emotions in tragic spectatorship. In an October 28, 1645, letter, for example, Elisabeth noted to her friend that

we naturally love to be moved [*emeus*, i.e., *ému*] by them [i.e., the passions] and to follow their movements; only the inconveniences proceeding from this path teach us that they can be harmful. And this, in judgment, is what makes trag-edies more pleasing the more they excite sadness, because we understand that it will not be violent enough to carry us to extravagances nor lasting enough to cor-rupt our health.[57]

Descartes's agreement is clear in the earlier letter from that month in which he compared emotional and physical exercise; the latter, he declares, demonstrates that even "fatigue and difficulty augment pleasure."[58] If the embodied subject experiences "contentment" when "crying while seeing some pitiable or disastrous action represented on the stage," the reaction derives from recognizing the soul's workings: the contentment "comes principally from its seeming to perform a virtuous action in having com-passion for the afflicted."[59] Therefore, the pleasure of tragedy resides partly in its capacity to incite sadness: just as exertion (such as "hunting, tennis, and suchlike") muscularly conditions the body that acts, so might the pas-sions that act upon the body exercise the soul, whose pleasure in the emo-tion "is not inseparable from the gaiety and ease of the body" that experi-ences it.[60] Indeed, this pleasure, Descartes claims, constitutes "true hap-piness" (*béatitude*)—a theory that he would formalize in *The Passions of the Soul*, in an article obviously inspired by this exchange with Elisabeth. There, he writes that

when we read of unusual adventures in a book or see them represented on a stage, this sometimes excites Sadness in us, sometimes Joy or Love or Hatred, and in general all the Passions, according to the diversity of the objects offered to our imagination; but along with this we have the pleasure of feeling them excited in us, and this pleasure is an intellectual Joy, which can originate from Sadness as well as from any of the other Passions.[61]

We can tie this article, which appears toward the end of the treatise's second part, to the definition of *générosité* that appears a few pages later, in the third. *Générosité* provides the model for how a spectator should react to theatrical events: with an emotional openness, but also with his or her emotions tethered to the guiding reins of reason.

As *Nicomède*'s heterogeneous cast of characters makes plain, however, not everyone is a *généreux*. Therefore, Corneille's 1660 confusion in the face of pity and fear—his sense that it had become difficult to imagine a purgation of the passions by means of these emotions—is telling.[62] For Descartes also argued, in ways that his culture would come to find persuasive, that these emotions could cause disordering effects. As Jean Émelina has noted, the diverse, subjectively determined physical reactions to these emotions would seem to engender "confusion and deviation" instead of the communal harmony we associate with catharsis.[63] Conceptually, the theory of tragedy offered in Aristotle's *Poetics* relies on the possibility of a universally shared experience of pity and fear for its audience. Yet the Cartesian model of emotion fundamentally disavows this possibility because of the individualistic nature of these emotions. It is true, as Corneille claims, that an audience is composed of people "not so severely entrenched in absolute virtue that they are insusceptible to emotions."[64] But each person's emotion—indeed, each instance of each person's emotion—is different because of the body's evolution during its ongoing emotional conditioning. No person can have the same experience of pity or fear precisely because each person is as unique in his or her emotional disposition as in the body that shapes it—because, to put it in the terms explored in the previous chapter, each person's body is conditioned by a different accretion of memories. Thus, Descartes specifically stresses in *The Passions of the Soul* that the same stimulus may incite fear in one perceiver and its opposite in another: "The same impression that the presence of a frightful object forms on the [pineal] gland which causes fear in some men may excite courage and boldness in others. The reason for this is that all brains are not disposed in the same manner."[65] Unlike Aristotle, Descartes—and the dramatic theory that followed him—cannot presuppose a universally fearful object. The problem of subjectivity imposes itself.

The Greeks and many since, including Corneille, have assumed that the purpose of tragedy is to create a bond of commonality among its audience; in Descartes's time, for example, the Abbé d'Aubignac recognized this social potential in the first chapter of *La Pratique du théâtre* (The practice of theater), written at Richelieu's command.[66] But tragedy could hardly rely on inherently subjective experiences such as pity and fear to do so. The difficulties would be multiple. First, no stimulus could accurately be presumed to instill fear or pity in all spectators, with their radically different memories and self-representations. Second, weak-souled spectators—unlike those Descartes and Elisabeth presume in their October 1645 exchange of letters—would merely indulge in the emotional experience without engaging their self-understanding and thus refining it. In another letter to Elisabeth that I take up in the next chapter, Descartes worries that such a spectator could even damage her body, since the physiological transformations effected by emotion—as the animal spirits reshape the channels through which they pass—would be unmitigated by her soul, the site of her native reason. Deriving no knowledge from her experience, the spectator who "occupies herself only in considering objects of sadness and pity . . . represented before her in tragedies," would "move her imagination without affecting her understanding [*entendement*]."[67] Recall that, as Descartes had described them, both pity and fear are constituted by the awareness of a muscular reaction occurring in the body because of the movement of animal spirits. Without "understanding," these unavoidable movements would merely cause bodily perturbations that further constrain the rational workings of the subject. As Elisabeth highlighted, these movements could result in being carried to "extravagances" or in the "corruptions" of one's health.[68]

Nicomède sketches such disturbances at various times in its poetry, which moves moral agents out of their subject positions and makes them the objects of driving passions. It is Arsinoé's hatred, for example, that purchases her assassins.[69] It is Laodice's furious rage that, seizing her soul, defeats her respect and generosity (however briefly).[70] Even Nicomède, acknowledging that he had disobeyed the king in returning unbidden to Bithynia, understands his disobedience in these terms: "My love for you committed this offence," he claims.[71] By Cartesian emotional logic, for a playwright to move a spectator to pity and fear may be to move him or her to disorder, with no guarantee that he or she would experience the emotional refinement that, Descartes claims, is possible in all emotional experience. (Indeed, in this regard, fear might be particularly noxious: Descartes specifically emphasizes that it is never "commendable" or "useful" since it diminishes the subject's agency to resist the evils that are near. For this reason, perhaps, he and Elisabeth dwell on pity or sadness in their discussions of stage tragedy.[72] And for this reason, perhaps, Corneille finds martyrs to be exemplary heroes, since their pitiable misfortunes occur "through no fault of their own." They "give us nothing to fear.")[73] The vital role of the emotions in ethical life, after all, derives from their becoming aligned with the correct moral valences, as reason judges whether the emotional stimulus is beneficial or detrimental to the subject, and therefore whether it should be loved or hated. As Descartes explains in his treatise, the passions' utility consists "in their strengthening thoughts which it is good that the soul preserve and . . . causing them to endure in the soul" just as their harm derives from their "strengthening and preserving others it is not good to dwell upon."[74]

In light of these theoretical problems, Cornelian catharsis substitutes pity and fear (unreliably fomented, too subjectively experienced) with the only emotion, wonder, that can be conceived of as universal and that can serve precisely to encourage the feeler's agency. Whereas pitiable or fearful stimuli are unreliable because of the varied experience of spectators—and, attendant on this experience, their self-representations—wonder is by definition conditioned anew every time it is experienced. And, therefore, it is not prone to the problem of subjective memory: any stimulus that could not reliably induce this emotion in a heterogeneous crowd would be, ipso facto, unwondrous. Wonder, we recall, is by its nature novel and physiologically unperturbing:

When the first encounter with some object surprises us, and we judge it to be new, or very different from what we knew in the past or what we supposed it was going to be, this makes us wonder and be astonished at it. And since this can happen before we know in the least whether this object is suitable to us or not, it seems to me that Wonder [*Admiration*] is the first of all the passions. It has no opposite, because if the object presented has nothing in it that surprises us, we are not in the least moved by it and regard it without passion.[75]

The emotion is not constituted by a muscular response. Instead, the animal spirits form an indelible impression on the brain "to fortify and preserve" the impression of the object, "rare and consequently worthy of being considered"[76]—an image not haunted by its remembered predecessors. The response to this image is still subjectively determined, of course: all who feel wonder are compelled to engage reason in order to judge whether the wondrous stimulus is beneficial or detrimental; and, if the stimulus is beneficial, a subsequent encounter will cause joy, and love for the object will be habituated, while if the stimulus is detrimental, a subsequent encounter will cause sadness, and an aversion for the object will be habituated. But the stimulus, at least, is universal—wonder's essential nature exempting it from the vicissitudes of our wildly varying subjective memories. As evidenced by its unique failure to produce changes in the heart or the blood, wonder thus relates physiologically only with the brain; its primary purpose is knowledge of the wondrous stimulus.[77]

It is wonder that Nicomède inspires when he returns in the play's final scene, having escaped, with the disguised Attale's aid, from his Prusias-ordered imprisonment. Confronting his family, he declares (with a serendipitous Cartesian resonance): "I come as a good subject [*en bon Sujet*] to restore the peace / Which other interests have unreasonably disturbed."[78] It is clear that blame for the disorder lies partly with Prusias, whose vacillations have set no example for a restive populace, as the play's 1660 frontispiece demonstrates (Figure 2.2). Outraged by the prince's unjust imprisonment, the bodies of Prusias's subjects are disordered, a disorder mirrored in the posture of a king who has yet to exercise his reason. Corneille describes the crowd as "émeuë" (*ému*)[79]—Elisabeth's word, too, and a word that beautifully captures the relationship between emotion and disorder, denoting as it does both "moved" and "riotous." The emotional movements of the crowd, unharnessed to understanding, have violently carried them to "extravagances," as Elisabeth would have it.

Nicomède, however, not only instills but embodies wonder, the only emotion that causes no physiological perturbation. Thus he subverts genre expectations by forgiving his father, Prusias, rather than killing him: "I removed from my scene the horror of [this] catastrophe," Corneille writes.[80] For, in contrast to his father, he is the paradigmatic reasonable subject—as he demonstrates in both his plea for forgiveness on behalf of the revolting citizens and in his bestowal of forgiveness on his once-wicked stepmother. "Pardon the people's fervor, / Which aroused their compassion for my misfortune," he requests of his father before telling

FIGURE 2.2. In the 1660 frontispiece to *Nicomède*, the disordered bodies of Prusias's subjects mirror the posture of their ruler. The composition reminds us of the onstage spectators at the Hôtel de Bourgogne, who would have looked, too, at the king. From Pierre Corneille, *Le theatre [sic] de P. Corneille, reveu & corrigé par l'autheur*, 3 vols. (Paris: Guillaume de Luyne, 1660), 3:362. Courtesy New York Public Library.

Arsinoé, "I know the reasons you were so hostile to me: / Your maternal love wished to see my brother reign."[81] As maternal love had led to disturbance, so does wonder at the stepson's emotional generosity lead to peace, as Arsinoé comes to love instead of hate him. Her valuations are realigned to serve her own benefit, which Descartes described as the purpose of the emotions: love, for example, arouses desire for the things that stimulate them; Nicomède is no longer greeted with hatred, an emotion properly reserved to "repel the things that harm and can destroy" the subject.[82] For Descartes this realignment accompanies a physiological change—as Arsinoé suggests with her potent metaphor of her stepson "triumphing" in her heart. Likening her heart to the three territories Nicomède had conquered in his military service for his father, she declares: "Join this conquest to three conquered sceptres / And I will think that in you I have gained a second son."[83] At least one critic reads Arsinoé's final-act conversion as just another dissemblance.[84] The cynicism of such a reading, however, reveals it as a product of the twentieth century. Our faith in Descartes's rationalist project has wavered, but Corneille's did not. The calmness and reason that seize Arsinoé, however surprising, reflect the physics of wonder, whose bifurcated etymology, Erec R. Koch astutely reminds us, "includes marveling or wondering at and reflecting or mirroring back": *ad-miror.*[85]

In wonder's twin peculiarities—its essential novelty and failure to perturb the body—resides the utility for the spectator and, by extension, the tragic playwright. Its effect is calming, as the protesting crowds discover. Upon the prince's release, "all is tranquil. The first sight of [him] / Suddenly calmed the people."[86] And in this, too, they mimic their king, whose exposure to his son leads to emotional refinement (and concurrent moral improvement) and not, as the historical sources would have it, attempted filicide. The moment of disorder represented in the *Nicomède* frontispiece precedes the stillness and order that we see in the frontispiece for *Cinna,* in which the regarding subjects assume the pacific emotional demeanor of their—and the play's—generous hero, Auguste (Figure 2.3). Wonder has given way to knowledge and, concomitantly, love for the emperor who benefits his subjects. Put another way, wonder provides an experience of epistemological refinement and emotional habituation because it bypasses previous, subjective memories and begins a new set of

FIGURE 2.3. The contrasting frontispiece to Pierre Corneille, *Cinna, ou La clémence d'Auguste* (Rouen: Toussainct Quinet, 1643), ai^r. Courtesy Bibliothèque nationale de France.

associations with the wonder-inducing object, not previously seen but now never forgotten.

With the 1690 representation of Auguste and Cinna with which I opened this chapter, Charles Perrault reminds us that mid-seventeenth-century French public theaters sat some audience members on the stage: Perrault's upper-left-hand tableau shows more spectators than actors present (see Figure 2.1). And it is certain that, for the premiere of *Nicomède* at the Hôtel de Bourgogne, men would have cluttered the wings and breached the playing space. The onstage characters regarding Nicomède, in other words—Prusias, Arsinoé, Attale, even Flaminius—would have been visually paralleled with the group of onstage spectators similarly regarding him. Whatever Corneille's claims and those of his critics, it is impossible to know whether the spectators were similarly quelled: as I detail in Chapter 4, onstage audiences tended toward misbehavior. But moving outward from one set of subjects (his characters) to another (his audience), Corneille seeks to effect a response in his spectators similar to that effected in Nicomède's antagonists, whose passions are refined by means of catharsis: the love that wonder inspires in us, he asserts, gives us hatred for the contrary vice and the passionate upheaval it causes.[87] The "mind of the spectator"—as he explained in his third discourse, the "Discours des trois unités" (Discourse of the three unities)—is left "serene."[88] His 1660 "Examen" to *Nicomède* attests that through the emotion of wonder spectators apprehend the dangers of the emotions of cowardice and ingratitude. "The greatness of Nicomède's courage leaves us averse to cowardice," he writes, "and the enormous gratitude of Héraclius who risks his life for Martian, to whom he owes his, plunges us into the horrors of ingratitude."[89]

In *Nicomède* father, brother, stepmother, and crowd are transformed by emotion and not, it must be reiterated, rational persuasion. So, too, does Corneille make clear in the "Examen" that wonder is merely a catalyst for its audience and not itself pedagogical. Wonder at Nicomède "leaves us" (*nous laisse*) with an aversion to cowardice. Similarly, rather than representing the horrors of ingratitude, the playwright uses wonder in his 1647 *Héraclius* to "plunge us" (*nous jette*) into its dangers. Emotional wonder in these cases is a positive causal factor for moral improvement but neither a necessary nor a sufficient cause. Corneille's choice of verbs (*laisser, jeter*) thus forestalls the understanding that the spectator is didactically taught by the spectacle and, consequently, both expresses his faith in emotional wonder and distinguishes his view of catharsis from the moralist view claimed (probably disingenuously) by Racine, whose preface to *Phèdre* alleges that it intends not to arouse passions but rather to "visually present" them, "only to show all the disorder they create."[90] The moral improvement engendered by *Nicomède* in its spectators—as per academy stipulations[91]—is inextricably connected with, but merely facilitated by, emotional wonder. Thus Corneille's usage of the term *wonder* is consistent with that of Descartes, which Jean Émelina and Ferdinard Alquié both relate to the modern sense of "astonishment" (even if Descartes is careful to distinguish *admiration* from *étonnement*, which overwhelms the subject and leaves her "frozen like a statue").[92] Certainly Descartes's writings would hardly support a didactic use of the theater, since a spectator's response to the play would depend entirely upon her subjectivity.[93] Rather, Corneille like Descartes leverages the emotional power of things that seem to us "rare and extraordinary" (in the philosopher's terms) in the service of refined understanding.[94] The playwright thus anticipates eighteenth-century theorists of the sublime, who would discover in Longinus a way to validate the emotional response to art in much the same way that Italian critics had discovered such a basis in Aristotle three centuries earlier.

In this way Corneille discovered one (but by no means the only) solution to the cross-pressures of tragedy after Descartes, which needed to understand a collective of subjective perspectives (as demanded by Cartesianism) as a universal audience (as required by the genre). Corneille fully realized cathartic tragedy and established a new paradigm for the form, as Nicolas Boileau would later corroborate. One of Charles Perrault's adversaries in the quarrel of Ancients and Moderns, Boileau had once (in an unkind misformulation) criticized those who would stir the tragic spectator with cold reason (*froids raisonnemens*).[95] But he would later concede to Perrault that Corneille "gave rise to a new genre of tragedies unknown to Aristotle. . . . He never dreamed like poets of ancient tragedy to rouse pity and fear but rather to excite in the soul of the audience, through sublime thoughts and beautiful sentiments, a certain wonder [*admiration*], which many people, and the young above all, adapt to much better than the real tragic passions [of pity and fear]."[96] Note that Boileau represents the spectators as having a collective soul before the wondrous stimulus, which would be inconceivable before a fearful or pitiable stimulus, according to Descartes. Moving the audience members from emotion toward reason, the Cartesian hero brings them closer to self-knowledge, closer to the self. By its emotional workings, *générosité* begets further *générosité*—a word, and a concept, that encapsulates the intimate connection between reason and the passions, between the subject and others. In this way the tragic spectators, whose passions are raised by the play's twists but then quelled by their experience of wonder, are much like Arsinoé, who after four and a half acts of emotional upheaval is stricken with calm—the agitation in her heart subdued—in the wondrous glow of her stepson's unlikely forgiveness.

The Drama *Of Dramatick Poesie*, June 3, 1665

Wonder was not entirely new to discussions of tragedy. In the *Poetics* Aristotle had noted that plot events better invoke wonder (*thaumaston*) when they are "unexpectedly interconnected" as opposed to "accidentally and by chance." (He later notes that epic "has greater scope for the inexplicable, at which men marvel most" because the characters are not embodied as before a spectator. "The circumstances of the pursuit of Hector in the *Iliad* . . . would appear ridiculous on the stage," he observes, "but in the epic this incongruity goes unnoticed.")[97] So, too, can the related Latin concept of *admiratio* be traced, through Minturno, to Robortello and possibly earlier critics, as Martin Herrick demonstrated in a landmark essay.[98] But Corneille is correct to set himself starkly apart from his predecessors in dramatic theory and practice. Corneille understood wonder not as an ancillary dramatic effect but rather as the prime tragic emotion, whose power could be leveraged in a *tout court* reconceptualization of tragedy. Whereas Aristotle subordinated the arousal of wonder to the "complete action" of "such things as stir up pity and fear,"[99] Corneille, in the expanded "Examen" to *Nicomède* first published in 1660, boldly evaluated his new tragic model thus: "In the wonder [*admiration*] that we have for [Nicomède's] virtue, I find a way to purge the passions of which Aristotle did not speak, and which is perhaps more reliable than that which he prescribes for tragedy by means of pity and fear."[100] If Corneille's theory and practice could, for the first time, excise pity and fear and in their place elevate wonder, it is precisely because of the playwright's proximity to and consonance with Descartes, who had come to reconceptualize the concept of wonder in philosophy.

In his earliest published work Descartes had described wonder with some ambivalence. At the beginning of his *Météores* (*Meteorology*)—which he had offered, along with the *Dioptrics* and the *Géométrie* (*Geometry*) as samples of his philosophical method—Descartes had appealed to the reader's wonder by noting that the experience is induced by looking at the skies.[101] But by the end of the treatise he wishes it away. "I hope those who will have understood all that was said in this treatise will see nothing in the clouds of the future whose cause they cannot easily understand or that will give them grounds for wonder [*admiration*]," he concludes.[102] The eminent Descartes scholar Geneviève Rodis-Lewis notes that *Meteorology* was produced in an era whose theatrical output was dominated by the baroque machine play, which so frequently represented rainbows and other celestial marvels through its elaborate scenic effects.[103] And she thus inspires a potent analogy. Descartes abandoned his admiration for natural wonders—explained with patient application of his scientific method—as he came to redefine and elevate emotional wonder to "the first of all passions" in *The Passions of the Soul*. Similarly, the French theater eventually turned its attention from the astonishing spectacles of the *salles des machines*, which provided technical marvels for its audiences; instead, the appropriate cause for wonder became the metaphysical truths of good and evil—of living well and living badly—wrapped in ingenious fictions such as *Nicomède*, the play in which Corneille most fully realized his catharsis of wonder.[104]

In his philosophical dialogue *Inquisitio veritatis per lumen naturale* (*The Search for Truth by Means of the Natural Light*), discussed in my epilogue, the classical point of view is shown as one that suspects wonder: Descartes has the character Epistemon (a Scholastic foil to the Cartesian Eudoxus) fret about the beguiling force of "wonder [*admiratione*] at something unknown."[105] Early in the seventeenth century, the English stage, too, had tended to dramatize this old paradigm of wonder, in which it erodes reason instead of facilitating knowledge. See, for example, the song of Hymen in *As You Like It*, which exhorts the audience to "Feede your selues with questioning: / That reason, wonder may diminish," or Prospero's remark, in *The Tempest*, that the Italian lords "so much admire / That they deuoure their reason."[106] (Shakespeare here uses *wonder*'s English synonym, *admiration*, loaned, the *OED* tells us, from the French word used by Corneille and Descartes.) But the picture became more complicated after the restoration of Elisabeth of Bohemia's cousin Charles II, who spent much of his exile in Paris and was pivotal to the migration of French models into England, for the king's prevailing taste inevitably drove tastes more broadly. ("The Court," as John Dryden obsequiously noted, "is the best and surest judge of writing.")[107] On one hand, the wonders of the French machine play were directly imported, by Dryden and others, into theaters newly designed to realize them. Lincoln's Inn Fields Theatre, the Theatre Royal at Drury Lane, and others still to follow—with their deep stages, flying scenery, and perspectival stagecraft—could provide precisely the meteorological and other wonders that Prospero conjures but that audiences at technologically primitive theaters such as the Globe were made to imagine. On the other hand, Dryden began to follow Corneille in situating a different kind of wonder at the center of a new paradigm of heroic tragedy, one that worked to display and foment the sort of emotional generosity whose benefits *Nicomède* had showcased.

That the period in English theater was transitional—suspended between contradictory forces—is suggested by the June 3, 1665, snapshot provided (at least according to its conceit) by Dryden's *Of Dramatick Poesie, an Essay*. A closet drama like Descartes's *The Search for Truth*, Dryden's *Essay* claims to relate the dialogue performed on that date by four dramatic critics, pseudonymously called Eugenius, Crites, Lisideius, and Neander. The quartet floats on a barge in the Thames, not far from where the "vast floating bodies" of the English and Dutch navies contest the "command of the greater half of the Globe," and thus the unmoored nature of the English theater in 1665 is unsubtly highlighted.[108] In theory Dryden spends the *Essay* building a suitable foundation for an English dramatic theory and practice, implied by the retrospective publication of the dialogue three years later—after his success with the heroic tragedy *The Indian Emperour* and after England's attenuated victory over Holland. In practice, and specifically in Dryden's theatrical practice, matters were less resolved, as expressed in the curious mingling of different species of wonder, some

of which facilitate and some of which inhibit understanding: the mingling of "genuine admiration" and "blind wonderment," in the astute later
assessment of William Wordsworth.[109] *The Indian Emperour*, for example,
inserts its hero, Cortez, whose stolid magnanimity clearly owes a debt to
French tragedy of the midcentury, into spectacular (and frequently changing) settings meant to stupefy its audiences—from the Royal Chamber to
a "pleasant Grotto" with its "Fountain spouting."[110] In view of this con-
junction, "'tis an irregular piece if compar'd with many of *Corneilles*," as
Dryden concedes in the dedicatory letter.[111]

   Of Dramatick Poesie, an Essay was inspired by Corneille, too. This
inspiration seems paradoxical in light of the *Essay*'s apparent intent to
assert the supremacy of English over French writers, but Dryden's anxiety of influence is unmistakable.[112] In the words of one critic the *Essay*
must have been written "with a copy of the 1660 edition of Corneille's
plays . . . by his side."[113] The *Essay* directly quotes Corneille's discourses
seven times ("This Corneille calls," "Corneille says judiciously," "I will
alledge Corneille's words," etc.)[114] and invokes the playwright or his plays
as positive examples a further six times.[115] Other borrowings are stealthier,
as for example when Dryden addresses the unity of action and notes that
in Euripides's *The Suppliants*, "he has made *Theseus* go from *Athens* to
Thebes, which was about 40 English miles, under the walls of it to give
battel, and appear victorious in the next Act; and yet, from the time of
his departure to the return of the *Nuntius*, who gives the relation of his
Victory, *Æthra* and the Chorus have but 36 Verses; that is not for Mile a
Verse."[116] The analysis (even its sarcasm) is directly lifted from Corneille's
third discourse—Dryden's only amendment being the helpful linguistic
and metric translation of the French "twelve or fifteen leagues" (*douze ou
quinze lieues*) to "40 English miles."[117]

   While the *Essay*'s four diverse characters each assumes a different
stance vis-à-vis Corneille, the French poet's consideration of dramaturgical questions in the three discourses clearly delimited the terms of the
Essay's debate. Indeed, we might see the quartet's polyphony as embodying the very cross-pressures that Corneille attempted to reconcile in his
univocal theory—cross-pressures that were also felt in the early Restoration and manifested in its unsettled theater practice. Crites, like Descartes's Epistemon, represents classical learning, mimicking the hectoring

voice of Richelieu's academy by obsessing on unities to an extent that no classical writer had; and Lisideius praises the separation of tragedy and comedy that *The Sentiments of the French Academy on the Tragicomedy of Le Cid* had so strictly effected, even as Eugenius extols—as Charles Perrault would come to do—the virtues of modern writers whose creativity had transcended that of their ancient teachers. Meanwhile, Neander's contribution to the *Essay* articulates his own syncretic theory of drama, which purports to adjudicate the claims and counterclaims of its day. (One additional demand was nationalism, revealed in Neander's praise of Jonson and Shakespeare and, rather more tenuously, his claim that "old Comedies before *Shakespeare* . . . were all writ in verse of six feet, or *Alexandrin's*, such as the French now use.")[118]

Threshing the neoclassical rules to separate wheat from chaff, Neander thus does as Corneille had done but, facing no threat of academy opprobrium, with less inhibition. For example, he endorses the tragicomic form put to such powerful effect in *Le Cid*, finding that "contraries when plac'd near, set off each other."[119] Thus, of the four characters in the *Essay*, he comes temperamentally closest to Corneille even as he voices the *Essay*'s only criticism of Corneille's practice, judging his comedy *Le menteur* (*The Liar*) overrated, for example, and his dramaturgical design sometimes "flat."[120] It is telling that Neander's harshest criticism of his French predecessor—a tendency to write plays "as long discourses of reason of State" or "in matters of Religion . . . as solemn as the long stops upon our Organs"—is attributed squarely to the unreasonable strictures of Richelieu, thanks to whom "long Harangues were introduc'd, to comply with the gravity of a Churchman."[121] Whereas the unwavering Francophile Lisideius sees Corneille's work in unabashedly positive terms—

the Muses, who ever follow Peace, went to plant in another Countrey, it was then that the great Cardinal of *Richlieu* began to take them into his protection; and that, by his encouragement, *Corneil* and some other Frenchmen reform'd their Theatre, (which before was as much below ours as it now surpasses it and the rest of *Europe*)[122]

—Neander is more nuanced and, to later judgments, more discerning. Concurring that Corneille had rehabilitated the French stage, Neander blames his predecessor's limitations on the rigid external forces that had imposed them. Meanwhile, trying himself to plot a new course forward without undue fealty to his forerunners, Neander attempts to honor his modern name, "New Man,"[123] and thus suggests his affinity with elements of the Cartesian revolution then exercising its influence in England.[124]

We know that Neander represents Dryden's own views in the *Essay*. And Dryden clarified his regard for and temperamental harmony with Corneille in his own words: in the preface to *Of Dramatick Poesie* he defends his use of heroic couplets by calling on Corneille's authority, noting that "I am sure my Adversaries can bring no such Arguments against Verse, as the fourth Act of [Corneille's] *Pompey* will furnish me with, in its defense."[125] (In the prologue to his 1668 play *Secret-Love*, Dryden notes his borrowing of "Scenes unbroken; and a mingled chime / Of *Johnsons* humour, with *Corneilles* rhyme."[126] Dryden's contemporary Thomas Shadwell saw it less generously: "Read *Dry—ns* plays, and read *Corneille*'s too, / You'l swear the *Frenchman* speaks good *English* now.")[127] We see Dryden's veneration—his word[128]—of the French playwright also in his "A Defence of an Essay of Dramatique Poesie," published later the same year as a preface to the second edition of *The Indian Emperour*. There, Dryden explicitly reiterates his regard for Corneille, whom he (twice) classes with Aristotle, Horace, and Jonson in the dramatic pantheon.[129] And he elaborates further on some of the critical points from the 1660 discourses that were raised in the *Essay*. For example, in the "Discourse on the Three Unities," Corneille had defended his breaches of unity of place and demanded a less onerous standard: the scene should only change between acts, he argued, and the change should not bridge too-remote locations, since such a change "would serve to deceive the spectator."[130] Eight years later, Dryden concurs, noting that "imagination being Judge of what is represented, will in reason be less chocq'd with the appearance of two rooms in the same house, or two houses in the same City, than with two distant Cities in the same Country, or two remote Countries in the same Universe."[131]

Dryden's considerable elaboration suggests the extent to which his dramaturgical arguments were shaped by the nascent Enlightenment discourse of his day, grounded in fundamentally Cartesian terms—even if he invokes a longer tradition of reasoning, one "used by *Socrates*, *Plato*, and all the Academicques of old," as the context for his inquisition and its "Sceptical" tenor, written in imitation of "the Royal Society" (of which he was a member).[132] Descartes had argued that playgoing held reason and imagination in a productive counterbalance, manifested in a kinesthetic tension: the spectacle engages the imagination (and the passionate bodily sensations it causes), but reason counterengages the imagination in order to control these sensations (since the imagination's self-representations will counteract the course of animal spirits). This ability to quell the passion's "extravagances" (in Elisabeth's terms) accounts for the particular pleasure of theater, whose "intellectual joy" derives from the "diversity of objects presented to our imagination" (in Descartes's).[133] Put another way, reason licenses the imagination by consenting to a controlled emotional openness—as, indeed, the emotionally generous Nicomède had modeled. Dryden, in turn, argues that "Imagination in a man, or reasonable Creature, is supposed to be participate of reason, and when that governs"—as it does when we suspend disbelief in regard to the play before us—"reason is not destroyed"; rather, it "suffers it self to be so hood-wink'd, that it may better enjoy the pleasures of the fiction."[134] He caps this argument with recourse to the same freedom/enslavement dichotomy that pervades Descartes's *Passions of the Soul* (whose first English translation appeared more swiftly than that of any other Descartes text, only months after its French publication)[135]—even if the colonial resonances are much riper in Dryden, with his near-fetishistic attraction to exotic encounter and its inherent drama. Reason, Dryden asserts, "is never so wholly made a captive, as to be drawn head-long into a perswasion of those things which are most remote from probability: 'tis in that case a freeborn Subject, not a Slave, it will contribute willingly its assent."[136]

Dryden certainly knew Descartes's work. He would have read the philosopher (at last supplanting the Ancients) at Cambridge;[137] his aptly titled poem *Annus mirabilis* (*The Year of Wonders*) relies in small part on a Cartesian theory of oceanography;[138] and he refers to Descartes by name in "A Discourse Concerning the Original and Progress of Satire."[139] The dawning of Adam in his 1677 libretto *The State of Innocence*, moreover, is expressed in a vocabulary redolent of Descartes:

> What am I? or from whence? For that I am
> I know, because I think; but whence I came,
> Or how this Frame of mine began to be,
> What other Being can disclose to me?[140]

But whether or not Dryden understood fully the Cartesian resonances of his "Defence of an Essay of Dramatique Poesie," it is significant that the text reiterates the *Essay*'s most pointed Cartesian borrowing from Corneille. *Of Dramatick Poesie* had mangled Corneille's theoretical gloss on Aristotle by retroactively attributing Cartesian insights to a classical forebear. There, Dryden had written that "the end of Tragedies or serious Playes, sayes *Aristotle*, is to beget admiration, compassion, or concernment"—a strange misformulation that lists (and gives precedence to) Cornelian *admiration* before Aristotelian pity and fear, here weirdly subordinated as "compassion" and "concernment," and with the fear that had troubled Corneille and Descartes tamed to a more tepid and decidedly less passionate state.[141] Thus, Neander's definition of tragedy had reiterated that of the moderns-loving Eugenius, who on the barge had defined the "objects of a Tragedy" as "pleasing admiration and concernment."[142] In the "Defence," by contrast, Dryden abandons Aristotle altogether, stating (and then restating) that tragedy serves to "affect the Soul, and excite the Passions, and above all to move admiration."[143]

Nicomède, we recall, had raised the passions by representing its hero's clash with his antagonists, including the vengeful Arsinoé, before lenifying both passion and antagonism in the face of his emotional wonder. Thus its audience was like the crowd represented in the play's 1660 frontispiece: riotous (that is, moved) but then duly pacified. Dryden saw the purpose of his tragedy in just these terms: "The Passions rais'd and calm'd by just Degrees, / As Tides are swell'd, and then retire to Seas," as he put it in the epilogue to his tragedy *Aureng-zebe*, which premiered in 1675.[144] But by then—only a decade after his putative barge ride on the Thames—Dryden's interest in wonder (and, indeed, tragedy) was waning. The performance of his mammoth *The Conquest of Granada*, which debuted in two parts in 1670 and 1671, may represent an apotheosis. The play centers on Dryden's most Cornelian character, Almanzor, a sui generis hero without known origin or parents (at least until a tenth-act revelation). His Cartesian self-sufficiency is noted by his sometimes rival and sometimes ally Abdalla, who claims that Almanzor "acknowledges no pow'r above his own," having been "rais'd by Valour, from a birth unknwn [sic]."[145] Abdalla's assessment makes manifest the perlocutionary effect of the earlier speech act by which Almanzor had expressed and performed his independence from the play's many warring factions. He proclaims: "Obey'd as Soveraign by thy Subjects be, / But know, that I alone am King of me."[146] The echoes of *Cinna* are presumably intentional; Dryden had noted in his essay "Of Heroique Playes" (prefaced to *The Conquest of Granada*'s first edition) that the heroic play had "heightn'd" its characters "from the example of *Corneille* and some *French Poets*."[147]

Almanzor's striking show of self-assertion precedes by only minutes of stage time his equally striking suppression of unrest in the kingdom:

> Lay down your Armes; 'tis I command you now.
> Do it—or by our Prophets soul I vow,
> My hands shall right your King on him I seize.
> Now, let me see whose look but disobeys.[148]

In two couplets and forty syllables Almanzor accomplishes what King Boabdelin and the skirmishes of various factions have failed to do, and peace is restored. But the peace is short-lived. Indeed, it lasts only four couplets, after which a Messenger heralds the arrival of the Duke of Arcos, forcing the Granadan moors, united under Almanzor, to fight the Spanish; and then some of the Granadans, under Abdalla, to overthrow Boabdelin, who will later squelch the insurrection of Abdalla and his now-ally Zulema. These plot twists, leavened or weighted with numerous scene-changes and songs, take us to the end of the fourth act. (Both the appearance to Almanzor of "the Ghost of his Mother" and the spectacular scene-change to "Vivarambla . . . *fil'd with Spectators*" will have to wait until the play's second part.)[149] Although Almanzor's incredible capacity to invoke wonder and quell discord appears inexhaustible—he is on the winning side of every battle, even if (as it was with Nicomède) this success doesn't keep him out of prison—the passionate stillness he engenders is always temporary. Another complication, another wave of discord, always awaits. The interests weighing on and in Granada are finally too many and too heavy. We might understand this fact of the play, which propels it through its lengthy ten acts, in various ways. We might say that the cross-pressures on Dryden's dramatic theory were also finally too great and took him to the breaking point of his dramatic practice, now surfeited. Certainly Almanzor's self-declared Cartesianism sits uneasily alongside his mercurial shifts of allegiance, which begin to look like turncoatism however much Dryden's play defends them. Similarly, Dryden's attempts to model Cartesian *générosité* sit uneasily not only alongside his desire to pay homage to the Ancients but also alongside his desire to "endeavour an absolute dominion over the minds of the Spectators" (in his words)[150] by "glut[ting] the publick with dramatick wonders" (in Samuel Johnson's).[151]

Or we might say that the radically individualized audience that Cartesianism presents, with each spectator entirely unique in emotional temperament and experience, in his or her accretion of bodily memories, finally can exhaust even the most accommodating playwright—or, indeed, the most wonderful hero, for *The Conquest of Granada* centrally features the proliferation of its characters, tribes, and factions (the Abencerrages and the Zegrys, but also by the Maças, the Alabezes, the Gazuls, and the Gomels, each driven by particular interests). And in this sense the play's final-act scene-change to a place overwhelmed with spectators may be particularly apt. Wonder, Corneille seemed to discover, was the sole emotion that could provide a universal stimulus in the Cartesian theater. But faced with a proliferating audience that could no longer be conceived as cohesive, perhaps wonder, intrinsically reliant on novelty, was bound to find its dramatic possibilities exhausted. We are left with an overstuffed mise-en-scène, a *Wunderkammern* or Cabinet of Wonders (popular in the period) that paradoxically provides no wonder at all, just a glut of inexplicable curiosities for an insatiable audience seeking sensation but no knowledge.

By the time of his 1678 play *All for Love*, Dryden had essentially abandoned the idea of a catharsis of admiration, retraining his remaining tragic efforts squarely on "compassion" or pity and, more generally, shifting his output toward epic poetry and retrenching toward the Ancients, whose thrall he could never leave.[152] His exploration of wonder in epic poetry, meanwhile, would recede closer to the Aristotelian *thaumaston* from which, despite Dryden's Cartesian sympathies, he had never fully disengaged. He explained in (appropriately) his Dedication to the *Aeneid* (1697):

To raise, and afterwards to calm the Passions, to purge the Soul from Pride, by the Examples of Humane Miseries, which befall the greatest; in few words, to expel Arrogance, and introduce Compassion, are the great effects of Tragedy. Great, I must confess, if they were altogether as true as they are pompous. . . . An

Epick Poem is not in so much haste; it works leisurely; the Changes which it makes are slow; but the Cure is likely to be more perfect. The effects of Tragedy, as I said, are too violent to be lasting.[153]

It is an apposite retreat, justified with yet another appeal to Corneille, who "after long Practice, was inclin'd to think, that the time allotted by the Ancients was too short to raise and finish a great Action."[154] The possibilities of Cartesian plotting *for* the stage, as inaugurated by Corneille, were finally limited *by* the stage, not only by its neoclassical pressures (with their backward tug to the Ancients) but also by the material production conditions of the day and especially an acting style that history would come to find rearguard and that—as we will see in Chapter 3—chafed against the Cartesian spirit now making its presence felt in stage performance as in the performance of everyday life. In other words the mode of performance that *The Conquest of Granada* demanded (so mercilessly lampooned in George Villiers's play *The Rehearsal*, which would appear later the same year and which I take up in the next chapter) would find itself fundamentally out of step with a new way of conceiving dramatic agency and a new style of acting even more indebted to Cartesian physiology than the wonder-filled plots of Dryden and Corneille had been.

Coda: *Nicomède*, le Louvre, October 24, 1658

Corneille, we know, wrote all of his late plays for the troupe installed at the Hôtel de Bourgogne where *Nicomède* premiered, a troupe acclaimed for the rhetorically complex stage declamation and well-codified gestures and postures it used to represent tragic stage emotion. But Corneille's fidelity to the Bourguignons and their highly stylized acting, as I will soon demonstrate, is incompatible with the Cartesianism of his later plays and especially with Nicomède, who emblematizes a new model of subjectivity. This tension—between Corneille's plot and the acting style for which he designed it in 1651—might be glimpsed in a performance that (its records being so few) we can scarcely reconstruct: Molière's first command appearance before Louis XIV. For it, Molière paired his farce *Le docteur amoureux* (The doctor in love) with *Nicomède*, wishing, no doubt, to showcase his comic gifts while signaling his deference to France's reigning tragic dramatist, whose favorite troupe were in the audience as guests of the monarch.[155]

Molière's provincial company, we know, lacked the Bourguignons' facility for declamation and gestures, and in fact he was already developing a more naturalistic style of acting later characterized thus by Perrault: "the performances seemed less like plays than reality itself."[156] Because the surviving accounts are so few, we can merely speculate about the troupe's inaugural court performance in Paris. The first page of the register kept by Molière's actor La Grange (i.e., Charles Varlet) records only that "the troupe started at the Louvre, before His Majesty, the 24th of October 1658, with *Nicomède*."[157] Did they give the court an aesthetic taste of what was to come? Or did they try to adapt to Bourguignon standards? Perrault noted only that "the troupe didn't succeed this first time."[158] La Grange noted more ambiguously that the "new actors did not displease, and the charm and the acting of the women were very satisfying."[159] One can imagine that the villainous Arsinoé, presumably in the hands of Molière's leading actress, Madeleine Béjart, stole the show. But of Molière's performance, La Grange, like members of the court audience, recorded nothing. It is not even clear which role the director took for himself. It may have been Prusias, whose comic undertones would have suited Molière's temperament, or it may have been the leading role, which best suits a natural style of delivery.[160] We know only that the performance ended with a fawning apology. La Grange records that the leader had bemoaned the "imperfections" (*deffauts*) of his troupe compared to the Hôtel de Bourgogne actors:

The play having been finished, Molière came onstage and, after having thanked His Majesty very humbly for the kindness he had shown in excusing his imperfections and those of his entire troupe, who trembled to appear before such an august audience, he told him that their pleasure to have had the honor of diverting the greatest King of the world had made [the troupe] forget that His Majesty had at his service such excellent originals, of which they were but very weak copies.[161]

Whether he acted as *Nicomède*'s transparently virtuous hero or the father in whom virtuous change is effected, it is clear why the play's Cartesian elements would have appealed to Molière, whose career we can read— as we can read *Nicomède*—as emblematizing the eventual triumph of a threatening new paradigm over an old one. For the acting style developed by Molière in the 1660s, as I detail in the next chapter, reveals his Cartesian sensibility, his attunement to a new understanding of the modern subject. If, in 1658, Molière did in fact choose to act Corneille in a new style, it is tempting to read this choice as psychological wish fulfillment: the upstart takes on, and then converts, the father figure. (He did not, of course; Corneille's Bourguignon loyalties were unflinching during his career.) However, the older playwright's Cartesianism reveals him to have been on the wrong side of the artistic feud that would be initiated by the quarrel of *The School for Wives* in 1662, in which the Bourguignons' ad hominem attacks on Molière were answered by his uncharitable burlesques of their acting. For example, in one of the sallies in the quarrel—Molière's 1663 play *The Versailles Impromptu*—Molière specifically parodies the actor Montfleury in a tenor that anticipates *The Rehearsal's* lampooning of the heroic drama's excesses.[162] Indeed, Molière uses Corneille's words verbatim, parodying Montfleury's portrayal of Prusias in *Nicomède* (a role the actor performed from the play's 1651 premiere). In the hindsight of intellectual history we see more clearly two different Pierre Corneilles. On one hand, there is the playwright mocked by Molière, who would take part in the Hôtel de Bourgogne actors' attacks on their rival. On the other hand, there is the playwright whose later plays—I am thinking also of *Rodogune*, *Théodore*, and *Héraclius*—reveal philosophical insights that fit ill with the Bourguignon style. It is no accident that, whatever their personal animosities, Molière stuck with Corneille as he persevered in his new style of tragic acting, even in the face of public disapproval: between 1658 and Molière's death in 1673, 166 performances of Corneille by Molière's troupe are recorded.[163]

Because of Molière and others like him, acting theory would abandon the codified gestures they inherited in order to follow the natural bodily expressions of the actors' subjective agency—to align body and mind by aligning Cartesian physics and metaphysics, as *The Birth of Peace* had done so elegantly. This alignment was, of course, one of Descartes's philosophical goals—the purpose, too, of appending *Meteorology* to *Discourse on Method*. Saint-Évremond noted in 1684 that Corneille had pushed beyond the tragic playwrights who preceded him. They saw drama as a series of actions, he claimed, whereas Corneille "went into their [i.e., the characters'] souls to find the principle behind their actions; he descended into their hearts to see the passions forming there, and to discover what was most hidden in their actions."[164] Note the echoes of *The Passions of the Soul*. What Saint-Évremond discovers in Corneille's tragedies is his dramatic consonance with Cartesian psychology—one reason, perhaps, for his success in England after the Restoration, as it registered the impact of its Francophile king, a French cultural influence, and a new philosophical paradigm. As Saint-Évremond would write to Corneille in 1666: "no reputation has been so well established in England and Holland as yours."[165]

In a recent book Dominique Labbé promotes the tenuous hypothesis that Corneille wrote Molière's best plays, whose lexicon he finds Cornelian.[166] I would counter that Corneille's interest in the self reveals him at his most *moliéresque*. In 1640, when Corneille had Auguste declare "Je suis maistre de moy comme de l'Vniuers: / Je le suis, ie veux l'estre,"[167] he closely followed Descartes's debut on the philosophical scene, three years earlier. Exploiting the pun *suis*—the first-person singular form, in the present tense, of both *to be* and *to follow*, *être* and *suivre*—Corneille illuminated the Cartesian method by foregrounding the self that *is* alongside the self that *leads*: "I" *is* the self ("I am master of myself as of the universe. I am, I wish to be") as "I" *follows* the self ("I am master of myself as of the universe. I follow it, I wish to be"). But the Cartesian model of subjectivity concerns not only thoughts but the actions thoughts engender, not only the mind that governs but the body that is governed. In thus affirming the primacy of the self in *Cinna*, Corneille limned a question on the page that would be fully, bodily, articulated by his rival on the stage. For a new wonder awaited audiences of the 1660s: the performances of Molière, which pointed to his own timely understanding of what it means for the Cartesian subject to act.

3

Cartesian Acting; or, Interiors

Sometime in 1668, probably on April 7,[1] Charles Le Brun addressed the Académie royale de peinture et de sculpture to deliver the text now conventionally known as the *Conférence sur l'expression générale et particulière* (*Conference on General and Particular Expression*). In it he translated the physiology outlined in *The Passions of the Soul*—specifically, the "movements of the blood and spirits" that proximately cause the physiological expression of emotions[2]—into terms accessible to the assembled painters, whose investment in "natural" emotional representations he had encouraged as chancellor of the academy. His accompanying drawings, executed over many years, augmented this work by presenting a literal alphabet of emotional expressions: each of Descartes's paradigmatic emotional states appears. (Le Brun's "A," for example, is *Admiration*, the "first of all passions" for Descartes.)[3] Collectively, Le Brun's work on expression would set the standard for emotional representation in the visual arts well into the eighteenth century—to the degree that later art historians could characterize members of the Royal Academy as "Cartesian painters" (*peintres cartésiens*).[4] Not that Le Brun's influence was restricted to France. After the lecture was published, it was soon translated and widely disseminated, reaching receptive audiences in England, Germany, Holland, and Italy. Nor was Le Brun's influence restricted to painting and sculpture; it permeated the theater, too. (This is perhaps unsurprising in light of his repeated employment of theatrical metaphors and even dramatic theory: for example, in a lecture one year earlier on the topic of a Nicolas Poussin painting, Le Brun had lauded the painter's unity of dramatic action and even his use of Aristotelian *peripeteia*.)[5] Indeed, Le Brun's drawings and his lecture on "general and particular expression" came to serve as the basis for entire systems for representing stage emotion. Thus, according to scholarly convention, it is through Le Brun that Descartes came to occupy a central position in theater history: consider, for example, the assertion of David Wiles that Descartes's theory of the passions—"mediated by the drawings of Le Brun"—made the philosopher a "seminal figure in the history of western theatre."[6] This narrative is fundamentally correct. After all, Descartes had provided unusually detailed descriptions of the physical perturbations attending each of the emotions that he so assiduously taxonomized in *The Passions of the Soul,* and these descriptions were directly translated by Le Brun, through whom the relationship between body and mind came to have its mechanistic articulations pictorialized, codified into an influential semiotics of emotion for use by artists. We can situate this project squarely in the picture drawn in my first chapter: in light of the late seventeenth-century vogue for codification in the fine arts, a vogue that gave rise to academies such as the Royal Academy of Painting and Sculpture in the first place.

But I have also traced the complicated relationship of these academies to Cartesian thought: how their scrupulous adherence to Descartes's "objectivity" coupled with their willful excision of his subjectivist nuances helped to evolve a doctrine of "Cartesianism" in strange tension with some of the philosopher's own writings. Similarly, by advancing the view that Descartes's emotional theories could be systematized into a semiotic code, critics (both then and now) elide substantial complications, which I take up in this chapter. Some of these complications concern the representational imperatives involved in acting, so radically different from those of painting—the differences, in other words, between canvas and the human body as artistic media. Other complications concern a more general incompatibility between Descartes's descriptive physiology and Le Brun's prescriptive aesthetics—an incompatibility glossed over when, for example, modern editions of the philosopher's work incorporate the artist's drawings as if the fit between Le Brun and Descartes were completely seamless, their projects fully consonant.[7] A précis of Le Brun's thesis might hold that the passions are expressed physiologically and that these physiological expressions, once properly anatomized, can be straightfor-wardly represented by the mimetically faithful artist, and convention sug-gests that Le Brun's method and Descartes's theory have been understood in this way. In his *Ut pictura poesis*, for example, art historian Rensselaer Lee promoted the view that "behind the categorical exactitude with which [the academicians] formulated the visible manifestations of these invisible states of the soul lay not only the rational thoroughness of the Cartesian method, but also the central concept of the Cartesian physics that the whole universe and every individual body is a machine, and all movement, in consequence, mechanical."[8] As I addressed in my first chapter, however, claims like Lee's understand the "Cartesian body" in an oversimplified manner, and this oversimplification corrupts their view of Le Brun's Car-tesian leanings. For the expressions of the body, however mechanically effected, reflect vicissitudes of the soul that cannot be understood in either universal or semiotic terms.

The reason inheres precisely in the representational character of emotion that I discussed in Chapter 1: the way that emotional bodily effects work as external signs to represent, to the outside world, passions that previously have been represented in—and to—an interior. That is, while each emotion might have a basic, universally shared physiological expression, for Descartes the experience of emotion (and especially the cir-cumstances under which it might be felt) is subjective and each emotional expression unique. Its feeling depends not only on specific objects but also on specific self-representations, through which the perceptual appa-ratus conveys an object to the soul (an object whose emotion-worthiness is assessed from a highly subjective and not universal basis) and through which the soul conveys its volitional assent or dissent to the body's pas-sions. In other words we are returned to the fact that our interior repre-sentations need not resemble the objective reality of what they convey at all, even if these self-representations lead to the legible emotional expres-sions of bodies and faces; rather, they reflect a subjective understanding marked by the subject's individually determined point of view. This prob-lem of Cartesian representation, as Foucault identified it, shines a par-ticular spotlight on actors, to whom the problem pertains with a special urgency. In theater after Descartes, actors came to be evaluated not only for their outward abilities to represent emotion but also for their interior perceptual, emotional, and volitional apparatuses, which determine these outward abilities and shape their performative expression. After all, the desire for "natural" representations demands something quite different from an actor than it does from a painter. While the latter is asked to strive for objective looking, to recognize a specific emotional expression and to duplicate it faithfully on a canvas, the former is asked to conjure a legible emotional expression by means of modifying his or her physiology through a controlled act of volition. By Cartesian logic, then, an actor's stage performance suggests to the audience something of this actor's interior self, since it is this otherwise invisible subjectivity that guides the self-representations that make effective emotional expressions possible.

Thus can two phenomena of the theater after Descartes be explained. The first is the period's emphasis on characters' interiority, by which I mean the acute interest in their mental landscapes—as seen, for example, in Racine's *Phèdre*, which I treat at length in Chapter 4 and whose famous frontispiece Le Brun had himself drawn. The second phenomenon is the rise of the celebrity actor in the late seventeenth and early eighteenth centuries, which we can understand as an acute interest in actors' own mental landscapes or interiority. The connection between these interests, and between the emotional landscapes of character and actor, is plainly expressed in the then historically novel vogue for metatheatrical plays about actors, who, in a bit of appropriate subjectival blurring, lent to their characters their own names (in addition to their own minds and bodies). The connection between the actor's and the character's emotional interiors is expressed, too, in the concomitant rise of the *jeu naturel*, the acting style whose principles are described in Molière's 1663 play *L'impromptu de Versailles* (*The Versailles Impromptu*). Molière, we will see, advocated a method of stage representation that, forgoing the semiotic conventions of stage declamation, instead promised to reveal something of the actor's interior self to the audience, to make visible the invisible. Such a playing style might have been more "simple and natural" (to invoke Le Brun's lecture) than the style it displaced; certainly its physiological expressions were less florid than the gestural emblems and rhetorical tropes previously used for stage representation, and which began to fall out of favor in the late seventeenth century. But the demands it made of its actors were undoubtedly greater.

Académie royale de peinture et de sculpture,
April 7, 1668

Le Brun's lecture itself adumbrates many of the tensions and complications taken up in this chapter, especially in the dense opening remarks
that attempt to define its subject:

In the last Assembly you approved my project to discuss Expression with you. It
is necessary, then, in the first place, to know what this consists in.

Expression, in my opinion, is a simple and natural resemblance of the
things one has to represent: . . . it is this which indicates the true characteristics [*veritable caracteres*] of each thing; it is by this means that we distinguish the
nature of bodies [*la nature des corps*], that figures seem to have movement, and
[that] everything imitated appears to be real. . . .

That is, Gentlemen, what I set out to demonstrate in earlier Lectures;
today I will try to make apparent that Expression is also that which marks the
movements of the soul, which makes visible the effects of the passions.[9]

Le Brun begins by arraying his key concepts in seemingly uncomplicated
terms: "expression" is "a simple and natural resemblance" of whatever the
artist would "represent"—in this case, human subjects in various states
of emotional perturbation. But in *The Passions of the Soul* Descartes had
stressed that habituation differently shapes the emotional expressions of
different subjects.[10] These qualifications would seem to erode the claims
to universality and naturalness that undergird Le Brun's project. In spite
of them, however, it is not impossible to conceive of a painting's "natural resemblance" to, say, a fearful expression. Many of the mechanistic
expressions of the body caused by the animal spirits—the curl of the lip,
the flare of the nostril—do seem to originate in nature for Descartes insofar as they are physiological and described by him in universal terms. But
it is significant, too, that Le Brun's codified "expression," however "natural," denotes only a single resemblance, marked by an indefinite pronoun
that suggests the greater complexity of things to be represented and thus
the inadequacy or partiality of any "resemblance" between object and representation. Indeed, Le Brun highlights this inadequacy more strongly
by immediately complicating his definition in terms that surely unsettled
an audience expecting practical tutelage in the craft of painting. "Expression," he claims, is "also" a reflection of the invisible "movements of the

soul," which in turn "make visible the effects" of the passions. In his orature Le Brun thus limned a relationship between visibility and invisibility that would haunt performance theory's considerations of representation into the twenty-first century.

Le Brun's Cartesianism is clear enough. For Descartes, an emotion—love, for example—comprises some physical perturbations, visible in facial changes and also palpable in the "muscles around the intestines and stomach" where the animal spirits are guided during the emotional sensation.[11] These spirits are the proximate cause of the body's sensational movements, whose ultimate cause is the object of love. At the same time, this object is perceived by the body, which represents it to the soul (also by means of animal spirits). When these representations are apprehended by the soul, it counters or intensifies the body's passionate movements by an act of volition: the soul consents to or repudiates the actions solicited by the body as the subject indulges in or tries to repress the feeling. On one level, then, love is a series of bodily changes that Le Brun could represent both as a generalized paradigm for painters and in the drawing of a particular amorous instance (as we see in Figures 3.1 and 3.2). (Le Brun focused primarily on faces, since he believed that the face showed the passions most keenly because of its proximity to the soul.)[12] But to contemplate his definition of the passions—as the visible effects of the invisible soul's movements—is to reveal the centrality of interiority in the passions' workings. Whether wittingly or not, Le Brun's convolutions make clear that the picture, and the very notion of codifying the Cartesian passions, is not nearly so simple as he might imply. The reason resides in our distinction (*on distingue*) between "the nature of bodies," a phrase whose conflicted grammar, which attempts to reconcile the singularity of nature with the plurality of bodies, suggests a problem at the heart of Le Brun's project, especially as it was taken up by theorists of acting. For what Le Brun's theory must ignore is precisely that which makes each person expressively individual and therefore unlike the painter's pictorial semaphore: the union between mind and body so thematically central to *The Birth of Peace*, which, tellingly, the ballet could represent only with recourse to allegory.

While the mechanisms of bodies may be universal in theory, the unique soul is embodied. And the union of body and soul finds physiological

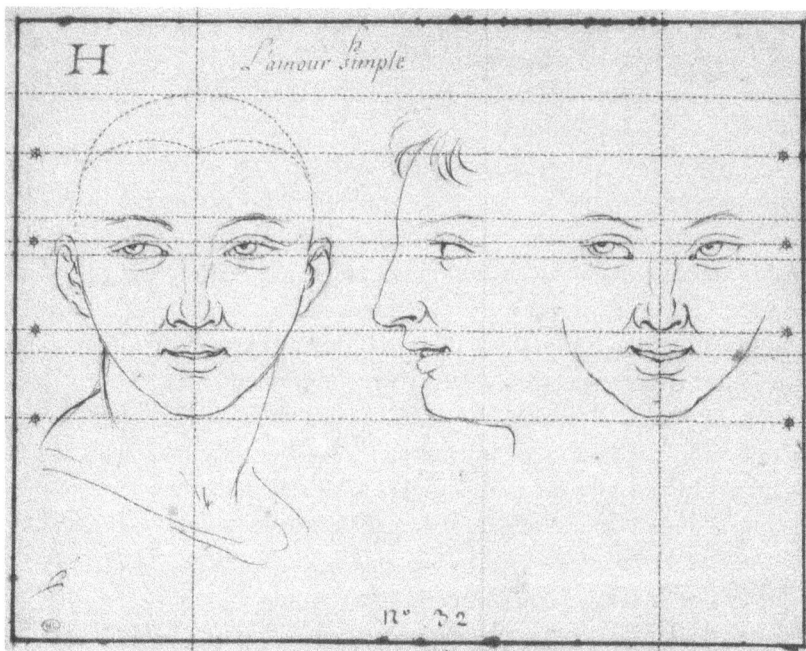

FIGURE 3.1. Charles Le Brun's drawing of passion "H" (*l'amour simple*). The drawing is catalogued as 6454, but not reproduced, in Jules Guiffrey and Pierre Marcel, eds., *Inventaire général des dessins du Musée du Louvre et du Musée de Versailles, école française*, vol. 8 (Paris: Librairie centrale d'art et d'architecture, 1913), 69. Courtesy RMN-Grand Palais/Art Resource, NY.

expression precisely because it shapes each person differently, because of disposition but also because of habituation, as the animal spirits are canalized through the body's memory-shaped channels—hence the physical resemblance between one person's crying and another's laughing.[13] The particular expression of "love" in this or that instance is always unique. It is determined by the other emotional resonances alloyed to it (for emotions always come with secondary shadings) and, while expressed in ways consonant with its general physiological mechanisms, it is shaped by the lived experience of the emotional subject—shaped, in other words, by the memories carried in his or her body. Recall that, for Descartes, memory is constituted by the patterns of animal spirits that signify it. And, because the pores through which the animal spirits move during the remembrance

FIGURE 3.2. Le Brun's finished head showing the subject in love (although frequently, following an eighteenth-century error, catalogued as showing wonder or *admiration*). The drawing is catalogued as 6452, but not reproduced, in Guiffrey and Marcel, *Inventaire général*, 69. Courtesy RMN-Grand Palais/Art Resource, NY.

are reshaped by this motion, bodily matter alters as memory changes. Princess Elisabeth of Bohemia sketched these complexities in a letter of April 25, 1646, in which she noted that "love is always accompanied by desire and joy, or by desire and sadness, and as it grows stronger the others also intensify."[14] Significantly, she continued by reminding Descartes that the physiological movements of the passions differ according to a person's temperament, modulated or intensified, of course, by experience. "Mine is such that sadness always decreases my appetite," she wrote—in keeping with Descartes's teachings, she uses her own experience as evidence—"so long as it is not mixed with any hatred, which comes to me only with the death of some friend" (a distressingly common occurrence for the princess).[15]

Le Brun's theory is unable to account for such particularities of mind-body union, a deficiency diagnosed already by his contemporary and fellow academician André Félibien, who believed that Le Brun's prescriptive method alone could not generate satisfying visual representations of the human. What is missing, Félibien writes, is the "je ne sais quoi"—that which cannot be properly expressed, which he analogizes, in an unmistakable Cartesian echo, to "the secret knot that joins the two parts of body and spirit [*esprit*]."[16] In the practice of painting, the *je ne sais quoi* can be seen in the subject of the representation—that is, a painter's model—especially if this painter has honed an objectifying gaze. And, according to Félibien, that "which cannot be properly expressed" in aesthetic theory could be imparted to the canvas by a master painter, who would supplement his technical knowledge with an untheorizable aesthetic of grace.[17] But the situation is substantially different for the artist who would represent onstage, through acting. After all, for the actor, both the means of representation (her paint and brushes) and the effects of representation (her finished canvas) are coextensive with her own body, which is meant to stand in for—to represent, even to surrogate—the subject of the representation and its own unique subjectivity: Phaedra, for example. As a result the actor's subjectivity is granted a curious primacy in dramatic expression, a primacy that is historically novel and inseparable from the origins of mind as a concept.

The Cartesian concept of mind has been famously characterized by Richard Rorty, in *Philosophy and the Mirror of Nature*, as the "inner arena."[18] It is just such an interior agency that will be understood to animate a good performance in the theater after Descartes. But to understand how this agency can do so requires contemplating some complexities of Descartes's physiology, his notion of mind-body union, that I rehearsed in Chapter 1. First, we must understand how self-representations work to blur the distinction between actions and passions (a blurring, we will see, that is vital to the actor's craft as he skillfully convinces the audience that he is vivified by emotional forces beyond his control). The simplest forms of self-representation are actions of volition, by which the subject can cause all manner of bodily movements, according to Cartesian physiology. If, while walking in the woods, for example, I see a wet patch of earth, I may direct the animal spirits that control my muscles to alter my path and to move my feet away from it. For Descartes this movement is inaugurated and made possible by a mental representation: the thought that stepping on a wet patch of earth could be slippery or messy. This thought attends my assessment that the risk is best avoided; it is represented to the muscles by the animal spirits. Moreover, both this assessment and its physiological effect (changing my path) are shaped by my experience, for just as I once did not know the dirty dangers of mud, so, too, did I once not know how to walk at all. By means of self-representations, volitions cause movements: actions.

A more complicated kind of self-representation is involved in the passions. When, during my walk, I see a bear, my body reacts as fearful bodies do, according to Descartes—including "a disturbance and an astonishment of the soul, which takes away its power to resist the evils it thinks are near."[19] But even as my perceptual apparatus conveys the image of the bear to my mind (via a representational process), and even as my fear and its constituent bodily sensations perturb my body and are apprehended by my soul (via a representational process), my mind assesses the fear as legitimate and thus represents the bear as dangerous—if, that is, the soul can overcome the immobilizing passion in the first place, "which takes away its power." Various kinds of self-representations are overlaid even before my body is affected by the representations of my volition: for the mind, if strong enough, might direct its fearful body to run away, for example, or—if past experience has taught that bears love a good chase and run extraordinarily well—to quell the body's fearful paralysis entirely and, instead, calmly play dead.

Two central aspects of this general picture need to be highlighted. The first is that, in the Cartesian model, habituation shapes all of our actions and passions, starting with the impressions received in utero and rendered increasingly complex with each and every experience: as I walk differently as I age, so do I think differently, and so do I love differently. Significantly, just as the muscles of every subject-body are different, so too does each subject-body experience the passions differently (and not just in response to different stimuli). The second aspect is that some of this habituation is not only beyond the subject's control but also deliberately clouds her view of her own agency: the passions, after all, take their name from a Latin etymon meaning "to suffer" and are so called because they happen *to* us. They are caused by movements in the body, but we cannot perceive the interior workings that constitute their proximate cause. This is what Descartes meant when he wrote, in *The Passions of the Soul*, that the passions are "among the perceptions which the close bond between the soul and body renders confused and obscure": because our feeling of them is the same, we have difficulty distinguishing the different kinds of movements, of bodily representations, experienced.[20] As Lilli Alanen explains in *Descartes's Concept of Mind*, "the passions present us with the illusion of being the autonomous agents of our spontaneous evaluations and actions—an illusion that is not dissipated until one becomes aware of their true nature and origin, in finding oneself overcome by them, unable to control or alter them."[21]

Alanen's explication sketches a central facet of our consideration. A Cartesian acting theory aligns neatly with a Cartesian moral philosophy, since both foreground the importance of emotional control and restraint—mastery, in other words, over the emotional "illusion." One is master of one's passions to the degree that one can successfully counteract the flow of animal spirits that constitutes them and (perhaps more crucially) to the degree that one can resist consenting to the actions solicited from the soul by the passionate body. The bar is thus higher for the actor than for others: while a person must quell her anger in the face of a petty provocation, an actor must foment anger in the service of a good performance—to deliver precisely the "illusion" that he is not in control of his passions—but he must also control its bodily perturbations so as to avoid overstepping the emotional limits imposed by the role and by the practical exigencies of stagecraft. Performing in, say, Corneille's *L'illusion comique* (*The Theatrical Illusion*), an actor playing Pridamant (or at least an actor seeking to do so naturalistically) must conjure and give expression to a sorrow that is mingled with love for his estranged son Clindor, an emotional cocktail Descartes describes thus:

The other cause [of tears] is Sadness, followed by Love or Joy or in general by some cause that makes the heart drive a lot of blood through the arteries. Sadness is needed, because in cooling all the blood it contracts the eyes' pores. But because it also diminishes the quantity of vapors—which must pass through them—in proportion as it contracts them, this does not suffice to produce tears unless the quantity of these vapors is simultaneously increased by some other cause. And there is nothing which increases it more than the blood sent to the heart in the passion of Love. We see too that those who are sad do not shed tears continually, but only intermittently, when they make some new reflection upon the objects they are fond of.[22]

While consenting to these passionate movements of his body, however, the actor must also regulate them, for, Descartes tells us, these physiological workings will also cause groaning or sobbing, an excess of which would inhibit the actor's ability to deliver lines, to follow blocking, to remember cues. In other words, it would be laudable for the onstage actor convincingly to resemble a person wracked with grief; it would be emotionally incontinent for this actor to actually become one.

Descartes's description—wherein he notes that tears are interrupted whenever crying persons "make some new reflection upon the objects they are fond of"—ties bodily habituation to imagination in a knot central to both acting theory and moral philosophy. The principal tenet of Cartesian moral philosophy, after all, is that one can learn to control the flow of animal spirits with practice—the French word is *habitude*—by means of precisely the sort of imaginative and habituating exercises that actors must perform in their rehearsals. Thus, actor training and moral exercise are conceptually consonant, as intimated by Descartes himself. In a 1645 letter to Elisabeth he compared two hypothetical subjects: one, "a person who would have every reason to be content" but who "occupies herself only in considering objects of sadness and pity" that she sees "represented before her in tragedies"; the other, a person "who has infinite real sources of displeasure" but who "takes great care to turn her imagination from them so that she thinks of them only when necessity obliges."[23] Because of her passivity in the wake of bodily sensation, the former person, warns Descartes, may "accustom her heart to restrict itself and to emit sighs," ultimately damaging her spleen and lungs, even though her emotional stimulus is only the feigned events of the theater.[24] By contrast, the latter person—he means Elisabeth herself—acts: she corrects the sadness-induced damage to her spleen and lungs by exercising her imagination and building up her capacity for contentment and joy. Thus, he directly prescribes to Elisabeth that she not only "clear her mind of all unhappy thoughts" but also occupy herself by "imitating those who, looking at a green wood, a flower's colors, a bird's flight, convince themselves that they are thinking of nothing."[25] Descartes's use of the verb *imitate* (*imiter*) is telling, for he prescribes the path of the actor, right down to the virtuosic final step, which is to internalize the work of rehearsals so that she can finally play the performance in the moment, as if thinking "of nothing." Far from excessively indulging in the "dreadful events" (*actes funestes*) of the theater as Descartes's morose, passive spectator does, the actor habituates her body precisely by engaging her imagination.[26]

It is important to stress that Descartes does not impugn spectators: the weak-souled person his letter describes, too carried away by the passions, would be very rare, her soul "enslaved" (*esclave*).[27] But the morally upright person, in the theater as in the performance of everyday life, resists the deleterious perturbations of the flesh by counteracting them with acts of volition. Such acts, as his letter to Elisabeth suggests, are those exercised by the actor, who uses the strength of her moral character, paradoxically, in the service of dissemblance. Descartes writes in *The Passions of the Soul* that "generally all the actions of both the face and the eyes can be changed by the soul, when, willing to conceal its passion, it forcefully imagines one in opposition to it; thus one can use them to dissimulate one's passions as well as to manifest them."[28] The hypothetical tragedy-obsessed spectator merely indulges her bodily sensation "without affecting her understanding," while the actor uses imagination not only to induce but also to control her emotional perturbations.[29] Doing so, she in effect conditions her body as a dancer or an athlete does. Just as the moral subject habituates himself by generating passions that are congruent with the desires of reason, so does the actor habituate herself to experience emotions more easily but never to give over to them, which would undermine her performance. Such habituation, which engages the "understanding," is salutary, and Descartes's yoking of aesthetics and ethics in this letter is of a piece with his larger philosophy. The ethical body is aestheticized insofar as its ethical conditioning reshapes its corporal material, as the movements of the animal spirits alter its flesh.[30] Recall that Descartes wrote to Elisabeth in October of the same year to explain that experiencing pity while watching a play is related to being more compassionate outside the theater and that, in general, the soul is "pleased to feel the passions move within it, regardless of their nature, provided that it remains in control."[31] We find Descartes prefiguring Bertolt Brecht, who derided passive spectatorship and demanded its active equivalent, the individual spectator engaged in mind as well as body.

The reader employing even a modicum of Cartesian skepticism will have already mounted a counterargument: surely the seventeenth-century actor is merely mimicking certain emotional expressions and not trying to conjure the emotions themselves, a conjuration more popularly associated with the twentieth century, with Konstantin Stanislavski and his ilk. But the Cartesian model of habituation and imagination—as well as Descartes's understanding of actions and passions—makes clear that one can induce emotional states by bodily manipulation as easily as one can perturb the body with emotional thoughts, since each is an operation of the animal spirits that both constitute perturbations and convey mental representations between body and mind. In other words, to distinguish the mimicking of emotional expressions from the conjuration of emotional states is to misunderstand the physiology of Descartes, for whom there is no distinction to be drawn. We do well to remember the opening gambit of *The Passions of the Soul*, in which the philosopher establishes that "the Action and the Passion never fail to be the same thing, which has these two names because of the two different subjects to which we can relate it."[32] The passions of the soul are simply the actions of the body, and vice versa. To exercise volition is to gain greater power over both.

Descartes described such exercise in another 1645 letter to Elisabeth, where he writes of "imprinting" (*imprimer*) something "in our mind [*esprit*] so that it becomes habit" (*habitude*).[33] Because of the workings of mind-body union, to imprint in the mind is also to carve into the body—as with

Descartes's lute player, whose hands carry the memory of lute-playing "for the ease of bending and positioning his fingers in various ways, which he has acquired with practice [*habitude*], helps him to remember the passages for which he needs these positions."[34] Such memory acquisition through habituation works, too, in the theater: the actors' emotional responses, conveyed through their bodies by the animal spirits, habituate them to emotional stimuli, but their memory of these responses strengthens and transforms them. The first instances of "natural" acting in the post-Cartesian landscape involve fusing the subjectivities of actor and character so that the imprinted body and *esprit* of the actor can perform the actions demanded by the role. For in surrogating the subjectivity of a character, the actor must not only imagine this subjective position but also supply the body that shapes and is shaped by it—to provide and to perform, too, the mysterious union that inextricably binds body and mind. In English theater history we tend to associate such acting first with David Garrick, whose emotional control was such that "the moment he entered on the stage, the character he assumed was visible in his countenance; the power of his imagination was such, that he transformed himself into the very man."[35] Garrick has been said to represent a shift between one paradigm, with its gestures of calculated, universal signals, and another, in which gestures spontaneously arise in action from the actor's felt passion. But we can find earlier examples of such "natural" acting—even, indeed, in France, where traditional so-called declamatory styles are sometimes held to have persisted into the eighteenth century.

L'impromptu de Versailles, Versailles,
October 14, 1663

If mind-body union provides the *je ne sais quoi*, the impossibility of naming it—of capturing its ephemeral essence—suggests this union's consonance with performance. For performance, we know, evanesces. It leaves few traces, unlike drama with its artifactual scripts or even theater with its design plans, costumes, props. Accordingly, if the debate about the relative naturalism of late seventeenth- and eighteenth-century acting styles is "tiresome" (in the assessment of Joseph Roach),[36] it is in part because the debate is never-ending, continuously generating itself for lack of evidence.

Roach must partake of the debate, too, of course, and his triumph is to force theater critics to historicize their understanding of what, exactly, "natural" would mean in this or that historical context. *The Player's Passion* emphasizes the links among acting, rhetoric, and physiological doctrines, an emphasis that helps us to see the history of acting theory in more nuanced evolutionary terms: to understand, for example, John Bulwer's famous treatises on expressive movement, his 1644 *Chirologia* and *Chironomia*,[37] not as providing a manual of gestural hieroglyphics but rather just as rooted in Bulwer's understanding of "nature" as Le Brun's is rooted in his own. (As Roach explains, "outward significations attain universality, Bulwer believed, because they flow naturally from the inner workings of the body—an undeniable part of the common experience of all humanity.")[38] Nonetheless, Roach underestimates the differences between Bulwer (and his predecessors) and his post-Cartesian successors by largely ignoring a central aspect of the Cartesian revolution, which does more than disentangle the debate from ancient authorities, more than remove acting from the framework of classical rhetoric. In theater history after Descartes, *natural* comes not only to signify a fidelity to the body's physiological mechanisms but also to emphasize the interpenetrations—the union—of body and mind. And thus the very notion of a legible standard for acting, regardless of the basis for its conventions, becomes crucially undermined. An invisible *je ne sais quoi* of individuality fills the void. It is no accident that, concurrent with the Cartesian revolution, both the French word *caractère* and the English word *character* began to shift: originally referring to a mark on a page, the word began to acquire a third dimension, a denotative deepening that is hard to separate from the discursive emergence of interiority.

Accounts agree that Molière's troupe developed an increasingly naturalistic style, a *jeu naturel*, during the playwright's career, which flourished after his return to Paris from the provinces, in 1658, for a command performance of Corneille's *Nicomède* (whose Cartesian resonances we saw in the previous chapter). For example, two descriptions from the period note of Molière's troupe that "their acting is hidden in nature so well that one cannot distinguish truth from mere appearance"[39] and that "the characters were so well drawn that the performances seemed less like plays than reality itself."[40] As Roach cautions, there is no way of knowing precisely what kind of acting might be described as a *jeu naturel* by such a witness, especially one accustomed to the more stylized Hôtel de Bourgogne actors, with their emphatic playing or *jeu emphatique*. Nonetheless, we can contextualize such accounts with other textual artifacts, which help us understand the extent to which Molière's "natural" style emphasized, as Le Brun's lecture emphasized, an alignment between interior and exterior so that "everything imitated appears to be real."[41] One such artifact is Molière's 1663 play *The Versailles Impromptu*, written (in a metatheatrical gesture toward the playwright's court debut five years earlier) to dramatize the anxieties of a troupe, led by a character called "Molière," about to perform before Louis XIV.[42] An extended contemplation of its theoretical insights and theatrical power can help us to speculate about Molière's understanding of the acting style he helped to pioneer in France.

As its title indicates, *The Versailles Impromptu* debuted at court. It was written at the king's express command that Molière respond to *Le portrait du peintre* (The painter's portrait), a play premiered shortly before at the Hôtel de Bourgogne and credited to Edmé Boursault—although believed by Molière, probably accurately, to be the collective work of various *antimoliéristes*. Thus, the *Impromptu* continued the yearlong war of words between Molière and the Bourguignons, the so-called *querelle* or quarrel of *L'école des femmes* (*The School for Wives*):[43] the play rebutted the ad hominem attacks on Molière made in *The Painter's Portrait* while also allowing him to take shots of his own, with uncharitable parodies of the Bourguignon acting style, which he found (in an assessment vindicated by history) outmoded. The *Impromptu*'s defensive and offensive maneuvers are, however, much slyer than those of the earlier plays in the quarrel, facilitated as they are precisely by Molière's new style. The maneuvers are framed by the play's sophisticated ontological structure: the plot concerns a troupe of actors (Molière's) meeting and rehearsing with their author/ director ("Molière") in the *salle de la comédie* of Versailles, before a performance commanded by the king. "Molière," having been unable to rehearse his play properly—but also espousing the virtue of naturalistic performance—coaches his troupe in the art of improvisation. As the pressure of the impending curtain builds, various digressions and obstacles, none more serious than the actors' resistance, set back the rehearsal. Then, in a resolution as bold as that in his *L'avare* (*The Miser*), Molière receives a report that the king, out of his "unique goodness" (*bonté toute particuliere*) has agreed to postpone the play. Molière calls this deferral the "greatest favor in the world" (*la plus grande grace du monde*).[44]

Albert Bermel, who translated the play into English in 1962,[45] declared it "the first utterly realistic drama (ahead of Hebbel by some 200 years)."[46] This assessment is accurate. Molière anchors the play's realism, which goes hand in hand with the naturalistic performance style it espouses, in several ways. First, its structure is looser than that of other plays about actors, or *comédies des comédiens*, of the period, its governing self-reflexivity presented more casually and less self-consciously.[47] Second, this self-reflexivity—the play is a diversion commanded with insufficient time by the king, unfolding at the theater in Versailles—is neater, because the conditions of production within the play perfectly mirror those of the play: the detailed register kept by Molière's actor La Grange (i.e., Charles Varlet) notes that the troupe had to leave for the palace "by order of the King" on October 11, 1663, a week or so before the performance and very soon after the opening of *The Painter's Portrait*.[48] Third, the *Impromptu*'s dialogue is (and would have been to seventeenth-century ears) startlingly conversational, as if improvised. This improvisational quality would become a distinguishing generic feature of the "impromptu," defined as a short circumstantial work giving the illusion of having been composed spontaneously.[49] (In 1660's *Les précieuses ridicules* [*The Ridiculous Young Ladies*], Molière had already noted the generic distinctiveness of the impromptu, when Mascarille—played in the troupe's performances by the playwright—catalogues his literary output, which includes sonnets, epigrams, and madrigals. "I am fiendishly good at impromptus," he boasts.)[50]

Bermel's rendering of the title as *The Rehearsal at Versailles*, which retroactively aligns the play with the English rehearsal burlesques it would inspire, therefore misses a key nuance: much of the play concerns not a rehearsal per se, since the dramatic script to be rehearsed seems not to be properly finished; rather, the impromptu is generated precisely through the actors' interaction with their troupe leader as they ostensibly prepare. Moreover, the translation of *impromptu* as "rehearsal" violates the neat self-reflexivity of the initial performance. Just as the characters ("Molière," "Béjart," "Du Parc," and so on) seem to partake in an impromptu within the world of the play, so, too, did Louis XIV and the court audience have an impromptu (and not a "rehearsal") performed for them by the actors (Molière, Béjart, Du Parc, and so on) on October 14, 1663.[51] Although the actors do not acknowledge their audience and feign that they are still "pre-show," this lack of acknowledgment—this breach in what Bermel calls the play's utter realism—facilitates the impromptu's conceit: the illusion of spontaneity. Onstage and offstage, at the debut performance at least, are meant to seem ontologically coextensive. As Georges Forestier notes, "the double enunciation [that is, of actor and character] in all theatrical discourse is reduced to a single enunciation."[52] This coextensivity serves as an analogue for that between actor and character in Cartesian-inflected acting theory.

The illusion that the *Impromptu* is indeed an impromptu is guaranteed by Molière's Pirandellian trick, since the lines putatively from the play-within-a-play are thrown into relief by the "spontaneous" discussion that surrounds them. For example, in a scene in which he and La Grange rehearse playing two marquises, Molière's lines as director are underscored as "real" (that is, unscripted) by the contrast to his lines as marquis:

MOLIÈRE.   Be sure to remember [he instructs La Grange] to come on as I told you, there, with that manner they call the *bel air*, combing your wig and muttering a little tune between your teeth. La, la, la, la, la, la. The rest of you, spread yourselves out, there has to be room for two marquises, and they're not the sort to present themselves in a cramped space, come on, speak.

LA GRANGE.   Good day, Marquis.

MOLIÈRE.   Good God, that's not at all the tone of a marquis, you have to raise it up a notch, and most of those gentlemen affect a particular manner of speaking to distinguish themselves from the masses. Good day, Marquis, start again.

LA GRANGE.   Good day, Marquis.

MOLIÈRE.   Ah, Marquis, at your service.[53]

The direction that Molière here offers La Grange points to another reason why we should understand *The Versailles Impromptu* as realism *avant la lettre*. In the play the natural diction of Molière functions self-consciously to advance a theory of naturalistic performance: La Grange ought to deliver his line as a real marquis would, and the other actors onstage ought, accordingly, to plan their blocking as if two real marquises had entered the room. Doing so serves to blur the distinction between real and feigned so crucial to Le Brun's definition of natural expression. This blurring is exacerbated, in the original published text, by the refusal to distinguish between the two ontological levels, a refusal that modern editions dishonor when they use quotation marks to set off scripted from putatively unscripted lines.[54]

However natural acting was understood in 1663, the *Impromptu* clearly sketches its difference from the stylized acting paradigms it displaced—paradigms strongly associated, by Molière and theater history, with the Hôtel de Bourgogne troupe. When Molière made his court debut in *Nicomède* in 1658, he had ended the performance with a fawning apology and an expression of gratitude to the king for "suffering their provincial style"—conscious as he was that the Bourguignon troupe, then the king's favorites, were in the audience.[55] The *Impromptu* revisits this scene from a 1663 perspective, by which time Louis XIV's attachment to Molière was secure. The play coyly celebrates Molière's unfamiliarity with Bourguignon conventions, noting that he had seen them perform only "three or four times since we have been in Paris" and had not "caught" (in the sense that one catches a cold) "their manner of delivery."[56] Winking at 1658, Molière explains one of his ideas for the command performance to Mlle De Brie, who, he says, will portray a member of a provincial troupe newly arrived in Paris. (She was one of five actors appearing in the *Impromptu* who had performed at court five years earlier.)[57] Proposing to cast himself as an established tragic poet—he has Corneille in mind— Molière describes how one of the troupe members would step forth and recite the following verse, as "naturally as he could":[58] "Shall I tell you, Araspe? He has served me too well / In adding to my power."[59] The lines are from *Nicomède*: Prusias in conversation with his captain of the guards. Molière's joke is unsubtle. The provincial actor's natural delivery of the lines shocks the unimpressed poet, who interrupts to give some Bourguignon direction, which prescribes a stylized pose and affected declamation. Molière thus acts Corneille, but while imitating the actor Montfleury: "You have to speak things with emphasis. Listen to me. Shall I tell you,

Araspe? . . . etc. *Imitating Montfleury, excellent actor of the Hôtel de Bour-*
gogne. Do you see this posture? Note that well. There, stress the last rhyme
as you should. That's what gets approbation and raises a brouhaha."[60] The
provincial actor's equally pointed retort, meanwhile, demonstrates his
moliéresque sensibility: "It seems to me that a king consulting privately
with the captain of his guards speaks a bit more humanly and hardly uses
this demoniacal tone."[61]

Note how carefully Molière folds even this parody into the *Impromp-*
tu's realistic frame: he is merely describing to Mlle De Brie an idea for a
comedy, and this description compels him explicitly to impersonate Montfleury and implicitly to critique Corneille's preferred acting style. He deliv-
ers his attacks under cover of an offstage impromptu—a contrast, he highlights, to his *querelle* rivals' ad hominem clumsiness. Moreover, whereas
the *Impromptu*'s printed 1682 stage directions explicitly indicate the actor
targeted in the parody, Molière's 1663 performance would have relied on
his celebrated skill at mimicry to ensure that the audience understood the
joke.[62] The subsequent parodies in the *Impromptu*, of all of the major Bourgogne actors except Floridor, also make use of Corneille: Molière quotes
variously from *Horace, Le Cid, Sertorius,* and *Œdipe.* Pointedly, though, the
fact that the *Impromptu*'s suite of parodies begins with *Nicomède* reminds
us, and would have reminded Louis XIV, that Molière's success in Paris
also began with *Nicomède.* Playing both sides in the exchange between the
provincial actor and the Cornelian author would have allowed Molière not
only to demonstrate his versatility as an actor but also to set up the crucial stylistic difference that undergirded his feud with the Hôtel de Bourgogne. Just as the *Impromptu*'s "spontaneous" dialogue throws into relief its
"scripted" dialogue, so, too, does the sincerity of Molière, espousing a *jeu*
naturel, throw into relief the pretensions of the Hôtel de Bourgogne. Thus,
the play connects its two suites of inset theatricality (that is, its Bourguignon
caricatures and its play-within-the-play marquises) by metonymically link-
ing Bourguignon acting with one of his favorite targets for ridicule: affecta-
tion. The shared quality is, of course, falseness. This metonymy revisits that
of *The Ridiculous Young Ladies,* in which Mascarille notes that he intends to
send his play to the Hôtel de Bourgogne, because they know how to "make
the poetry whirr, and stop at a beautiful spot."[63] ("The others"—those who
"recite like people talk"—are ignoramuses, he claims.)[64]

Mascarille's approval of the Bourguignons satirizes more generally the popular taste of the time: theatergoers in general, for whom the Hôtel de Bourgogne represented the pinnacle of tragic acting, did not want to hear tragic alexandrines spoken with simplicity and naturalism.[65] It is useful to remember that, however celebrated he was as a comedian and especially as a *farceur* during his lifetime, Molière was mocked for his tragic acting, in which he dropped the comic mask both literally and figuratively. (Mlle Béjart pointedly notes in the *Impromptu* that "imitating an actor in a comic role isn't depicting the man himself, it's depicting his manner of playing his roles. . . . But imitating an actor in serious roles is depicting him by faults that are entirely his own, since those sorts of roles do not require either the gestures or the ridiculous tones of voice by which he is recognized.")[66] Underscoring the need for verisimilitude in performance, therefore, the director's advice in *The Versailles Impromptu* allows Molière the character to provide the poetics of Molière the playwright—one well described by Léopold Lacour as "a revolutionary doctrine of art."[67] This doctrine is best summarized by one bit of direction that Molière provides the troupe: "Try to take on all the character [*caractère*] of your roles and to make yourself appear as if you are who you are playing."[68]

The sentence repays close attention. If contemporary eyes miss how unusual the phrasing and formulation would have looked in historical context, it is precisely because our Cartesian worldview has been so decisively consolidated. In the play Molière uses several different meanings of the word *caractère*, some of them denotatively novel: for example, as "keynote," or as "assembly of traits that constitute an individual's personality."[69] *Caractère* is used to tell the actors the "type" they will play: for example, "a prude" in Mlle Béjart's case. Additionally, and more significantly, the word is used to delimit an interiority for the role: "Enter into this character," Molière tells Mlle De Brie.[70] As in English, the word had begun to acquire its third dimension. Molière also uses the word to denote the distinctive features—the figuration—by which the audience will recognize the sort of person being represented. (It is in this sense that Viola means "character" when she tells the Captain, at the beginning of *Twelfth Night*, that "I will beleeue thou hast a minde that suites / With this thy faire and outward charracter.")[71] Molière's various uses of the word—it appears eight times—mark his historically unorthodox acting advice: outwardly draw and therefore express that you *are* who you represent. The edict is analogous to Le Brun's instructions for the painter seeking natural "expression," but it is modified to fit the actor's medium. The actor is asked to fuse with the character through performance—or rather, to provide his or her unique subjectivity in the service of expressing that of the character, to make visible the invisible workings of not only the character's soul but also the actor's own. Thus the actor is meant to embody the ontological coextensivity (between real and represented) on which the *Impromptu* and Cartesian acting theory conceptually rely.

In response to this advice, Mlle Molière (played by the playwright's wife) quips to her husband that he ought to have devised a play for one actor: that is, himself.[72] Her sarcastic retort—as when the character Mlle Béjart (played by Madeleine Béjart) confesses that she can't play a part that she hasn't entirely rehearsed,[73] or when La Grange (played by the keeper of Molière's register) complains that the troupe cannot act in a style they don't know[74]—adumbrates how radical Molière's conception of acting is. He uses their (fictive) stubbornness to throw into relief his own radicalism; even his own actors, Molière suggests, remain insufficiently revolutionary in their method. Theater historians have made similar claims for Molière, confirming his self-aggrandizing vision of himself in the *Impromptu* as theatrically revolutionary.[75] It is more precise to say that Molière came to lead, and was the most important player in, a phenomenon in acting style that was not exclusive to him.[76] After all, it was some time earlier that Hamlet's advice to the Players had similarly steered them away from emphatic declamation and stylized gestures. But there is a telling ontological distinction to be drawn between "the Player Queen" and "Mlle Molière" as characters. My contention is that Molière does more than push for greater theatrical verisimilitude, and the *Impromptu* helps us better to understand his pioneering. *La critique de L'école des femmes* (*The School for Wives Criticized*), which he had written a few months before, also contains aspects of a theatrical poetics: "represent according to nature," Dorante famously advises.[77] But the *Impromptu* goes further—well beyond Hamlet, certainly—in providing a theoretical means and motivation for the performer to do so in performance. The individual actor is licensed to make himself or herself into a character, both in a literal sense (since Du Parc played "Du Parc," for instance) and in a philosophical sense (since the self of the actor, his or her own *caractère*, is to anchor that of the role). "How do you expect us to do that," Mlle Béjart asks, "if we don't know our parts?"[78] Molière's sincere response— "You will know them, I tell you"[79]—asserts that a scripted text is unnecessary if the actor has completely imagined, understood, and inhabited the character.

This assertion gives the actor primacy in dramatic expression. From the point of view of performance, it also casts aside the stylistic edicts typical in seventeenth-century acting, which reflected older pre-Cartesian paradigms, anchored in the prescriptions of classical rhetoric. In this way the *Impromptu* distills and potently fortifies Dorante's stance in *The School for Wives Criticized*, which endorses the modern subject's *bon sens* while denigrating rules and received conventions.[80] Foregrounding the individual as a thinking agent in both plays, Molière thus recapitulates the opening gambit of Descartes's 1637 *Discourse on Method* (in which he proposes that the reasoning ability or *bon sens* of the individual should guide philosophical investigation)[81] and his 1641 *Meditations* (in which he resolves to sweep away all of his preconceived knowledge and begin anew, from the ground up).[82] For the Cartesian actor, not rules or conventions but the "I"—her or his own subjectivity—shall be the actor's guide. Thus, Molière commands Du Croisy to fill himself with his role, Mlle Béjart to keep the character in front of her eyes, Mlle De Brie to enter into her character.[83] He echoes Descartes's epistolary advice to Elisabeth when the director commands the entire company to imprint their characters strongly into their minds.[84] Molière considers a role to be a two-dimensional textual construct, awaiting animation by the actor's agency or *esprit*—tellingly, the same word Félibien had used in describing what is knitted to the body in the *je ne sais quoi* of graceful naturalistic painting. In acting this animation is effected by an interpenetration of the actor's mind and the character's interiority—an interpenetration signified by Molière's spatially contradictory directions, which demand that the actors both fill themselves with, and enter into, their *caractères*.[85] According to this model, the actor's mental conceptualization of the *caractère* leads the bodily business of acting a role; that is, the performer is the empirical (and grammatical) subject, charged with a process in which mental representation precedes physical representation—a process, indeed, that Descartes exhaustively theorized. Molière ends his instructions by using the word *caractère* in yet another novel way. Cleverly violating the denotative distinction between *caractère* and *rôle*, he "tells them all their characters."[86] Doing so, he at once directs the actors and casts the play.

The *Impromptu*'s emphasis on the performer's mental agency does have implications for casting: stressing mind over body, it foregrounds the actor's own character and deemphasizes physiognomy.[87] (It is useful to recall that Molière's critics repeatedly, and to modern eyes unfairly, deemed him ill suited for tragedy because of his physique. He was said to lack the necessary "physical gifts" [*dons extérieurs*].)[88] He reinforces this implication with a pointed in-joke, giving Mlle Du Parc an unsympathetic role. When she protests that she is herself nothing like the affected character she is assigned, he demurs: "That is true."[89] The demurral, however, is coy. The original audience would have remembered that Mlle Du Parc had piqued Molière's ire by leaving him for another company for one season.[90] (She would deal a crueler blow just a few years later, leaving him again for the Hôtel de Bourgogne.)[91] More generally, Molière's evolving understanding of casting was reflected in the evolution of his company, which initially resembled a *commedia dell'arte* troupe but came to rely less on physical types.[92] Moreover, his facility with casting was recognized quickly by the critics; as early as 1696, for example, Charles Perrault had written that Molière "understood the ways of the actors so well, in giving them their true character, and in addition he had the gift of assigning the roles so well and then directing so perfectly that they seemed less like actors in a play than the real people [*vraies personnes*] they were portraying."[93] It is noteworthy that Perrault cites not only the believability of the portrayals but also the verisimilitude of the characters, who seem like "real people." Molière's commitments to more naturalistic acting and to verisimilitude are indeed closely interrelated, as his gradual abandonment of monologues attests.[94] So, too, attests his stubborn defense of prose during his dramatic career: significantly, in the *Impromptu* he notes that prose is easier to improvise, as it is more natural.[95]

The ontological trick of the *Impromptu*, and of naturalistic acting more broadly, allows a spectator to forget the difference between an actor and a character, or between a character and a real person—to effect the confusion between real and feigned that Le Brun had prescribed. This trick was made possible by the philosophical moment in which Molière lived. If this moment is manifested in Molière's understanding of *caractère* and in his assertion of the actor's agency, it is also reflected in the shifting denotations of the word *acteur*. At the beginning of the seventeenth century the word means, simply, *"personnage"* or "role," and the two appear interchangeably at the top of dramatis personae in printed plays.[96] By the end of the century, however, *acteur* had come to signify *"comédien"* or "actor,"[97] the sense in which Molière uses the word—three times in the text and once in the stage directions—in the *Impromptu*.[98] I have already noted how the playwright foregrounds the actor's agency; it is in this sense that the denotative displacement of *comédien* (from the Greek *komoidia*, "comedy") by *acteur* (from the Latin *agere*, "to do") is most resonant. Martine Clermont has beautifully detailed how such a shift in meaning emerges with appropriate simultaneity alongside new theoretical reflections on the art of acting.[99] The particular line of theoretical reflection that Molière sketches in the *Impromptu*—about the experiential reality of the actor and its relationship to his or her portrayal of a three-dimensional character—is made possible by new modes of thinking about the self more generally.

We might amend Allardyce Nicoll's much-quoted line about authors and actors in the eighteenth century, then, by saying that the late seventeenth century was the age not of the *comédien* but of the *acteur*, a word on whose ambiguities Molière would seem to capitalize.[100] The opening printed matter of *The Versailles Impromptu* lists the following under "Noms des Acteurs": "MOLIERE, BRECOURT, DE LA GRANGE, DU CROISY, LA TORILLIERE, BEJART, Mademoiselle DU PARC, Mademoiselle BEJAR [*sic*], Mademoiselle DE BRIE, Mademoiselle MOLIERE, Mademoiselle DU CROISY, Mademoiselle HERVE."[101] Ten of these names are *acteurs* in the sense of "roles": "Molière" is a character name, and the performer portraying the character in a contemporary revival plays Molière. However, "Béjart" and "La Torillière" (i.e., La Thorillière) are *acteurs* only in the modern sense: their characters are not Béjart and La Thorillière but, respectively, a "man of quality" and a marquis. Thus the "Nom des Acteurs" list cleverly exploits its own denotative ambiguity. This sly joke, of course, appears only in the (posthumously) printed drama, but it provides a textual analogue for the *Impromptu*'s first moment in theatrical performance. Sitting down to Molière's retort to *The Painter's Portrait*, Louis XIV would have seen Molière call eight members of his troupe into the *salle de la comédie* to discuss their impending, unfinished, improperly rehearsed performance. Explicitly naming each of the eight one at a time, Molière (and "Molière") would have clarified for the audience that the troupe members were playing themselves. He would have established the play's realistic conceit—a conceit violated and thus underscored in the second scene when La Thorillière entered as a "real" marquis, as opposed to the "pretend" marquises that "La Grange" and "Molière" briefly play. The desired theatrical effect, Bermel's "utter realism," would have been underscored, too, by the sheer number of bodies onstage[102] and by Molière's squabbling with his new wife during the scene. (This squabbling, in turn, alludes to *The School for Wives* and the origins of the feud. Thus, the ontological ambiguity between actor and character serves also to make the *Impromptu* more pointed as a parry in the quarrel.) Meanwhile, the semiotics of the play's staging captures its ontological multivalence: the onstage bodies, including M. and Mlle Molière, are dressed not as themselves but "fully costumed" (*tous habillez*) for the impending play.[103] This play, of which we see a few interrupted scenes in rehearsal, is that ostensibly anticipated by Louis XIV. It never arrives. Molière, although dressed as a marquis, acts as Molière.

English Rehearsal Burlesques, 1671–1747

Molière's trick in the *Impromptu*—the way that his "real-life" personality and his three-dimensional performance as himself overwhelm his marquis costume and his apparent role—serves as an analogue for what Felicity Nussbaum has called the "interiority effect," an epiphenomenon of performance by which actors create the impression that their interiority can be known.[104] Nussbaum reveals how eighteenth-century British actresses exploited such interiority effects to enhance their currency in the theatrical marketplace, which was increasingly reliant on a kind of inwardness whose other cultural expressions included the epistolary novel and the suddenly voguish autobiography; they promised to make visible interior workings considered as private, invisible. (In this way these actors prefigured the conceptual hook of much contemporary performance art, predicated as it is on the play between visibility and invisibility.) But such interiority—and, in some crucial way, the nascent concept of celebrity[105]—is conceivable only because the Cartesian revolution makes it possible. Thus, the strictly gendered effects that Nussbaum catalogues rely, paradoxically, on the ungendered notion of interiority that Cartesian thought articulated. Interiority effects (both as Nussbaum theorizes them and as eighteenth-century actors cultivated them) presuppose a unique personal agency—call it mind—that, while invisible, governs the body and through it finds performative expression by means of a *je ne sais quoi* for which Le Brun and his successors could not account. It is therefore unsurprising to find instances of the phenomenon several decades earlier than Nussbaum's examples, and in France as well as in England. Even in a court performance (very slightly) removed from market considerations, Molière could practically school his troupe in how to align interior and exterior and thus make interior visible. Or at least seem to: because Mlle Du Parc's role as "Mlle Du Parc" in the *Impromptu* apparently required her to act out of character, Molière facetiously jokes that "sometimes violence to ourselves is necessary"—a delectable phrase, in light of Descartes's view of corporal aestheticization, of the body's transformation in light of its actions and passions, and one that limns the specific cultural pressures that led to female actors' self-fashioning of their interiority effects, so unlike those of their male counterparts.[106]

The extent to which playgoers after Descartes could believe themselves to know actors' interiority, to conceive of them as celebrities, is registered in rehearsal burlesques of the late seventeenth century—a genre predicated on the personalities of the putatively rehearsing actors and a genre, we know, whose fashion in the London theater was generated by *The Versailles Impromptu*.[107] For example, *The Rehearsal* by George Villiers, Second Duke of Buckingham, which premiered on December 7, 1671, mimics Molière's ontological maneuver by showing actors rehearsing at the Theater Royal in Drury Lane in a play written to be performed there. The play's metatheatricality relies in part on its "Three Players," whose dimensionality as characters throws into relief the thinness of the roles they are assigned in the play-within-a-play, written by the laughable playwright Bayes:

Enter three Players upon the Stage.

1 PLAY.   Have you your part perfect?

2 PLAY.   Yes, I have it without book; but I do not understand how it is to be spoken.

3 PLAY.   And mine is such a one, as I can't ghess for my life what humour I'm to be in: whether angry, melancholy, merry, or in love. I don't know what to make on't.

1 PLAY.   Phoo! the Author will be here presently, and he'l tell us all.[108]

But if *The Rehearsal* is not as radical as Molière's *Impromptu*, it is precisely because its players largely remain generic, as their speech prefixes indicate—however keenly they would have been animated by the company. (So, too, does their absurd author, Bayes, remain generic, standing in for a number of playwrights satirized by Villiers—however particular the attack on John Dryden, and specifically *The Conquest of Granada*, and however much the actor John Lacy emphasized his Dryden impersonation in performance.)[109] In spite of these qualifications, the fundaments of an interiority effect are glimpsed in several throwaway moments during which the play relies on specific, real-life players. There are the play's offhand mentions of "Mr. Cartwright"[110] and "Mr. Ivory"[111] (twice each) and "Mr. Wintershull"[112]—references to William Cartwright, Abraham Ivory, and William Wintershall, members of the Drury Lane company and of *The Rehearsal*'s cast. These references, which rely on the audience's recognition of the actors as people, anchor *The Rehearsal* in the real world even more decisively than Konstantin's reference, in Anton Chekhov's *The Seagull*, to his actor mother's contemporary Eleanora Duse: after all, unlike William Cartwright in *The Rehearsal*, Duse never actually turns up.[113]

Consider, too, this metatheatrical moment in act 2:

Enter Shirley.

SHIR.   Hey, ho, hey ho: what a change is here! Hey day, hey day! I know not what to do, nor what to say.

Exit.[114]

The character, absent from the dramatis personae page, is neither a fictional composite like "Bayes" nor generic like the "Three Players." He is George Shirley, another member (since 1668) of the Drury Lane company. (He returns in the play's final scene, after Bayes's play is abandoned, to dance with another company member, Joe Haines.)[115] As his speech prefix indicates, Shirley is not a character within Bayes's play-within-the-play. Rather, he appears in the rehearsed scene as himself, and from within this frame he reaches across the proscenium to the audience in order to comment—in a move that was surely designed to seem unscripted—on the absurdity of the situation and also on the texts (both Bayes's and Villiers's) that can neither contain nor script him. In print Villiers's play therefore can only hint at its appeal in performance. By a mechanism theorized as "ghosting" by Marvin Carlson, the onstage George Shirley could delight his audiences not really because of what he did or said (or didn't do or say, in this case) but precisely because he was already known to them (as La Grange or Brécourt were known by the court spectators at Versailles)— that is, not as a character but as a three-dimensional person, possessing an interiority and embodying the altogether unique history of his particular past performances, including Pedro in John Corye's *The Generous Enemies* a few months earlier.[116] Shirley's cameo has the same theatrical effect as the inappropriate giggles of an actor who breaches the theatrical illusion, what the British call corpsing: the character "dies" as a result of the overwhelming effect of the actor's own agency.[117]

As actors became celebrities, more pointed use could be made of them as onstage characters, as seen in *The Female Wits*, performed twenty-five years after *The Rehearsal*, in September or October 1696.[118] Whereas Villiers's satirical target was an assortment of writers, *The Female Wits* specifically lampoons Delarivier Manley and her play *The Royal Mischief*.[119] More significantly, it also lampoons an entire troupe of actors: the newly constituted company at Lincoln's Inn Fields, including Thomas Betterton, Elizabeth Barry, and Anne Bracegirdle. Manley had written *The Royal Mischief* for these actors while they were still at Drury Lane, under the management of Christopher Rich in the United Company.[120] But after the so-called Actors' Rebellion of 1695 sent them to Lincoln's Inn Fields, Manley's play was inherited by Rich's company, now dominated by George Powell, who had stayed behind.[121] The rehearsal process seems to have generated creative differences (as current parlance euphemizes them) between Manley and the actors, and eventually, in the spring of 1696, the play had to be withdrawn. But Manley successfully premiered it instead, with what was perceived as untoward speed, with Betterton's new company in April or May 1696, thus compounding the ill feelings between her and the Drury Lane troupe.[122] These ill feelings are vented in *The Female Wits*, whose author remains unknown but who obviously intimately understood the imbroglio. (One prime suspect is Joe Haines, who had danced with George Shirley in 1671 and whose fame would grow, in the decades following, because of his most celebrated role: *The Rehearsal's* Bayes, which he inherited after John Lacy's death.[123] Haines's celebrity and real name, in turn, would be leveraged to lovely metatheatrical effect in Elkanah Settle's 1697 play *The World in the Moon*, in which Haines played himself.)[124]

The play sought to settle a score with Manley, to be sure, but, more significantly, it sought to capitalize on public knowledge of both sets of actors: not only Betterton, Barry, and Bracegirdle (represented and lampooned as a rearguard) but also the Drury Lane troupe who did the lampooning and most of whom, significantly, played themselves: Powell, Letitia Cross, Benjamin Johnson, Frances Maria Knight, Jane Lucas, and William Pinkethman, all of whose real names serve as speech prefixes in the printed text. (Still other actors played conventional roles, such as the insipid and arrogant playwright, Marsilia, who stands in for Manley. But even this role relies in a sense on celebrity: according to the play's preface, only Susanna Verbruggen could ever have "play'd the Chief Character . . . as the Chief Actress in her Kind, who never had any one that exceeded her, or ever will have one that can come up to her, unless a Miracle intervenes for the support of the *English* Stage.")[125] Contemporary critics therefore mislay the emphasis when they claim, for example, that the play "reveal[s]" the Drury Lane actors' "own personalities with astonishing clarity."[126] The play may do so to us, but its dramatic action in 1696 depended precisely on the actors' personalities in the first place: the public knowledge of Lucas's love of coffee,[127] for example, or of Cross's hoydenish sass, later leveraged by John Vanbrugh when he wrote her the part of Hoyden in *The Relapse*. ("I have such a mind to kick him i'th'Chops," Cross told the audience of *The Female Wits* when the sycophantic fan Praiseall, played by Colley Cibber, asked to "kiss the Strap of your Shoe, or the Tongue of your Buckle.")[128] When Powell is revealed to be at the tavern despite the early morning rehearsal time, the joke relies not on the fact that the actor drank heavily but rather on the fact that his heavy drinking was widely known.[129] The play's robust audiences (it matched its progenitor *The Royal Mischief* in running for six consecutive nights)[130] confirm its success at capitalizing on the clarity and currency of public personae—not only those of its cast but also those of the Lincoln's Inn Fields troupe, as much targets of satire as Manley herself.

Despite its sometimes misogynist jokes about female playwrights—for Mary Pix and Catherine Trotter also come under unkind scrutiny[131]—*The Female Wits* offers profound insights into the era's conception of actors. Written in a time still apparently obsessed with prescriptions for "good" acting, it reveals two growing understandings. First, actors are seen to act with their own bodies, as particularized by their own experience. Second, successful performances are seen to deploy and express these bodies' particularities rather than to accord with universal standards. Take, for instance, a moment when Marsilia directs Pinkethman by exhorting him to "Fetch large Strides; walk thus; your Arms strutting; your Voice big, and your Eyes terrible."[132] The joke would have crucially relied on the audience's recognition of Betterton, whose mannered acting style it parodies, but, equally crucially, on the particularities of Pinkethman's short and clownish body, so unlike that of the six-foot Betterton.[133] *The Female Wits* uses the structure of this joke twice more, in jokes that highlight the gendered expressions that constituted the actors' public performances of interiority. Within the play-within-the-play Cross cheekily parodies the virtuous Bracegirdle, whose reputation for virginity was carefully cultivated and has been called a "public obsession" of the period.[134] And Knight is directed to affect the heroic acting style of Barry, over two decades her senior. Marsilia asks, for example: "Dear Mrs. *Knight*, in this Speech, stamp as Queen *Statira* does, that always gets a Clap. . . . Now Stamp, and Hug your self, Mrs. *Knight*: Oh! The strong Exstasie!"[135]

The structural symmetry of these three jokes—Betterton's body contrasted with Pinkethman's, Bracegirdle's temperament contrasted with Cross's, Barry's acting style contrasted with Knight's—is apt. The three jokes work in tandem precisely to align body, mind, and acting style in just the manner proposed by Molière and, indeed, acting theory after Descartes. Imagine the final moments in *The Female Wits* in 1696. When Verbruggen (playing Manley) lost her temper and declared, "I desire to go directly into *Lincoln's-Inn-Fields*. . . . I'll never set my Foot agen upon this confounded Stage," the following response ensued: "*Enter Mr. Powell, Mrs. Knight, Mrs. Cross, &c. Laughing.*"[136] The troupe members entered as characters, laughing within the world of *The Female Wits* at Marsilia's tantrum. But, recalling Shirley's cameo in *The Rehearsal,* they entered, too, as actors, laughing with the audience at Manley's misbehavior and in celebration of their own successful lampooning of it. The ontological status of this laughter—imitated or real—would have been less ambiguous than irrelevant, since the difference between real and fake has been collapsed as decisively as the difference, for Descartes, between laughter induced by muscular reflex and laughter induced by a funny thought. In other words the lack of difference is more than phenomenological: it is not only that the audience apprehends either laugh in the same way but also that the laugh is in either case physiologically identical.

It has been presumed that comic and tragic stage practice were fully separate in the period, and much theory of the day, saturated with neoclassical influence and with the authority of the ancients that Descartes had derided, bears this presumption out. Practice was changing, however. Molière's ideas in *The Versailles Impromptu,* a comedy that explicitly considers tragic acting, represent a shift that extends beyond the limits of dramatic genre. Consider, for instance, the fact that Charles Macklin—known to his age and our own as a paradigmatic naturalistic actor[137]—seems to have introduced Molière's insight into his own tragic method: having opened the first acting school in England, Macklin counseled students to first speak their lines exactly as they would in real life and then to practice projecting the same effect while onstage.[138] Laying Molière and his descendants alongside Le Brun and his own yields exegetical benefits. Braiding together these strands, we recognize how Descartes's notion of subjectivity also came to exercise an influence on acting, and we can thus supplement the usual narrative of Descartes's influence on theater history. For the Cartesian model of interiority—with each agent's unique self shaped by and shaping the unique physiology of his or her body—was equally pivotal to this history, even if its impact is harder to trace in the straight lines we can draw from his physiology, disseminated via Le Brun.

Another juxtaposition may be instructive. In 1747 Macklin's student Samuel Foote produced not only a Cartesian tract on tragic acting (*Treatise on the Passions*) but also began performing his *Diversions of the Morning,* lampoons of public figures tied together in a plot structure derived from the rehearsal burlesque.[139] In his treatise Foote had "calculated to open the Eyes of the Injudicious" by explaining the passions, foregrounding the Cartesianism of his theory by rooting it in the agitations of the soul as felt in the body; in light of this explanation, his injudicious readers could "judge how far the Imitation of those Passions on the Stage be natural."[140] But Foote left the finer physiological details "to the Determination of the Physicians," emphasizing instead the interiority that makes stage emotion (and the many guises of his stage performances) possible.[141] As he stresses:

The word Passion is applied to the different Motions and Agitations of the Soul, according to the different Objects, that present themselves to the Senses; how or by what means this mutual Action, or Communication between Soul and Body is effected, remains a Secret to us; all our Attempts to resolve it into any thing prior, or more simple have been fruitless and ineffectual, except we refer to the immediate Will and Agency of the first Cause itself.[142]

Orienting us to the subjectivity that determines all emotional experience (and therefore all emotional and physiological expression), Foote's treatise thus reiterates the lesson of his comic parodies, where he realized the goal of Molière, who had licensed the actor to make himself into a character and who had asserted that a scripted text would be unnecessary if this character were completely inhabited.[143] Foote's improvised entertainments relied entirely on the *je ne sais quoi* of performance, and the show's advertisements self-consciously emphasized the interiority effects that would bind him to his audience. Reads one: "On Saturday Noon, exactly at Twelve o'Clock, at the New Theatre in the Hay-Market, Mr. Foote begs the favour of his Friends to come and drink a Dish of Chocolate with him; and 'tis hoped there will be a great deal of good Company, and some joyous Spirits; he will endeavour to make the Morning as Diverting as possible."[144] His own interiority—here offered, in false intimacy, to "his Friends"—was made visible in his uncanny physiological transformations but also cemented his celebrity (substantial enough that he could ultimately lampoon himself, when he turned a libel suit brought against him into an entertainment and sold the show bluntly as *The Trial of Samuel Foote*).[145] In other words Foote demonstrated the lessons of *The Versailles Impromptu*: like Molière he impersonated other actors by mobilizing

their unique characteristics, but he also exploited his own three-dimensional character and foregrounded his own bodily particularities, including, eventually, his leglessness, which came to be one of his most important signifiers.[146]

It is telling that Foote makes reference, early in his treatise, to Molière,
his acknowledged predecessor.[147] For he saw (as many acting theorists of his
day did not) that, finally, "the Effects of the Passions, are so very different
in different Men, and often so complicated and mixed, that it would be
almost impossible, to trace their several Connections, and describe their
various Effects."[148] Compare a passage of *The Passions of the Soul*, apparently overlooked by Le Brun, in which Descartes had argued that the movements of the face in different emotions "differ so little that there are men
who have almost the same look when they cry as others when they laugh.
It is true that there are some that are quite recognizable, like a wrinkled
forehead in anger and certain movements of the nose and lips in indignation and mockery, but they do not seem to be natural so much as volun-
tary."[149] Descartes's philosophy in general and his theory of the passions in
particular are governed, I have said, by his subjectivist nuances, his insistence that each person's emotions are unique: because of his or her unique
lived experience, because of the unique self-representations that determine
emotional expressions, and because these expressions have shaped his or
her body uniquely. Honoring this conception, Foote's treatise highlighted
the limitations of Le Brun's *Conference on General and Particular Expression*, which had encouraged a universalizing view of the movements of the
mind. Foote's *Diversions of the Morning*, like the rehearsal burlesques it
resembles, helps us to look beyond mechanistic prescriptions and toward
the individualized complexities of the mind's movements, made visible in
the subject's body—to see clearly the limitations (and the anti-Cartesian
elements) of Le Brun's theory and those of his followers, like Aaron Hill,
whose plans for a Royal Academy for tragic acting foundered in 1735 and
whose *The Art of Acting* appeared in 1746,[150] or James Parsons, whose 1746
lectures to the Royal Society extended the influence of the Le Brunian for-
mula in England.[151] Both are well represented in the usual theater-historical
narrative about acting theory after Descartes.

To recognise the consonance between Foote's treatise and his comic
practice, then, is not only to suggest the importance of comic documents

like *The Rehearsal* or *The Female Wits* in analyzing acting in the period. It is also to see how the limitations of Le Brun's theory were supplemented by performance practice: in the work of Macklin, for instance, or of his best-known protégés, Foote and Garrick. In Garrick, theater history tells us, the actor's subjectivity and body fused with those of his characters so completely that his "passions rose in rapid succession, and before he uttered a word, were legible in every feature of that various face." Thus, "the audience saw a most exact imitation of nature."[152] We should see Garrick as an apotheosis, and not an originator, of such naturalistic acting—advocated by Molière before him and predicated on a Cartesian model of the body in which the passions of the soul equate to the actions of the body, in which the mind's volitions master and control both the body (to which it is united) and its feelings.

Descartes wrote to Elisabeth, on July 8, 1644, that "the construction of our bodies is such that certain bodily movements follow naturally from certain thoughts: as seen in the blushing that follows from shame, the tears from compassion, and the laughter from joy."[153] His faith in this view—in the strength of volition and mental representation—was so strong that he could suggest that the princess bring her exceptional intelligence to bear on her ill health, thus leveraging "the force of nature": "when one has an illness, one can recover solely by the force of nature, particularly when one is still young. This conviction is without doubt more true and more reasonable than that of certain men, who, following the advice of an astrologer or a doctor, make themselves believe that they will die at a certain time, and by this alone become sick and even die often enough."[154] For Descartes the fleshy exterior and the invisible interior are knotted together and performed by the *je ne sais quoi* of mind-body union. They are as inseparable as actor and character in Cartesian acting. Theater history (or, more accurately, theater-historical lore) would confirm Molière's achievement in such acting in an ironic twist on Descartes's letter: instead of safeguarding his health, Molière's well-trained volitions could endanger it when he inhabited the subjectivity of Argan, the titular hypochondriac of *Le malade imaginaire*, on February 17, 1673. (In an uneasily metatheatrical moment, the role had required Molière, as Argan, to feign his own death, despite the worry that Argan himself poses: "Isn't it dangerous, pretending to be dead?")[155] Fusing with his character, as he had instructed his troupe to do ten years earlier, Molière became the sort of man who is convinced he will die, and, doing so, experienced the ontological coextensivity promoted by his acting theory. In a fatal inversion of corpsing—with character instead overwhelming actor—he fomented too well the psychosomatic symptoms that wrack the hypochondriac and, after suffering an onstage seizure, eventually succumbed. Or so legend has it.[156] In his death, too, then, Molière revealed the porous boundary between comedy and tragedy, even as he performed his difference from the rhetorical school whose actors he had supplanted. The Hôtel de Bourgogne's Montfleury (the rival parodied in *The Versailles Impromptu*) had died onstage six years earlier, but not of psychological commitment or volitional physiological transformation. He burst a blood vessel while playing the perfectly healthy Orestes in Racine's *Andromache*: overacting to the end, or so it would be seen in the retrospect of Cartesian theater history.[157]

4

Cartesian Design; or, Anatomies
of the Theater

The medieval worldview, we know, was not mapped by the latitudes and longitudes that we associate with Cartesianism and through which we locate and navigate our positions in the world: inner/outer, self/other, subjectivity/objectivity. Indeed, the very notion of a fixed self locatable in a cartographic world is a modern one, incompatible with the picture presented by medieval art, for example, in which the constituent elements float spatially unmoored, their sizes not relative to one another. There is no ontological unity, no fixed perspective, and this is precisely because the illusion of a spatially locatable beholder remains inconceivable and unconceived in both the medieval aesthetic and ethos. Reconstructing a medieval theatrical mise-en-scène, we observe the same immersive quality, as performer and spectator (sometimes the same person changing roles midplay) ambulate to, from, and through areas used variously for playing and watching: mansions that represent places in the mystery cycles—hell, for example, or Gethsemane—without being locations in the Cartesian sense or having fixed positions within an ontologically unified whole.

However much the vogue for environmental and promenade productions in the last fifty years may try to revivify it, the kinesthetic and emotional memory of such an experience of theatergoing is now dead. But for theatergoers in the seventeenth century, especially at Paris's Hôtel de Bourgogne—built in 1548 for the staging of mystery plays—it was still palpably alive and, indeed, embedded in the playhouse just as Cartesian memory is embedded in the body of the subject: the *mémoire du corps*. Recall that, for Descartes, each act of memory contains and revises its antecedents as the animal spirits are canalized anew through the body. In this chapter I anatomize the theater design and architecture of the day, imagining the canalization of bodies through specific theatrical spaces: over the stage, through the parterre, into the loges. As the seventeenth century crept toward the eighteenth, these patterns of movement extended the collective but ever-fainter memory of a medieval aesthetics of immersion, but this memory was now haunted by the distinctly modern ghosts I identified in Chapter 1: first, the epistemological dilemmas of Cartesian subjectivity and, second, the cultural anxieties about intersubjective contamination that Cartesianism exacerbated. Invoking these ghosts, I here consider three productions of Racine's *Phèdre* in three different venues: the 1677 premiere at the Hôtel de Bourgogne; the 1689 production that inaugurated the first permanent home of the Comédie-Française, designed by François d'Orbay; and the 1707 London premiere at the Queen's Theatre in the Haymarket, designed by the playwright John Vanbrugh. Racine's play braids together two models for subject-object contact, as tropes of literalized consanguinity (in which subjects and objects threaten to bleed into one another) sit alongside tropes of ocularity (in which the spectating subject visually apprehends the performing object). And so it testifies to the interrelationship between the perceptual and circulatory apparatuses, as Descartes sees it: as images are conveyed via optic nerve to the brain, their emotional significations are disseminated by the animal spirits passing through the blood vessels, making and remaking the body. As we will see, however, Racine's play signifies differently depending on how the bodies of its actors and spectators inhabit the space in which it is acted, how they move through the space and perform the dynamics it structures. Each of the three productions I examine provides different answers to Racine's questions about Cartesian subject-object relations, and these differences emerge precisely because, in each case, the theater architecture— through its spatial articulation of these relations—serves either to amplify or to muffle Racine's sanguinary and ocular discourses.

 A rich vista into the problem of theatrical subject-object relations is provided by Pierre-Narcisse Guérin's treatment of Racine (Figure 4.1),

FIGURE 4.1. Pierre-Narcisse Guérin, *Phèdre and Hippolyte*. Musée des Beaux-Arts, Bordeaux, France. Courtesy RMN-Grand Palais/Art Resource, NY.

believed by some to represent an early nineteenth-century performance of *Phèdre* at the Comédie-Française starring Catherine-Joséphine Duchesnois.[1] The painting seems to offer two oppositions: between bodily failure and bodily integrity, on one hand, and between display and spectation, on the other. We see Phaedra, whose passionate failures of corporal self-dominion are represented in her entanglement with Oenone and Theseus. The dubious postures and agonized aspects of all three mirror one another, and their garments overlap as if they were continuous, tethering them in a fatalistic, sinister knot at the bisellium's curved armrest, where Phaedra's left arm meets the left hands of her husband and her nurse. Phaedra's visual ties to her husband are further highlighted by their perfectly paralleled right legs and right arms, the latter both primed for violence in spite of an obvious lack of defenses: Theseus's shield and helmet sit unused; his and Phaedra's recumbent positions, like Oenone's severe crouch, underscore their shared physiological vulnerability. Guérin thus pictorially extends Racine's most famous *gestus*: "She sits" (*Elle s'assit*).[2] (In the play there is only this one stage direction, offered immediately after Phaedra first enters, lamenting her body's failures—and her mind's—under her emotional burden.) By contrast, Hippolytus stands alone, his arm held ramrod straight in a gesture of rejection or repudiation. Meanwhile, opposing display and spectation, the painting elevates the enmeshed objects of Hippolytus's disregard on a dais, as if on a stage, and orients them perpendicularly to the recessed space in which he stands before them, a shallow parterre. They are passionate performers, each one's face betraying emotional disturbance; he, a stoic spectator, refuses to watch. (Indeed, in the play he ardently wishes never to see Phaedra again [*de ne la plus revoir*].)[3]

But details bedevil these oppositions. Hippolytus's parted eyelids suggest tantalizingly that his resistance to watching may flag—a reminder that he is neither entirely blameless nor entirely divorced from his family. After all, for Racine (unlike his classical forebears) the prince's taboo love for Aricia implicates him in the very treachery he condemns in Phaedra, which imperils the state and violates ties of blood. Moreover, the ostensible separation of Hippolytus from his father and stepmother is compromised, as both Hippolytus's left arm and Theseus's right foot breach the boundary between stage and parterre, and as the softened position of Hippolytus's left leg inches him closer, both figuratively and literally, to those whom he would reject. However firm his apparent rejection, Hippolytus is yoked to them: to his father by blood and to his stepmother by his own sword, which she holds and whose status as a conduit for intersubjective contact the play confirms. ("If not your arm, lend me your sword," Phaedra demands of her stepson, and, after she has apparently grabbed it, Hippolytus is physically transformed, left pale and dumbstruck.)[4] Moreover, Hippolytus's height, stance, and, indeed, pictorial prominence lend him a suspiciously theatrical air, belying his apparent status as a spectator. They remind us that in Guérin's title—*Phèdre and Hippolyte*, which was also Racine's title in 1677—Hippolytus is paralleled, conjoined, with Phaedra. He is certainly an object of observation: note Theseus's intense ocular concentration. Guérin's painting, then, seems to pose an opposition between the distanced spectator who watches and the objects of watching, who are cross-contaminated, entangled, physically manifesting the unhealthy dependencies that the French aptly call *relations fusionnelles*. But Guérin finally undoes this opposition, threatening to pull not only Hippolytus but even the painting's implied viewer—it positions us as the object of Phaedra's own intense gaze—through the frame, across the proscenium, and into kinesthetic and emotional fusion with her. Guérin thus succinctly captures Racine's thesis: to have dominion over the passions is in part to declare oneself independent, as Hippolytus seems to do. But, as he knows well from his experience of Aricia, the pull to intersubjectivity is strong. "You love, you burn; / You perish from a malady that you hide," Theramenes declares to Hippolytus, correctly guessing that Hippolytus's disdain for love is just a show.[5]

Racine thus dramatizes the central tension of the stage after Descartes (whose portrait, incidentally, was among the playwright's belongings).[6] As a collective endeavor and a communal experience, theater has always served to inculcate and manifest our interconnectedness—to stress our inextricability from one another and from the world outside, as Descartes does in his writings. For example, he wrote to Elisabeth on September 15, 1645:

One must nevertheless think that one does not know how to subsist alone, and that one is, in effect, one part of the universe, and more particularly still one part of this earth, one part of this state, of this society, of this family, to which one is joined by his home, by his oath, by his birth. And one must always prefer the interests of the whole, of which one is a part, to those of one's person in particular.[7]

The tension arises because of the success with which Descartes had established the self-sufficient empirical subject in the first place: the individual "I" that governs the *Meditations*, and within which, according to the *Discourse on Method*, all knowledge can be found.[8] Indeed, Descartes's writings so vigorously conjure the individual agent of Cartesian thought that it can here speak out of turn; in the letter to Elisabeth it seems to assert its independence even at the expense of the passage's central claim. One must "nevertheless" be mindful of one's interconnectedness, Descartes must exhort, precisely because one is not by nature mindful of it—because "each of us is a person separate from others"[9] and because the tug of solipsism is so strong in a "first philosophy" that elevates inner experience above all else. This tug became inexorable in theater architecture as the seventeenth century ceded to the eighteenth: playhouses asserted more and more strongly the independence of spectators from spectacle and from one another, and these spectators were each encouraged to take a single, objective viewpoint.

Phèdre and Hippolyte, Hôtel de Bourgogne, January 1, 1677

As Guérin's painting represents, the subject's autonomy is fragile. The anxiety attendant upon this fragility suppurates through Racine's play. And it would have been particularly strongly felt in the play's first production, which debuted on January 1, 1677. The playwright wrote *Phèdre and Hippolyte* for the troupe installed at the Hôtel de Bourgogne on the Right Bank's rue Mauconseil, on the southern edge of what is now the second arrondissement of Paris.[10] The space retained, more than any other in Paris, the memory of the immersive experience of playgoing that we associate with medieval theater. Indeed, the Hôtel de Bourgogne had begun as the site of mystery plays in Paris: the Confrérie de la passion, the organization that built the theater in 1548, had had a monopoly on the production of mystery plays since 1402, by order of Charles VI.[11] Accordingly, the space had no formalized separation between performers and spectators, and, despite various renovations, its features recalled a time before such a division—what David Wiles pointedly calls the "Cartesian theatrical dichotomy"—could be conceived.[12] Significantly, its interior was modeled on a tennis court or *jeu de paume* (Paris's other public theaters of the day, such as the Théâtre du Marais, were literally installed in tennis courts), and the interaction between the players in a tennis game provides an analogy for the interplay between the performers in one-half of the space, that is, the actors, and those who performed as spectators opposite them.

The space was intimate, even cramped; its maximum size, measured from the outside of the walls, was 109 by 44 feet (Figure 4.2). Somewhat less than half of this length was given over to stage space, the rest to a large parterre in the front and a raked seating gallery or *amphithéâtre* in

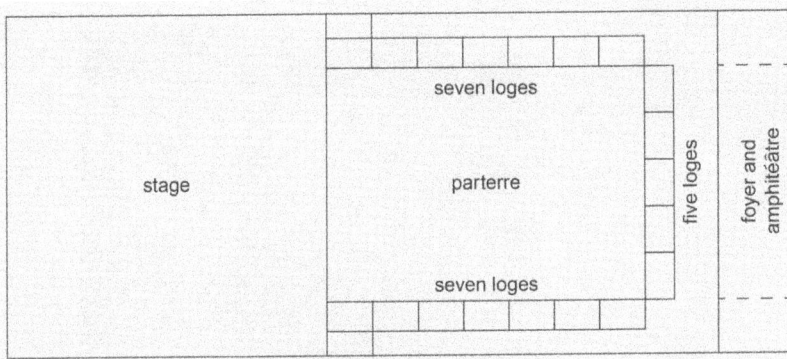

FIGURE 4.2. Floor plan for Paris's Hôtel de Bourgogne theater after its 1647 renovations. Rendering by Anna Szczepaniak based on the plan of D. H. Roy, "La scène de l'Hôtel de Bourgogne," *Revue d'histoire du théâtre* 14 (1962): 227–35, at 231.

the very back.[13] Lined by loges (for the more bourgeois and for most of the female spectators), the flat and capacious parterre would have housed by far the greatest number of spectators, standing and milling, whistling and shouting, drinking and eating.[14] The unruliness of this hundreds-strong parterre audience has been documented by nineteenth-century theater historians such as Eugène Rigal and Eugène Despois; not for nothing was carrying swords, poniards, and pistols in the Hôtel de Bourgogne expressly banned by the order of Louis XIII in 1641.[15] T. E. Lawrenson, in *The French Stage and Playhouse in the XVIIth Century*, attributes the crowd's behavior to the spectacle's having been "shorn . . . of any collective social purpose such as the mystery play possessed."[16] However, this attribution seems to miss the point—or, to put it more precisely, to reveal its own anachronistic, post-Cartesian position—for the goings-on in the parterre, the drinking and whistling and even brawling, were vital elements of the theatergoing experience, not aberrant deviations from it and, accordingly, as essential as any actor's blocking or actress's costume. The social purpose of gathering at the Hôtel de Bourgogne had been secularized since the days of the mystery plays, of course, but a social purpose persisted nonetheless; and in its interactivity the audience performed its communal obligation. The layout of a *jeu de paume* suggests how integral

FIGURE 4.3. The onstage spectator takes center stage. From Raymond Poisson, *Le zig-zag*, in *Baron de la Crasse, comédie représentée sur le théâtre royal de l'Hostel de Bourgogne* (Paris: Gabriel Quinet, 1667), 22. Courtesy Bruce Peel Special Collections Library, University of Alberta.

the parries of the parterre were in seventeenth-century French theater; a play without them would be as infeasible as a tennis match with only one player. Moreover, the performance of the spectators in the parterre was as much the object of spectacle as whatever was onstage at a given time, as the placement of the loges suggests.

In 1677 the Hôtel de Bourgogne provided a visual emblem of the audience's centrality to the theatrical experience: the conspicuous placement of spectators onstage. The 1667 frontispiece to Raymond Poisson's *Le zig-zag* (Figure 4.3), which premiered at the theater, literally foregrounds this centrality by making its key figure—and the only one whose gaze addresses the viewer—an onstage spectator.[17] Seated in the chair farthest downstage, the seemingly bemused figure turns his attention outward, toward the parterre instead of toward the goings-on of three of the play's four young lovers, who are shown playing a scene. The frontispiece thus shifts the reader's focus toward this onstage spectator and his companions, some of whom seem to be engaged in conversation and none of whom, pointedly, is watching the play. Through one of the curtained wings, another actor peeks out, perhaps straining to hear a cue over the din or perhaps getting ready to navigate an entrance that could be tricky. After all, just three years before *Phèdre and Hippolyte*, Samuel Chappuzeau had attested that "the actors frequently have a struggle to enter the stage, since the wings are so full of gentlemen," whose presence he found (as it is in this frontispiece) a "rich ornament."[18] Others were less forgiving of the ornamentation: Molière, who would periodically satirize onstage seating throughout his career, is particularly cutting in his 1661 *Les fâcheux* (The bores), written during his first season at the Théâtre du Palais-Royal, a space that also allowed the practice. That play opens with its lead character, Éraste, metatheatrically describing his own experience at the theater that day:

> With a loud noise and full of airs,
> A man with large cannions entered brusquely,
> Shouting "Hola-ho! A seat at once!"
> And his huge ruckus surprised the assembly
> And disturbed the play in its finest moment.
>
> .   .   .   .
>
> The actors wanted to continue with their parts:
> But the man, in seating himself, made a new ruckus

As he crossed the stage again in long strides—
Although he could have been comfortable in the wings—
And planted his chair downstage centre,
His broad back blocking the spectators
In three quarters of the parterre from seeing the actors.[19]

Éraste complains of the restricted view from the parterre caused by his attention-seeking nemesis, one of the irritating people, or *fâcheux*, that the play addresses. But as the *Zig-Zag* frontispiece makes clear, the onstage spectator was part of the show.

From a present-day perspective such a spectator would violate the unity of the world represented by the play, and most contemporary productions that seat spectators onstage contrive to integrate them into a harmonious ontological picture: I am thinking, for example, of how the onstage spectators came to resemble jurors in the 2000 Broadway production of Michael Frayn's *Copenhagen*, directed by Michael Blakemore, or how they were positioned as parliamentarians, and therefore undistinguished from planted actors, in the 2012 production of James Graham's *This House* at London's National Theatre, directed by Jeremy Herrin. In both cases the set design incorporated the spectators such that their presence could be explained within the ontological reality of the world represented. But to think of the world of the play as distinct from the world of the spectating space is, of course, possible only from a Cartesian perspective; previously, such an ontological distinction remained unthought. As Henri Lefebvre has famously shown in his *La production de l'espace* (*The Production of Space*), space is socially constructed. And the conception of space of earlier, ambulatory, religious productions, which had been imported into the Hôtel de Bourgogne in the sixteenth century, had evolved but not radically changed by the early seventeenth. For this reason we should consider the practice of seating spectators onstage in 1677—it had begun decades earlier—as an evolution from, as well as a continuation of, an earlier notion of the theatrical space as unbifurcated.

It was precisely the introduction of Cartesian thought that troubled the picture and caused an epistemic rupture, one symptom of which was the controversy about space set off by Pierre Corneille's *Le Cid* in 1637, the same year that Descartes's *Discourse on Method* appeared in print. The *Le Cid* quarrel ostensibly concerned the classical unities in general and "unity of place"—never a classical idea to begin with[20]—in particular. But as George Kernodle astutely reminds us, at issue was not the changing of settings as such but rather the concomitance of two different staging practices.[21] First, there was the practice of mansion staging (which theater historians frequently declare "medieval," even though it persisted until well into the seventeenth century) in which a play's settings were juxtaposed in fixed positions on the stage, with no conventions of verisimilitude governing their relationship: a mansion inches away might represent a location far away in diegetic time or place. Second, there was the Italian practice of perspective, in which the places represented by the mansions were meant to stand in visually correct spatial relationship to one another. The introduction of perspective staging to France had been gradual, with elements imported from Italy mingling with various indigenous habits derived from royal entries, street theater, and mystery plays;[22] and this hodgepodge (tellingly nonpejorative in its Old French root, *hochepot*) had continued organically and unproblematically in theater practice. The currency of Cartesian ideas made such mingling untenable: the establishment of a subject/object dichotomy had led to a schism between the world of the representation and the world of the spectation. Thus, the practice of perspective staging, which served only an aesthetic function in its Italian Renaissance beginnings, came to serve an ontological function in the Cartesian era. By reinforcing the boundary around the onstage world, perspective staging seemed to promise the ontological security of the spectator. The Abbé d'Aubignac's call in *The Practice of Theater* that the playwright "reunite [onstage] times and places," for example, betrays a Cartesian worldview: with regulations such as those proposed by d'Aubignac, the object could be contained; the subject, defended.[23] To trouble the ontological distinction between Seville and Paris—as *Le Cid* did at the Théâtre du Marais in 1637, with its mansion staging and proliferation of onstage spectators[24]—threatened to trouble the ontological distinction between self and other.

If the crisis of theater history (and visual culture) that *Le Cid* represents was Cartesian, however, it was not solved by the end of mansion staging. The very space of the Hôtel de Bourgogne structured subject-object relations in a way problematic for the Cartesian mind-set, transgressing rather than policing the newly crucial categories of self/other, inner/outer, individual/collective. As such, the space was all too appropriate for *Phèdre and Hippolyte*, since the destabilizing of these categories provides the play with its central theme and with the anxiety that animates its tragedy. In the play's first scene Theramenes likens Hippolytus's forbidden love for the captive princess to a "yoke" (*joug*), rhetorically using the image to bind him also to his father and his legendary romantic entanglements. He asks:

> Are you no longer the proud Hippolytus,
> Implacable enemy of love's laws
> And of a yoke that Theseus has so often borne?[25]

In some sense, Racine suggests, the prince *is* no longer the proud Hippolytus, his self-definition having been compromised by the weight of love's yoke. Anticipating the famous speech of Phaedra in which she laments the "shameful yoke" (*joug honteux*)[26] of her own taboo love, Theramenes thus prefigures the play's philosophical system, in which the object-directed nature of emotions—we cannot feel an emotion without feeling it in regard to something else—serves to erode the subject's self-dominion by tethering him or her to an object and thus compromising both agency and bodily autonomy. Images of yoking and enslavement abound. For example, the play analogizes Aricia's literal imprisonment in Troezen with Hippolytus's captivity to her love, and it twice invokes the yoke of love that binds the two.[27] (Slyly, toward the end of the play, Racine has Hippolytus ask Aricia to "leave her enslavement" and elope with him, well after the playwright has definitively established that the bondage of love restricts more than Aricia's sentence ever could.)[28] Perhaps most tellingly, Oenone laments that Phaedra's yoke was imposed long ago.[29] She repeats Theramenes's gesture in the first act—when he conflated Hippolytus's amorous burden with those of Theseus—by aligning Phaedra's love with the impious desires of her mother and sister. After all, her family is, as Hippolytus assesses, "of a blood . . . fuller in all these horrors than [his] own."[30]

Racine thus hooks his yoking metaphor into a pervasive network of blood imagery that courses through the play. (*Sang* is the fourth most common noun in the text's lexicon, after *œil*, *cœur*, and *amour*.)[31] Through this imagery he invokes the Cartesian opposition between inner and outer and raises the specter of its collapse. Thematically, the playwright underscores that love is treacherous in the play because of the burdens of consanguinity: Hippolytus and Aricia are taboo objects of desire because of his shared blood with Theseus, and hers with her brothers. At the same time, Racine reminds us that we are not, finally, autonomous agents but inextricably tied to the decisions and desires of others, as Descartes had instructed Elisabeth in his letter of September 15, 1645. Blood, after all, is family—quite literally, in the word *sang*'s dual meanings—and therefore palpably both inside and outside. Aricia must be punished (and can claim the Athenian throne) because she is "the blood of Pallas," "the last of a fatal blood" that battled Theseus.[32] Hippolytus is an "enemy of [Phaedra's] blood" because of his mother, Antiope.[33] And Theseus, on learning of Hippolytus's alleged rape of Phaedra, laments that "all the ties of blood" could not hold his son back.[34] This line's irony is particularly bitter because it is precisely the "ties of blood" that are shown to erode reason and to imperil the authority of the self; blood is revealed as one more fetter on volition. Family ties are like the yokes of love, and a burden on the subject's sovereignty—an analogy that the play clarifies, and physiologically justifies, by blood's centrality in the process of emotional experience. After all, as Descartes theorized and as I analyzed in my opening chapter, blood is the first site of corporal perturbation, carrying the animal spirits through the body and disordering it when an object-directed emotion compromises the subject—as, for example, when Phaedra sees Hippolytus and uncomfortably feels "all [her] blood withdraw toward [her] heart."[35]

Phaedra's torments are initially a mystery to all but herself until she attempts to unburden herself on Oenone (and thus burdens herself further with her nurse's terrible persuasions). But from the play's very beginning, Phaedra's autonomy is undermined precisely by her blood, whose tormenting heat derives, in multiple ways, from outside of her: Hippolytus, as the object of her desire, causes her emotional and physiological perturbations, and her family bequeaths her an unfortunate sanguinary inheritance. (The gods have cursed "all of [Phaedra's] blood," the "blood of Minos.")[36] Racine's portrayal is more extreme, to be sure, but one finds in late Descartes a similar insistence that the actions and passions of others can be determinative for the subject. For example, one unsettling fact about Cartesian habituation is that it begins not in infancy but in utero. Thus the conditioning of our emotional reactions begins prior to consciousness, part of Descartes's explanation for the emotions' puzzling illogic. As he explains in *The Passions of the Soul*:

It is not difficult, for example, to think that some people's unusual aversions, which make them unable to tolerate the smell of roses or the presence of a cat or similar things, come only from having been badly shocked by some such objects at the beginning of life, or from having sympathetically felt the sensation of their mother who was shocked by them while pregnant. For it is certain that there is a relation between all the movements of a mother and those of the child in her womb, which is such that what is adverse to the one is harmful to the other. . . . The idea of the Aversion he had then for the roses or the cat may remain imprinted in his brain to the end of his life.[37]

Indeed, Descartes himself claimed to bear a bad inheritance from his mother, caused by her "unhappiness" and manifesting in him as a physiological deficiency that took him more than twenty years to overcome. He wrote to Elisabeth that "being born of a mother who died a few days after my birth of a lung disease caused by some unhappiness, I had inherited from her a dry cough and a pale color that I retained until after I was twenty."[38] Blood, then, both metaphorically and literally—as in the case of Descartes's childhood pallor—undermines the sui generis Cartesian subject and mitigates its self-determination in various ways, just as family mitigates the subject's freedom.

By this logic blood can compromise us, not least of all when it effects the physiological changes wrought in the body as a result of its ocular perceptions. Accordingly, in Racine's grim representation blood appears as the symptom of and testimony to the collapse of the subject—most dramatically in Hippolytus's final moments, when his body literally comes apart as it is dragged down the beach by his out-of-control horses, leaving a bloody trail for his survivors to follow. (The accident grimly revisits the play's thematic preoccupation with yoking: the axle of Hippolytus's chariot "groans" and "breaks," in Racine's personification, but the prince is entangled in the reins.)[39] In a gruesomely vivid image, Theramenes will report that "the traces of his noble blood led our way."[40] Surveying *Phèdre*'s network of blood imagery, we note its centrality to the play's principal subject: the structural collapse of self that Phaedra experiences, as immediately announced in her very first speech: "I cannot support myself."[41] The line and its supporting physical gesture—"she sits"—nicely encapsulate Racine's Cartesian thesis. It connects body with mind and shows the collapse of one as coextensive with the collapse of the other. Indeed, it beautifully prefigures one of the play's most famous speeches, when, after Oenone demands that Phaedra pull herself together in order to rule Troezen, Phaedra expresses the inextricable linkage of mind and body (and of personal and state sovereignty):

> Me, reign! Me, bring a state beneath my rule!
> When my weak reason no longer rules over me,
> When I have lost dominion over my senses,
> When under a shameful yoke I struggle to breathe,
> When I am dying.[42]

However poor her judgment in some regards, Phaedra's diagnosis of her trouble is correct, at least in Cartesian terms: her mind's inability to acquire dominion over her passions erodes her subjectivity. Love can thus undermine her bodily integrity, and, in a typically Racinian conflation of physiology and family history, Phaedra can proclaim that Venus "hounds her blood."[43] Struggling to regain her self-control, then, Phaedra rails "against all of [her] blood," as Oenone puts it, seeking to avoid the unhappy ends of her sister, Ariadne (abandoned by Theseus while she was sleeping at Naxos), and of her mother, Pasiphaë (cursed by Poseidon to mate with a bull).[44] But as the denotative multivalence of *sang* makes clear, to war against her blood is to war against her own body: by refusing to eat and refusing to sleep, Phaedra feeds her physiological disorder.[45] Racine makes clear that these, too, are actions dictated by her passions—in this case her all-encompassing guilt at her impious desire—and he thus reminds us of the weak-willed subject that Descartes described several decades earlier, whose body is turned against itself as it is moved in multiple directions by its proximate and ultimate causes: the emotional cocktails that constitute experience and the external objects causing these emotions.[46] Eventually, Phaedra will discover Hippolytus's attachment to Aricia and will be further undone by the obliterating effects of her jealousy, which, she claims, make those of love seem like a "weak foretaste" (*foible essay*).[47]

Imagining *Phèdre and Hippolyte* at the Hôtel de Bourgogne in 1677 requires asking how this blood imagery would have signified in a closed space where the arteries through which actors and audiences circulated were shared instead of discrete, as they are in modern theater architecture. (The space had been designed before William Harvey—whose importance to his own thinking Descartes acknowledged[48]—had "discovered" the body's circulatory system. This fact is not trivial if one considers Lefebvre's famous thesis in *The Production of Space*; one could connect the imminent changes in theater architecture to new understandings of the body's design.) A spectator taking his seat onstage would pass through the actors' backstage space and through the same wings they used for entrances and exits; if he felt like it, he could cross the stage. There was no lobby per se, with parterre spectators entering straight from the street into a meager vestibule, and a communal social space would have been superfluous since the socializing, we know, did not stop for the play. Male and female spectators alike could and would move from loge to loge during the performance, and men moved freely from downstairs up to the balcony, whose spaces were treated as private, like homes.[49] The circulation through the space in order to get to the concessions, moreover, would not have flowed more slowly simply because of actors onstage. And, as I have said, the layout of the space generally discouraged the distinction between actors and spectators, with little visual demarcation to guide their two different functions: even the lighting levels were identical.[50] My claim is that the constant circulation of bodies through the theater performed not only its spatial logic but also the collective memory of how the space had historically functioned, before the Cartesian schism between those meant to perform and those meant to observe. And this collective memory no doubt encouraged spectators' boundary-breaching behavior, from interrupting the play from the parterre to interacting with the actors onstage. (There is a marvelous anecdote about Molière's widow, Armande Béjart, being hit on repeatedly by an onstage spectator at the Hôtel de Guénégaud: the victim of a prostitute's prank, he believed himself to be having an affair with the actress. Not responding to his come-ons—"You have never been so beautiful! If I weren't already in love, I would be this afternoon!"[51]—Béjart probably understood one type of ontological confusion as another, presuming that he addressed her onstage character instead of mistaking her for another real-life woman.)

　　Phèdre and Hippolyte's Cartesian anxieties about intersubjective contamination must have signified strongly in a space that could not provide an ontological rampart to contain the world of the play. Indeed, if we follow Roger Herzel's understanding of this production, the scenic design in 1677 must have exacerbated these anxieties. It has been generally assumed that the play was produced with a universal set: the so-called *palais à volonté*, which we will encounter at the Comédie-Française in 1689. But Herzel's exacting research has shown that several of Racine's tragedies written for the Hôtel de Bourgogne required play-specific sets, which made his requirements of Michel Laurent, the theater's multitasking *décorateur*, greater than those of other playwrights.[52] In the case of *Phèdre*, Phaedra herself mentions the vaults above her in the third act, and Laurent was apparently required to furnish "a vaulted palace" (*un palais voûté*)[53]—a set that, atypically, was enclosed at the top. Such a setting, with its arches looming over the heads of the onstage spectators, must have exaggerated the confinement of the Hôtel de Bourgogne. Moreover, as Herzel reminds us, the play's setting is self-consciously described as liminal: Phaedra sets off, in her first entrance, toward the outdoor light, but she stops short, and the entire play unfolds in this ambiguous space between two locations.[54] That the scene deliberately signified both the liminal and claustrophobic elements of Phaedra's—and the audience's—positioning can only have amplified the suffocating dread of the tragedy, which moves with swift inexorability to the death of its two (in 1677) titular characters.

Phèdre, Comédie-Française, April 18, 1689

In his preface to the play Racine claims that it intends not to arouse passions but rather to "visually present" them, "only to show all the disorder they create."[55] In other words he offers *Phèdre* as an *objet*, a word with dual denotations in seventeenth-century French. In keeping with its etymology (the Latin *objectum*, "to present to sight"), it means "object" but also "spectacle."[56] In his emphasis on ocularity—he modifies the verb *presenter* specifically with *aux yeux*—the playwright seems to presume a detached subject, who, like Descartes or Kepler or Galileo, will observe and learn. His spectator must objectify the stage picture. In "Die Zeit des Weltbildes" ("The Age of the World Picture"), Martin Heidegger defines this process as "a setting-before [*Vor-stellen*], a representing, that aims at bringing each particular being before it in such a way that man who calculates [*der rechnende Mensch*] can be sure, and that means be certain of that being."⁵⁷ Racine's defense of the play, then, makes little sense with regard to the 1677 production, because the Hôtel de Bourgogne hardly emphasized visuality or facilitated objectification. Indeed, as d'Aubignac complained of the theaters of his day, seeing was "very inconvenient," with "the majority of the loges being too far off and badly situated, and the parterre having neither elevation nor seats."⁵⁸ The sight lines were terrible; especially with the proliferation of onstage spectators, the stage picture was too compromised, too enmeshed with its surroundings. Theater design of the late seventeenth century was undergoing a transformation, however: one that would separate the spectators from the actors—the stage from the house—and one that would therefore encourage in spectators the same objective detachment that Descartes had promoted in his philosophy. The first permanent home of the Comédie-Française (sometimes called, in documents of the period, the Théâtre des François or Français) represents an important step in this transformation.

The troupe had been formed by order of Louis XIV, who had gradually reduced Paris's public acting companies from three to one: in 1673 the Théâtre du Marais merged with Molière's troupe at the Théâtre du Palais-Royal, and, in 1680, the merged troupe absorbed the Hôtel de Bourgogne actors at the Hôtel de Guénégaud on the Left Bank, where Armande Béjart would encounter her amorous spectator. After playing in several venues in the intervening years, the consolidated Comédie-Française acquired, in 1688, a *jeu de paume* on the rue des Fossés-Saint-Germain-des-Prés, in what is now the sixth arrondissement. They opted not to install themselves in it. Rather, they demolished it and its two adjacent buildings and had a new space built directly to their specifications. Designed by the architect François d'Orbay, the house would open on April 18, 1689, with an inaugural performance of Racine's play, which had been brought to the new repertory from the Hôtel de Bourgogne (Figure 4.4).⁵⁹

Several features of the new theater seem deliberately designed to quell the dangers of actor/audience contagion that *Phèdre* uncomfortably evokes, and, indeed, these features were deliberate insofar as they strove to guarantee perspectival stagecraft in ways that the Hôtel de Bourgogne, despite its renovations, never could. As at the older theater, there were nineteen loges in each tier. But, as per the most radical design feature, these loges curved in a semicircle, providing the spectators in each box

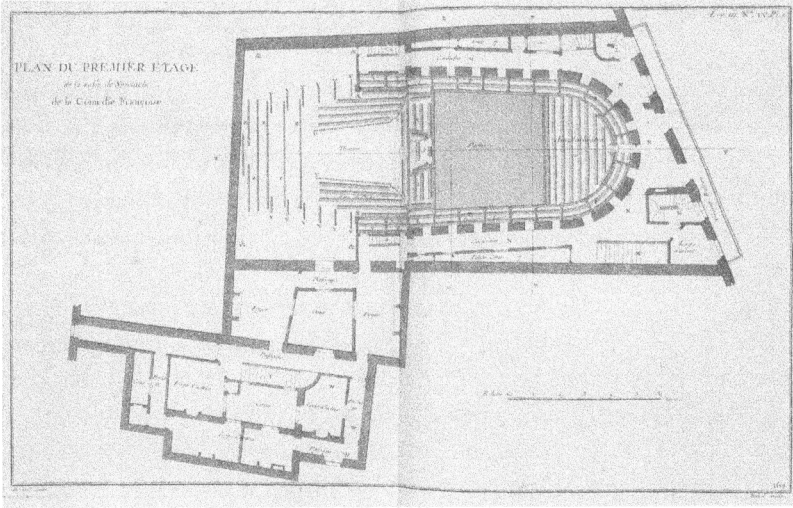

FIGURE 4.4. Jean-François Blondel's gravure of François d'Orbay's *salle de la Comédie-Française*. Note that the plan represents a later renovation: the *enceintes de la balustrade* that I discuss are here shown to contain four-and-a-half rows each; they were initially shorter and contained only two. The plate appears in Blondel, *Architecture française*, 4 vols. (Paris: Charles-Antoine Jombert, 1752–56), vol. 2, book 3, chapter 4, plate 2. Courtesy Rare Books and Special Collections, McGill University.

with a vista into the stage picture, which was perfectly centered for the tenth box. Historians have wondered why this curvature, common in Italian theater design, took so long to reach Paris, when the reasons were clearly not economic: in 1644, for example, after the Théâtre du Marais was destroyed in a fire, its troupe chose to rebuild it in the same rectangular *jeu de paume* configuration.[60] So-called Italianate design elements, like curved loges and proscenium arches, were inextricably bound to Cartesianism in France, so that its theater design—first in private playhouses, then public—evolved in tandem with Cartesianism's ascent.

In the second of his *Meditations*, Descartes defined the Archimedean point as that which is "fixed and immovable" and proposed its perspective as the best hope of discovering one thing that is "certain and unshaken."[61] Theater design could literalize this zero point. Accordingly, various critics have noted that the perfect vantage point for perspectival illusion came to represent the Cartesian ideal of objectivity: it is the "angelic 'I'," in Karsten Harries's terms; the "monocentric reality" (*vérité monocentrée*) that equates to rationality, in Jean-Joseph Goux's.[62] The word *perspective* derives from the Latin *perspicere*, which, Claudio Guillén reminds us, means not only "to see clearly" but also "to examine," "to regard mentally," and "to ascertain."[63] If the purpose of perspectival stagecraft is to help its audience not only to see clearly but also to examine, it is not coincidental that public auditoria took on rounder and rounder shapes. In my first chapter I noted the uncanny similarity between Descartes's diagrams of the eye in perception and the layout of Louis XIV's *salle des machines*, built in 1662 and considered the most technologically advanced theater of its day (Figures 1.2 and 1.3). The 1689 Comédie-Française represents only the first of many public theaters that would try to narrow the perspective of a spectating body into a single ocular line, giving each spectator as close an approximation as possible of the perfect vantage point enjoyed by royalty in private playhouses. (In light of these playhouses the perspectivally best box of the Comédie-Française was not reserved for the king, as was the practice in Italy.)[64] Thus was d'Orbay's theater "drawn and established according to optical forms" in order to encourage "the best way to see," as a document of the period puts it.[65] This vantage point passed through an elaborate and visually assertive proscenium arch, which we can liken to a cornea or—since the stage was now semiotically marked as another world—to the lens of a telescope.

During the performance of a tragedy, the perspective from offstage was intended to guide the viewer's eye to the center of the perfectly symmetrical set known as the *palais à volonté*, which came to be used for all tragedies at the Comédie-Française sometime after 1680.[66] The theater's wing structure, as can be seen in Jean-François Blondel's engraving, helped to compose and frame a universal setting that, however generic its design, was very precise in its signification: "not here." A function of a *Neuzeit* or modern age, in Heidegger's terms, the *palais à volonté* severed itself from the viewing subject, to whom it provided a picture for objectification.[67] The world of the house—the parterre, loges, aisles, and foyers—was now semiotically coded as the domain of the spectator, whose role was to observe. The world of the stage—as well as backstage spaces and dressing rooms—belonged to the characters and to the actors who inhabited them. Anatomizing the new theater, we see that it provided two separate systems for circulation, unlike the cross-contaminating Hôtel de Bourgogne. (Indeed, a small capillary joining the two systems, the last site of potential leakage, was blocked eight years after the theater opened.)[68] Joining with the proscenium arch to enforce and visually mark the separation of the two worlds was an orchestra, which could provide seating for the musicians who had sat in the rear loges at the Hôtel de Bourgogne.[69] If, for Guillén, "the idea of perspective can readily be associated with a growing epistemological dualism, with a rigorous split between subject and object," the design of the new theater attempted to map this dualism onto the theatrical space, encouraging spectators to objectify the picture before them, to behave as pure mind.[70]

The encouragement was in vain: the parterre continued to be the site of considerable misbehavior in the eighteenth century, as Jeffrey Ravel has shown in *The Contested Parterre: Public Theater and French Political Culture, 1680–1791*. But my thesis complements rather than contradicts Ravel's. If he claims that parterre standees of the 1680s grew more hostile vis-à-vis the stage, I claim that a necessary precondition for this hostility was a new design imperative that effected the mitosis of one group into two. (For T. E. Lawrenson this 1689 mitosis was definitive, after which "little or no semblance of the legitimate stage is to be seen," in his spirited assessment.)[71] If the sixteenth-century playhouse was a single pot in which all could mingle, the late seventeenth-century playhouse had firmly established—and structurally policed—its subjects and objects. And, as Heidegger theorized, the constitution of the former creates its opposition in the latter.[72]

Unlike the private playhouses such as the king's *salle des machines*, however, public theaters—and the stockholding troupes that managed them—had to deal with scores of theatrical consumers who demanded to sit on the stage as they were accustomed, regardless of the newly created ontological untenability. And whatever the actors' wishes, economics dictated that the practice would continue.[73] In response to the attendant problems both practical (e.g., spectator interference) and ontological (e.g., the breaching of the stage world), the actors devised an ingenious solution for their new space: wrought-iron balustrades were installed to surround the onstage spectators in two spaces called the *enceintes*. The floor and benches in these enclosures were covered in green fabric, and the railings were topped with golden knobs; this ornamentation, along with the *enceintes'* shape, visually incorporated the onstage spectators, along with three tiers of *avant-scène* loges, into the proscenium arch, as shown in Jean Le Pautre's 1690 frontispiece to *Les fables d'Ésope* (Aesop's fables) by Edmé Boursault, the credited author of the Molière-maligning play *The Painter's Portrait* that we encountered in Chapter 3 (Figure 4.5).[74] Collectively, this structure constituted a thick limen that enclosed the stage, effecting an aesthetic and ontological containment. The stage picture was properly framed. By means of the balustrades, a compromise was struck between the public theater's economic and its aesthetic/epistemological exigencies. But so, too, was the clear direction of theater design heralded, and in time theaters would conform to an even more rigorous Cartesian ideal, as we will see at the Queen's Theatre in the Haymarket in 1707. Standees in the parterre would be seated in rows, fixed and curved to mimic the retinal curvature of the loges, and (although it would take some time) onstage spectators would be banned altogether.[75] These features would further discipline theatergoing subjects into ocular objectivity, with each one's vista corresponding, as well as theater architects could muster, with the empirically best vantage point. Their patterns of movements through the space—like those of the actors in their own, separate circulatory system—would carve new cultural memories into the body of the theater, memories that differed notably from those of the Hôtel de Bourgogne.

Herzel bemoans the fact that "the distinctive individual settings for Racine's plays were sacrificed to expediency" when the Hôtel de Bourgogne troupe was folded into the new Comédie-Française and the *palais à volonté* became de rigueur; he presumes that the new need to run shows in repertory, with seven performances a week, made individual settings materially unfeasible.[76] But this change in set design practice resonates, too, with broader cultural pressures wrought by Cartesianism. The universalizing *palais à volonté*, along with other new staging customs, would have changed the signification of *Phèdre* on April 18, 1689. Performed in a theater that not only provided better sight lines but architecturally emphasized perspective and spectation, the production must have foregrounded Racine's thematic preoccupation with ocularity, which provides

FIGURE 4.5. The frontispiece to Edmé Boursault, *Les fables d'Ésope* (Paris: Theodore Girard, 1690), shows the *enceintes de la balustrade* (here unoccupied) in their original dimensions. Courtesy Division of Rare and Manuscript Collections, Cornell University Library.

an image-system as multivalent and richly integrated into the play as its blood imagery.

For, in keeping with Racine's claim that it is presented "aux yeux," the play obsesses on seeing: in its various conjugations, the verb "to see" (*voir*) appears eighty-four times, and "eye" (*œil*) is the single most common noun in the play's lexicon, with it or "eyes" (*yeux*) appearing sixty-five times. Hippolytus's eyes cannot leave Aricia; Oenone frets that her mistress will expire "before her eyes"; Phaedra's husband, thought dead, returns to "appear before [her] eyes," to list just a few examples.[77] When Theseus does return to Troezen, emerging into the play in its third act, he asks bluntly: "What do I see?"[78] So pervasive is the trope of sight in the play that even sleep is said to "enter the eyes" and Phaedra can claim that her (verbal) declaration of shameful love to Hippolytus was made to his eyes, rather than to his ears.[79] It is no surprise, therefore, that Phaedra's breakdown involves an ocular crisis. She explains to Oenone that her "eyes no longer saw" once she had seen Hippolytus; before her suicide her eye will no longer recognize her own servants, according to Panope's report.[80] More troubling, however, is the proliferation of false visual perceptions that Phaedra experiences. When Hippolytus confesses to Aricia that his eyes continually see her when she is not present, Racine means to underscore the prince's parallels to Phaedra, who sees her stepson "endlessly" in his absence.[81] Racine links visual perceptions with thoughts—mental images—just as Descartes does in *The Passions of the Soul*. Thus the playwright theatrically enacts the famous gambit of the second of Descartes's *Meditations*, where the philosopher contemplates the impossibility of the Archimedean point and supposes that his eyes might always be deceived.[82] Part of this deception inheres, of course, in the entanglement of perception with emotion, of the eyes with the body whose blood effects the physiological transformations that testify to subjectivity.

Racine vividly represents the subjective nature of seeing—as Guérin emphasizes in his painting, in which Hippolytus, Theseus, and Phaedra are shown in the act of looking. Guérin's Hippolytus sneaks a peek; his Theseus glowers; his Phaedra directs an anguished, piercing gaze out at her viewers. Thus the painter reminds us that people may look and see differently from one another. He pictorially translates one of *Phèdre*'s dramatic themes: in the play Aricia disparages Theseus's eyes, which alone cannot see Hippolytus's virtue, and Theseus retorts that love blinds her; Oenone wishes that Phaedra had had her nurse's eyes, instead of her own, to see Hippolytus, whom Phaedra can denounce as "a fearful monster in my eyes" only after Theseus's ill-timed return.[83] In each of these instances the character makes explicit or implicit reference to a correct view, and both Phaedra and Theseus will bemoan that their eyes had been deceived. But such allusions to objectively correct perception sit in productive tension with the play's abundant descriptions of emotionally colored, subjective perception, and Theseus's emphasis in particular is noteworthy: "What eye would not have been deceived like mine?" he asks.[84]

Visualizing the new space of the Comédie-Française on April 18, 1689—filled with spectators eager to see the new theater—we can imagine how this productive tension would have been performed by the assembled bodies. The theater's design attempted to enforce the spectators' perspective and to separate them decisively from the spectacle. By these attempts the theater's spatial logic sought to promote objectivity, to guard against the ocular deceptions that befall Phaedra and her husband. However, d'Orbay's design is inconsistent: note, in Blondel's gravure, how the partitions between the loges face the center of the house (and the possibly unruly parterre audience) instead of angling toward the stage and its actors. Meanwhile, the parterre spectators (still standing and looking in whatever direction they pleased)[85] and the onstage spectators behind their balustrades (forgoing the perspectivally correct vista in favor of a close-up side angle) both provide analogues for the competing points of view that *Phèdre* presents: for Racine substantially undermines the notion of objective seeing, or at least acknowledges the impossibility of an Archimedean perspective, in ways that d'Orbay does only unwittingly.

Once filled with people, the 1689 theater would have generated friction between the subject/object dichotomy that its design inculcates (in which the stage is objectified) and the heterogeneous, subjective perspectives that its practical functioning guaranteed. The collective of actors and audience would have performed the dynamics of Racine's play, which slyly inhere not in either its sanguinary or its ocular discourse but rather in their coexistence and even conflict. For ultimately the playwright collides these two image systems to powerful dramatic effect. Theseus will describe the "bloody image" (*sanglante image*) of his son, who has been so disfigured that (Theramenes reports) "even the eye of his father would not recognize" the "*triste objet.*"[86] Racine deploys the phrase in both of its meanings. The sad object, the sad spectacle, will not be enjoyed by the audience, which cannot judge for itself: Hippolytus's unrecognizable body, like his death, is described rather than shown. In his climactic fifth-act speech Theramenes will effectively usurp the audience's vision, and, invoking his own sight nine times in one monologue, he will describe the grisly chariot ride that has obliterated Hippolytus.[87] Longing to ocularly consume something that is withheld, meanwhile, the audience members would have found their objectifying impulses rebuked even as their thoughts drew mental images and their blood quickened at the horror. Indeed, the play uncomfortably aligns the spectator with its titular character. As it ends, *Phèdre* grimly recalls its own beginning, when Phaedra had entered with her eyes "dazzled by the light" and had wished that she was watching Hippolytus's chariot—following it with her eye, in the pointed French expression (*suivre de l'œil*).[88]

Phædra and Hippolitus, Queen's Theatre, Haymarket, April 21, 1707

The notion of subjectivity does not contradict but rather makes possible the notion of "perfect objectivity." This fact, claims Jean-Joseph Goux, stands behind both the practice of perspective in the seventeenth century and the Cartesian *cogito*.[89] But if subjectivity gave birth to objectivity, the longing for the latter is always shadowed by the biases of the former—a paradox performed in the tension between the design imperatives of the Comédie-Française's 1689 space, on one hand, and the experience of its spectators, on the other. Descartes's correspondence with Elisabeth of Bohemia testifies that both were attuned to the subjectivist nuances of "objectivity" in his philosophy—the impossibility of Archimedes's point—but many of these nuances were lost as Cartesianism developed as a philosophical doctrine after his death. Thus a too-rigid mind/body dualism would come to elide the complications of *The Passions of the Soul*, for example, and thus a philosophy with considerable emancipatory potential for women would come to reinforce sexist essentialisms—especially as rationality, never a gendered ideal in Descartes, came to be affiliated with the masculine. Whatever nuances concerning the limits of objectivity are expressed in Descartes's letters to Elisabeth, both Cartesianism and (relatedly) theater design would continue to strive toward unrealizable ideals as they developed. An apotheosis can be discerned in the first British production of *Phèdre*—adapted by Edmund Smith and retitled *Phædra and Hippolitus*—which premiered on April 21, 1707, at the Queen's Theatre in the Haymarket, London.

The journey that European theatrical architecture took in the seventeenth and eighteenth centuries proceeded in phases—as proscenium arches and stage curtains were introduced, as parterre standees were seated and onstage spectators were removed, as aprons dwindled and actors were moved behind the proscenium—but its direction was consistent. This journey served to press the imperatives of ocularity, which triumph in the playwright John Vanbrugh's design for the Haymarket theater. By 1666, when d'Aubignac had called for the abolition of standing in Paris's theaters, parterre audiences were already seated in all of London's.[90] However, in Vanbrugh's theater (which he opened with William Congreve in 1705) these seats—like the loges—rigorously followed the arc of the building's structure, which was planned around a sphere with a twenty-foot radius, as shown in Graham Barlow's reconstruction (Figure 4.6).

Critics like Barlow have noted that Vanbrugh's design bears the influence of classical and Palladian architecture, and, indeed, Samuel Garth's "Prologue Spoken at the Opening of the Queen's Theatre in the *Hay-Market*" praises these virtues.[91] However, by imagining the premiere production of *Phædra and Hippolitus*, we can see how these putatively classical features were now freighted with Cartesian significance. (In this regard they are like the libertine Loveless in Vanbrugh's most famous play, *The Relapse*, who enters, at the play's beginning, while reading. "How true is that Philosophy, which says, / Our Heaven is seated in our Minds," he declares, voicing an idea that the play's audience would have recognized as Cartesian.)[92] In his prologue Garth praises the theater as an example of reason's triumph in a new age that had decisively broken with an ignorant past. "In the good Age of Ghostly Ignorance, / How did Cathedrals rise, and Zeal advance?" he asks, before noting that "now that pious Pageantry's no more, / And Stages thrive, as Churches did before."[93] Significantly, he stresses that the modern project of the Haymarket theater outshines even its classical forebears. Thus

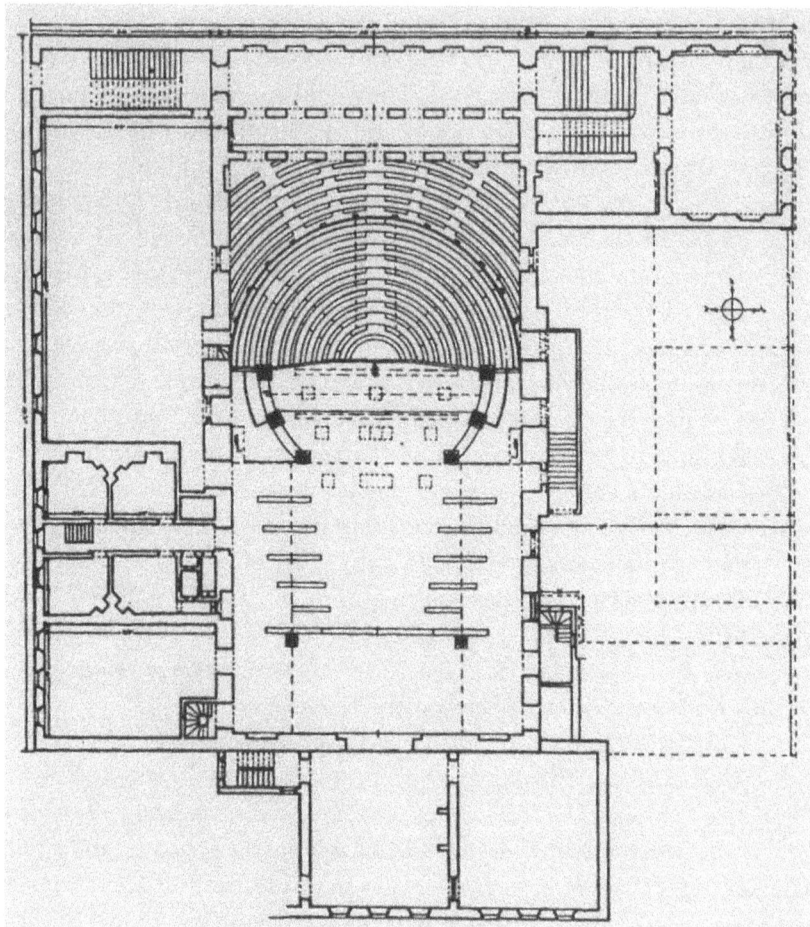

FIGURE 4.6. Reconstruction of the original Queen's Theatre in the Haymarket, circa 1707, from Graham Barlow, "Vanbrugh's Queen's Theatre in the Haymarket, 1703–1709," *Early Music* 17, no. 4 (Nov. 1989): 515–21, at 516. Reprinted with the permission of *Early Music* and Oxford University Press.

the prologue—spoken under Vanbrugh's elaborate proscenium arch and the theater's magnificent ceiling, designed by James Thornhill—can boast that "Descending Goddesses" have "quit their bright Abodes" for the "gilt Machines" in the Haymarket, and that the space could rival the sun itself. "*Shou'd* Jove, *for this fair* Circle, *leave his Throne*," the prologue hypothesizes,

He'd meet a Lightning fiercer than his own.
Tho to the Sun, his tow'ring Eagles rise,
They scarce cou'd bear the Lustre of these Eyes.[94]

As the last clause of the poem attests, ocularity triumphs. In fact, so all-encompassing was the visual focus of Vanbrugh's theater—with its "emphatic circularity"[95]—that an ironic problem arose. As at Louis XIV's eyelike *salle des machines*, the acoustics were terrible, the soaring ceiling causing the actors' voices to sound like "the Gabbling of so many People, in the lofty Isles in a Cathedral," in the words of Colley Cibber, who estimated that "scarce one Word in ten, could be distinctly heard in it."[96]

The visual triumphs, too, in Smith's rendering, which emphasizes Racine's ocular imagery and stresses the power of sight: Theseus's "joyful Eyes" may, upon his homecoming, greet his son, for example; graces can "dar[t] from [Phaedra's] Eyes"; and the "sight" of Hippolitus threatens to "kill" Phaedra.[97] This threat is, of course, potent. In one of Smith's closest paraphrases of Racine, Phaedra laments of her stepson: "Can I forget? Can I drive [him] from my Soul? / Oh! he will still be present to my Eyes."[98] But when Phaedra misrecognizes Theseus and stabs at him with Hippolitus's sword, her faltering vision can now stand in contrast to the unimpaired vision of the audience, whose vista is trained directly on the perspectival vanishing point. The sight lines in Vanbrugh's theater facilitated a disentangling of theatrical subjects and objects much more effectively than the Comédie-Française had, and there were neither standees nor onstage spectators to compromise the stage picture.[99] This picture can become fully objectified; the audience's seeing can dominate the scene. In this way Vanbrugh's theater seems to anticipate the engraving of Claude Nicolas Ledoux's theater at Besançon, France, in which the eye and the playhouse are represented as fully coterminous (Figure 4.7).[100]

Such an ocular view of Racine's play would become pervasive. For example, in his famous consideration "Racine et la poétique du regard" (Racine and the poetics of the glance), Jean Starobinski describes a play entirely dominated by an ocular poetics. He writes: "if the characters neither embrace nor strike one another on the stage, however, they see one another. Scenes, in Racine, are *interviews*."[101] While he understands that "seeing is an act of pathos" and that the characters' glances "disturb the soul," he nonetheless deracinates visual perception from its intensely corporeal effects.[102]

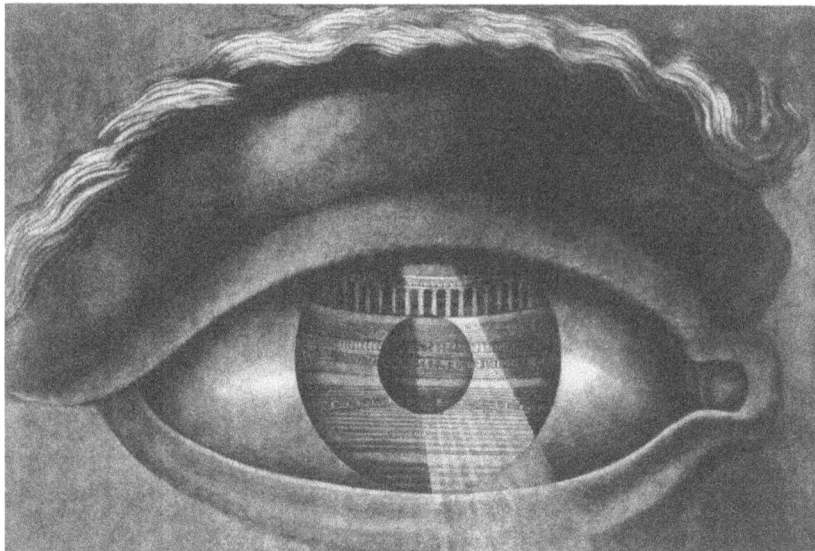

FIGURE 4.7. Ledoux's theater at Besançon, known for its superior sight lines. From Claude Nicolas Ledoux, "Coup-d'œil du théatre de Besançon," in his *L'architecture considérée sous le rapport de l'art, des mœurs et de la législation*, 2 vols. (Paris: H. L. Perronneau, 1804), vol. 1, plate 113. Courtesy Bibliothèque nationale de France.

And, unsurprisingly, he imagines Racine not in the Hôtel de Bourgogne with unique sets but in a later *palais à volonté* with its "stage, almost bare" of "porticos, colonnades, and marble panels."[103] The play's sanguinary imagery, so vitally emphasized by the blood-compromised space of its premiere performance, is forgotten to such an extent that the play's audience can be imagined only as a reading public; rather than risking intersubjective contamination along with the characters, these readers can achieve the objective detachment that Heidegger describes in "The Age of the World Picture." Likewise apprehending the play visually (and via the book), Starobinski sees "the word *voir*, itself almost invisible in its monosyllabic brevity," leading "the reader's eye to the heart of the essential relationship of characters united only in the exchange of glances."[104]

More than 250 years earlier, Smith, too, expunged *Phèdre*'s sanguinary discourse in emphasizing its ocular discourse. And just as the

Queen's Theatre in the Haymarket disentangled actors and audiences, so, too, the text of *Phædra and Hippolitus* disentangles the bloodlines that prove so treacherous in Racine. Aricia—her character has been collapsed into her servant Ismène and renamed Ismena—is no longer tainted by her brothers' perfidy, so the central hindrance to Hippolitus's love for her is removed; she represents no threat to Theseus's crown.[105] Meanwhile, the toxicity of Phaedra's lust for her stepson is mitigated by the spirit, if not the letter, of the law: the play repeatedly insists that she has not consummated her marriage to "wrinkled Theseus"[106]—who was played by Thomas Betterton, then well into his sixties, in semiretirement, and plagued by gout.[107] Indeed, the playwright thoroughly emasculates Theseus, erasing all reference to his epic virility and, pathetically, sending him to war in compensation for his impotent marriage. As Phaedra reports:

I still deny'd my Lord, my Husband *Theseus*,
The chaste, the modest Joys of spotless Marriage;
That drove him hence to War, to stormy Seas,
To Rocks and Waves less cruel than his *Phædra*.[108]

Smith thus attenuates Phaedra's incestuous desire and even suggests that Hippolitus might have been a more appropriate love-object all along. As one character rhetorically inquires, for example:

Why did she wed old *Theseus*? While his Son,
The brave *Hippolitus*, with equal Youth,
And equal Beauty might have fill'd her Arms.[109]

After Theseus's apparent death, even Ismena can encourage Hippolitus to "take to your Arms Imperial *Phædra*"—a choice that would seem disturbingly logical (love having been removed from the equation) from the perspective of politics and succession.[110]

In Racine's play he had represented how the emotions, as passions of the soul, could run riot over the undisciplined mind. Without mental discipline, he shows, the subject is divided against itself, made porous. "Do what you will, I abandon myself to you . . . I can do nothing for myself," his Phaedra wails, appropriately to no one in particular, for while she seems to address Oenone, she makes this declaration immediately after she sees Hippolytus.[111] As its original, binomial title suggests, the play extends the problems of the collapsing subject to Hippolytus, who, we must recall, meets a gorier end than his stepmother. For in offering him her love, Phaedra offers Hippolytus an unmoored subject position. The playwright makes this clear (and revisits his thematic preoccupations with consanguinity and sanguinary contamination) when stepmother courts stepson by reimagining her husband's fateful meeting with her sister, Ariadne. Perversely, Phaedra recasts son for father and sister for sister: "You would have slain the monster from Crete," she declares; "I, Prince, it is I whose invaluable assistance / Would have taught you the labyrinth's detours."[112] Note Phaedra's habitation of Ariadne's first-person singular pronoun. Remarking on how much the absent Theseus resembles his son—and, tellingly, not the other way around—she describes, for example, how she loved Theseus because Hippolytus's "noble modesty colored his face."[113] "He had your bearing, your eyes, your speech," she explains, and—even after recanting and then blaming her confusion on the "poison" of love—she tells Oenone that she wishes only that Hippolytus would become the father of her son by Theseus.[114] Representing intersubjectivity as a dramatic annihilation of a locatable subject-position, Racine implies that this annihilation is the effect of too-intense emotional experience.

Smith, however, lifts Hippolitus's yokes and disentangles him from the reins, and at the end of *Phædra and Hippolitus* he is quite unharmed. Removing the sanguinary impediments that stand between subjects and objects, Smith thus unbalances Racine's play and mutes its interrogation of the emotions. He consequently saps much of its strength. Smith's Phaedra proclaims that she "groan[s] beneath / The Pain, the Guilt, the Shame of impious Love," but, in fact, we see little evidence of this emotional burden.[115] In Racine the emotions' all-encompassing nature is shown to erode the subject's agency to the extent that Phaedra struggles, until the fifth act, even to commit suicide. Smith entirely tames this awesome power, and, accordingly, his Phaedra can snatch Hippolitus's sword and, in a gesture of self-assertion, try to stab herself. (Her impulse toward self-sacrifice—noble, by the logic of the play—is squelched by Lycon, Smith's masculinized version of Oenone and Phaedra's scheming "Minister of the State.") In Racine the emotions play the same role that Poseidon does in Euripides's version of the myth. They are given the power to obliterate

Hippolytus—a power that suggests, in keeping with Racine's Jansenist inflections, our overwhelming powerlessness in the face of sin and under the burden of our emotional tethers. However, in one of Smith's many substitutions, he ultimately bestows act 5's subject-shattering power on Theseus himself: his potency renewed by his reunion with his son, he condemns the villainous Lycon to be "wrackt and gancht, impal'd alive."[116] In Racine, Theramenes asks, "Are you no longer . . . Hippolytus?" when his friend is transformed by love for Aricia.[117] And in Smith, Hippolitus asks his stepmother: "Are you not *Phædra*?"[118] But when the contrite Phaedra confesses that "Another Soul / Informs my alter'd Frame," the emphasis is quite different from that laid by Theramenes.[119] She testifies not to the soul-destroying effects of her love for her stepson but, more banally, to the insidious counsel of the minister who informs her.

These differences manifest the adaptation's underlying logic. Relieving the emotions of their agency-sapping force, Smith presents them, instead, as artillery in the strategies of agents such as Lycon, who, for example, can soliloquize out of Theseus's earshot:

> Now, *Lycon*, heighten his impatient Love,
> Now raise his Pity, now enflame his Rage,
> Quicken his Hopes, then quash 'em with Despair,
> Work his tumultuous Passions with Frenzy;
> Unite 'em all, then turn them on the Foe.[120]

If Racine portrayed emotion and reason, and mind and body, as mutually imbricated—in a manner consonant with Descartes's writings—Smith shows each pair instead as fully dichotomized. Lycon, a clearer villain than Oenone, is curiously unemotional, motivated entirely by his thirst for power; he exploits the gullibility of both Phaedra and the emasculated Theseus as he jockeys for power and schemes to prevent Hippolitus, a clearer hero than in Racine, from ever ruling Troezen. The play's hero and villain become its clear subjects, contrasted in the play's final line: "Th'Accus'd is happy, while th'Accuser dyes."[121] The accuser is Lycon, who has entirely orchestrated Phaedra's play for Hippolitus and made the charge of rape; and the play's ending is managed so that this accuser gets impaled while the accused gets to "live for ever in *Ismena*'s Arms."[122] The audience, presumably, is meant to applaud this happy ending and, like

Theseus, Ismena, and Hippolitus before them, spend no time mourning Phaedra, finally dead by her own hand in the immediately previous scene. In Racine, Phaedra does not objectify Hippolytus but rather threatens, in her emotional dissolution, his very subjectivity. In Smith, Phaedra is recast as a clear object (usually of derision) and used to throw Hippolitus, as a discrete subject, into relief.

Forgoing Racine's poison for something showier, then, Phaedra stabs herself onstage, and the play's spectacularization of her corpse tells. She plays body to Lycon's mind, and she represents emotionality in contrast to his clever premeditations, which manipulate her feelings for strategic ends. By the play's logic, only Hippolitus and Lycon provide sites of identification for its spectating subjects—their eyes trained, per Vanbrugh's design, on Phaedra as suffering object. Ignoring her death, in other words, the plot replicates the functioning of the space itself, which tames the intersubjective potential that Racine's Phaedra represents and, instead, objectifies her. Anatomizing the Hôtel de Bourgogne, I noted its messy circulatory logic, how the passageways carrying actors and audience collapsed like Hippolytus on the waves. Here, the blood is missing. At the Queen's Theatre in the Haymarket, the audience would have sat back and, their gaze truly so called, watched the show. It represented the sort of picture that Heidegger describes as "the structured image [*Gebild*] that is the creature of man's producing which represents and sets before."[123] As Heidegger reveals, moreover, it is man who regards the picture, and the masculinized gaze at the Queen's Theatre in the Haymarket in 1707 mirrored the gendering that Smith effected. He relegates both Phaedra and the startlingly passive Ismena to object positions; he assembles the feminine agencies that had animated Racine's tragedy—Phaedra's burning desires, Aricia's hold over Hippolytus, Oenone's schemes—and concentrates them in Lycon's plotting. This concentration leaves a residue: for example, Oenone's duties as nurse to Phaedra are relegated to Ismena. But the play's saturated emotionality is dissipated, inappropriate as it is for the hyperrational hero, for the cool-headed villain, or, indeed, for an audience that is discouraged even from ruing Phaedra's spectacular death.

That *Phædra and Hippolitus* simplified Racine's *Phèdre* was clear even to its first audiences. For example, the early eighteenth-century periodical *Muses Mercury* noted tactfully that "there is so much Art and Delicacy in the Conduct of *Racine's Phædra* . . . that it would have been surprizing, if we shou'd have found all these Qualities in a young Poets *first* Play."[124] Smith's play is based on a seventeenth-century precedent whose complications are tidily resolved and whose misogyny is greatly exaggerated, and in this way it can serve as an analogue for Cartesianism as a discourse; Smith bowdlerizes his source by resolving all of its tensions, thus adumbrating the resolutions effected on Descartes's writings, which teem with contradictions and nuances. Crude dualisms—mind/body, emotion/reason—result. The tidy gendering of subject and object in *Phædra and Hippolitus*, for example, aligns precisely with the gendering of subject and object in Cartesianism.[125] And the objectifying force of Smith's adaptation—Phaedra is likened to Theseus's "yet warm Urn"[126]—does not reflect its source material so much as a cultural shift that took place after Descartes's death. Even more fundamentally, the hard distinction between subject and object that Smith draws, and that Vanbrugh's theater abets, aligns precisely with Cartesianism's separation of subject from object. Henri Lefebvre has claimed that "by conceiving of the subject without an object (the pure thinking 'I' or *res cogitans*), and of an object without a subject (the body-as-machine or *res extensa*), philosophy created an irrevocable rift in what it was trying to define. . . . The living body, being at once 'subject' and 'object,' cannot tolerate such conceptual division."[127] My claim is that Cartesianism created this problem precisely by simplifying Descartes's ideas—insufficiently attuned as Descartes's interpreters were to the nuances of his thinking and especially his late thinking. To invoke Irigaray, we need a careful rereading of Descartes to restore to the emotions their due power and to reevaluate the possibilities of intersubjectivity for Descartes's subject.

Phaedra's remark that she cannot govern "when I have lost dominion over my senses . . . / When I am dying" offers the bluntest retort to tooblunt dualisms: there can be no mind in a dead body.[128] Exercising the tragedian's prerogative and revealing his Jansenist biases, Racine dwells on the emotions' negative potential, but he also dramatically captures their capacity to connect subject and object. In response to Hippolytus, Phaedra experiences the gamut of physiological perturbations that Descartes itemizes in *The Passions of the Soul*, as the animal spirits course through the subject's body and send blood rushing here and fleeing there. She declares, for example, that

> my strength abandons me.
> My vision is blurred by the day's light,
> And my trembling knees buckle under me.

And, later:

> I saw him, I blushed, I turned pale.
> A trouble arose in my frantic soul.
> My eyes couldn't see, I couldn't speak,
> I felt my entire body freeze and burn.[129]

Even the weight of her hair brings pain as her mind breaks down. Significantly, however, Phaedra's loss of agency in Racine's play is not effected by her objectification but by her entanglement, not only with Hippolytus but also with the entire legacy of her family, her "deplorable blood."[130] Metaphorically and literally, she learns, this blood mitigates her self-determination.

The brunt of this lesson in Racine is borne by the Pallantide princess Aricia, enslaved because of her brothers' perfidy. And it was driven home powerfully to Descartes by the Princess Palatine Elisabeth, whose emotional upheavals invariably emanated from her blood relatives. For example, on November 30, 1645, Elisabeth wrote of her brother Edward:

I thought that a strong resolution to seek true happiness only in things that depend on my will would render me less sensitive to those that come from elsewhere when the folly of one of my brothers exposed my weakness. It [i.e., his folly] has troubled my body's health and my soul's tranquility more than all of my previous misfortunes. If you take the trouble to read the gazette, you could not fail to know that he has fallen into the hands of people who have more hatred for our house than affection for their religion, and has been caught in their snares so tightly as to change his religion and make himself a Roman Catholic.[131]

As we would expect, the Catholic Descartes was peevish in responding, reminding her that "those of my religion (who are, without doubt, the great number in Europe) are obliged to approve" of such a conversion.[132] But he does not question her mind-body logic, and, indeed, he is sympathetic to it, especially when she writes of her mental and physical upheavals after her uncle Charles I of England was executed in the Civil War (in which her brothers Rupert and Maurice fought)[133] or after her brother Philip murdered one of their mother's suitors.[134] A key difference, of course, intervenes between Descartes's presentation of the mind-body emotional connection and Racine's: the philosopher, unlike the playwright, sees the value in these emotions and in their role in decision making. As Elisabeth put it so succinctly in September 1645, "experience" shows "that there are passions that do lead to reasonable actions."[135]

In one of his most eloquent letters to the princess, Descartes wrote that "the most common cause of low-grade fever is sadness, and Fortune's persistence in persecuting your house continually gives you matters for annoyance that are so public and so explosive that there is no need to use conjecture, nor to be accomplished in these matters, to judge that the principal cause of your indisposition consists in them."[136] Elisabeth's ailments, he asserts, derive from her emotions, but, far from encouraging a stoic refusal of these emotions, Descartes sees them as emanating from her own good judgment. (The concerns that wracked her health were hardly trivial, and, as for Aricia, for Elisabeth the personal was also political: even her long search for a permanent home was directly caused by the Thirty Years' War, which exiled her family.) When Descartes reminded her to think that "one does not know how to subsist alone," in other words, he did not bemoan this fact but used it as the basis for an ethics that explicitly prefers "the interest of the whole, of which one is a part"[137]—an interest to which one is alerted, of course, by one's passionate interactions. It is appropriate, therefore, that in Racine's darker picture these interactions appear as ties of blood. Maximizing the denotative multivalence of the word *sang*, Racine marries the physiological perturbations of blood—engendered by the outside objects of emotion—to the burdens of filiation. In Smith's bloodless rendering something essential is lost.

Contemplating the intersubjective experience with Hippolytus that Phaedra seeks in Racine, we can mobilize and connect two strands of Racine criticism. The first is that the play is self-reflexive, thematizing the nature and effects of tragedy—an argument made most famously in Marc Fumaroli's *Héros et orateurs* (Heroes and orators) but encountered elsewhere.[138] The second is that the playwright, steeped as he was in the rhetoric of his Jansenist educators, worried about the porousness of the subject that he dramatizes. As I discussed in my first chapter, even non-Jansenist theologians like Jacques Bénigne Bossuet worried about the transformations effected in the actors (by the roles they played) and in the spectators (by the performances they watched), and we can see *Phèdre* as staging just such worrisome changes, as the body is reshaped by its emotional experience and by the coursing blood that constitutes this experience and traces its memory in the body. If we consider that blood is central to the processes of emotion and memory, Racine's blood imagery—his preoccupation with contagion and enmeshment, so beautifully captured in Guérin's painting—becomes clearer.

The Jansenist Pierre Nicole famously wrote that the playwright was a "public poisoner, not to bodies but to the souls of the faithful, who must be considered guilty of an infinite number of spiritual murders."[139] And Racine's most famous play ironically may have bolstered his former teacher's charge while simultaneously updating it with a distinctly Cartesian insight: the body and the soul (like the perceptual and circulatory systems) are not so separable as Nicole implies. It is appropriate, then, that Racine, having deployed several different images to represent emotional burdens, ends with the image of love as poison. Several acts after Hippolytus has refused to plunge his sword into her heart as she desired, Phaedra reaches for a poison that performs the same task. And the feeling she describes as the poison destroys her body is startlingly similar to the play's description of emotional effects. "I have sent flowing through my burning veins / A poison that Medea brought to Athens," Phaedra declares: "Already the poison has reached my failing heart / And into it sent a new chill."[140] The poison running through her veins to her heart reminds us of the physiological processes of emotion, and it reminds us, too, that the physical effects that Phaedra experiences are meant to align with the audience's emotional response to the chilling horrors of *Phèdre*'s last act. However dramatically effective, then, the moment seems to express all of Racine's ambivalence toward the theater, which would resolve itself with his withdrawal from the stage immediately after writing *Phèdre*.[141] The debilitations effected on characters in the play because of their emotional attachments, after all, seem to discourage the emotional encounters of theatergoing more forcefully than the play's preface would laud them.

At the Hôtel de Bourgogne, the space for which the play was written, *Phèdre and Hippolyte* visually and experientially transgressed boundaries, pushing the audience toward, and entangling it with, the object of its regard. The January 1, 1677, audience was placed in an ontological limbo, stuck between two locations, neither here nor there. On one hand, the immersive ideal of the medieval theater—before there were defined subjects and objects of watching—had been displaced, even as its collective memory lingered. On the other hand, the space was unsuitable for the baroque and Cartesian ideals, in which audiences could look on at Phaedra from a safer distance. A 1647 renovation of the Hôtel de Bourgogne, intended to accommodate deeper perspective sets, had extended the stage into the parterre but in so doing only further compromised the vista: now the parterre was more cramped than ever, a mass of hundreds of bodies pushed right up against the stage, in a space no more than fifty-nine by forty-two feet.[142] With the deepening of the stage, the view from the loges was worse than ever, and the proliferation of stage spectators on boards not designed for it muddied matters further.

Theater architecture would shortly begin more effectively to distance the spectator from the actor onstage, to disentangle subject and object as definitively as the play's title had, when—by the April 18, 1689, performance at the Comédie-Française—it had lost its *"et Hippolyte"* and trained the spotlight on Phaedra alone.[143] All eyes were to be on her, the object of the audience's gaze (and the embodiment of its moral, presented "aux yeux") and not merely one party in a reciprocal relationship of intersubjective possibility. Eighteen years later, on April 21, 1707, this objectification was effected with much greater ease at the Queen's Theatre in the Haymarket, abetted by Smith's plot amendments and Vanbrugh's architectural plan, which also diminished the communal feeling in the audience by individuating its parterre members and seating them. Later in the eighteenth century, Jean-François Marmontel would rue that a play was "more quickly felt" (*plus rapidement senti*) for a standing parterre, and Cartesians would not disagree.[144] In their view, however, objects are meant to be regarded dispassionately. And—to paraphrase Descartes's *Discourse on Method*—an object is all the more perfect when it is conceived by a single subject.[145]

For Descartes the theatrical encounter might be partially introspective insofar as the spectator judges the emotional experience and situates it within a moral perspective, as I discussed in Chapter 2. Does what I see induce bodily aversion and therefore teach and reinforce a hatred of those things that cause pain? Or does it bring joy and inspire love? But the encounter is also collective and interactive—breaching the divide between subject and object and offering the possibility of intersubjective experience. The "objective" spectator at a theater like the Queen's Theatre in the Haymarket might well be situated at zero point, his eyes trained along a perspectival line. But what such spectators watch is transformed by their watching, since the nonreproducible and fundamentally emotional exchange between actor and audience inevitably colors the performance. We do well, too, to remember that visual perceptions are for Descartes representational, thus raising the epistemological dilemma that I identified in Chapter 1 or, to put it less anxiously, mobilizing "the performative quality of all seeing," in Peggy Phelan's formulation.[146] This quality stands behind one of Phaedra's more desperate seduction attempts: to bypass the agency that won't requite her love and suggest to Hippolytus that "your eyes alone" could be persuaded "if your eyes could see me for a moment."[147] But Hippolytus sees with Hippolytus's eyes. It is impossible to separate the conveyance of the thing seen from the emotional impact of what is seen, and this emotional impact proves highly variable, conditioned differently as it is by individual spectators. In other words, as emotion changes—via the accretions of experience that, collectively, constitute memory—vision changes.

In Cartesian thought, we recall, the eyes and blood are connected as they are in Racine's play. Eyes apprehend images from outside of us, but the animal spirits, via the blood, convey these images to the mind as representations. Tying his characters' perceptual apparatuses to their emotional apparatuses, therefore, Racine reveals his Cartesianism most fully. When Phaedra remarks that Hippolytus's perception of his own sword changes entirely once she has grabbed it—it becomes "horrible in his eyes" (*horrible à ses yeux*)[148]—she provides an emblematic instance of the connection between perception and emotion, between eyes and blood, and thus she encapsulates the physiological view promoted by the play. It is anger that obscures Theseus's view of Hippolytus; it is jealousy that distorts Phaedra's perception of Aricia. Since visual perceptions are for Descartes representational, the apparent objectivity of perception is always already suspect. Descartes believed that an objective view was possible with the strength of the will, but Elisabeth of Bohemia's ill health and family problems led her to issue a frequent reminder in her letters: the concrete conditions of the subject's particular situation inevitably erode any possibility of true objectivity. Housed in a body, the mind is always located and materially bound.

Elisabeth's first critic—Alexandre Foucher de Careil, who discovered and published her correspondence with Descartes—noted already in 1879 that her letters, so full of rationalist determination, were themselves shadowed by an "unfathomable pain" (*douleur insondable*) that recalled, to him, Racine's most famous heroine. The analogy may seem strange, even accounting, as Foucher de Careil does, for the differences in "style" and "cause" in Elisabeth's and Phaedra's respective emotional perturbations.[149] But it is true that Elisabeth alerts us, as she alerted Descartes, to an inherently subjectivist tilt in his apparently objective philosophy. She reminds him of what he had intimated in the *Meditations*: the Archimedean point is only theoretical. For his part, in his counsels to Elisabeth, Descartes offers a way of understanding intersubjectivity as different from entanglement: as a way of celebrating her interconnectedness while distinguishing herself from the network of blood relations to which she was connected. A subject can be located, not unmoored, and yet still be moved by the emotional encounter, as Elisabeth may have discovered when she set aside Seneca's *De vita beata* (*On the Happy Life*) to care for her sick brother and asked Descartes explicitly, for the first time, "to define the passions, so to know them better."[150]

An epistolary exchange between Elisabeth and Descartes from 1643—early in their relationship—concerns a geometry puzzle, the so-called problem of three circles. In a test of the princess's intellectual mettle, the philosopher had asked her to identify the radius of a fourth circle whose circumference would be tangential to all three. In other words she had to locate an absent circle that would touch each of those already present to form a group of "kissing circles," as they are delightfully called. In general terms Cartesian geometry—and especially the Cartesian coordinate system that came to dominate not only Western science but also Western culture more generally—provided subjects with the latitudes and longitudes through which positions in the world could be navigated and through which problems, such as the problem of three circles, could be solved. By means of this system Descartes situated each of us at a zero point around which the universe circulates, and he thus initiated an objectifying worldview whose sometimes troubling ramifications have been exhaustively identified. But Descartes also illuminated our interconnectedness. There is something in the fact that the fourth circle—which Elisabeth easily calculated and called to presence—joins three that are otherwise disconnected. There is something, too, in Descartes's response to her having solved the puzzle so quickly and so well, thus launching their fruitful dialogue. Evoking the emotion whose absolute necessity he would explore both in *The Birth of Peace* and *The Passions of the Soul,* he wrote to her that he was "transported with joy."[151]

Epilogue: *Cætera desunt*

Phèdre, SilverCity Yonge-Eglinton Cinema,
September 23, 2010

Building on the success of their event of June 25, 2009—in which
a live performance of Racine's *Phèdre* at the Lyttelton Theatre was digi-
tally captured and transmitted via satellite to movie theaters around the
globe—London's National Theatre held what it called a "live rebroadcast"
on September 23, 2010. Audiences around the world streamed into movie
theaters whose designs would make the Queen's Theatre in the Haymarket seem intimate. In Toronto, for example, I walked down an aisle almost
all the way to the massive, looming screen before turning 180 degrees and
filing up the stairs of the steeply raked "stadium-style" space, built to provide an unobstructed view of the entire screen to every spectator. Settling
in, the global viewers—in their discrete groupings in their own cinemas
and own cities, but encouraged to think of themselves as a worldwide collective—were given a curtain-raiser: talking-head clips with, first, director
Nicholas Hytner, who praised the play, its translation (by Ted Hughes),
and the actors; and, then, with Emma Freud, posed with a microphone
and reporting "live" from the theater as these actors apparently took their
places. But, of course, she was not reporting live—and not because the
transmission was delayed to account for time differences, as it had been
for the 2009 broadcast. In fact, Helen Mirren, long having finished with
Phèdre, was not backstage at the Lyttelton at all (as Freud claimed) but

in Budapest, shooting the film *The Door* with Hungarian director István Szabó.

When the sound began cutting out, Freud's body arresting and blurring on the screen, the Toronto audience was reassured that it was all part of the "live rebroadcast," another hazard of the performance event in which, we know, anything can happen. In other words, without a film to project—without an archival document—we were experiencing the same difficulties and often thrilling unpredictabilities of performance, the same problems of satellite transmission, that other audiences were elsewhere in Toronto, in New York, in Chicago. The "live" actors for this performance—technicians in the United Kingdom, facilitating the digital transmission—were struggling with their roles or perhaps with the technologies of the theater, as when an actor trips on her hem or when a missing prop forces a spontaneous deviation from what is planned. And, as happens so often in the theater, the glitch was soon improvised around, and the performance got back on script in time for Hippolytus's first line.

In one of the play's most pivotal scenes, however—when, having learned of Theseus's death, Oenone convinces the apparently widowed Phaedra to make a play for her stepson: "Your love [*flâme*] becomes an ordinary love," Oenone reassures her[1]—the live rebroadcast experienced additional technical difficulties. The actors were suddenly mute, and the image of Margaret Tyzack froze. (Only her torso and head showed in the frame, already dismembered as she was by the camera operator.) Her body, fractured by the live editing of 2009 and by the camera angles (which switched from front to side views, from midrange shots to close-ups) smeared, disintegrating visibly. The pixilation that constituted her quickly ceded to visual static, prefiguring, in a way, the end that Panope would describe to Theseus four acts later: "the waves have forever taken her from our eyes."[2] Then Oenone's disappearing image gave way to a shot of gaily colored fish swimming in an ocean reef—and a stock digital image that was intended to signify "please stay tuned" seemed, instead, like camp mockery of Oenone's suicide by drowning. The house manager, in one Toronto cinema at least, materialized house left as the houselights came up. He reassured the audience—some of whom were demanding that the live broadcast be "rewound"—that "everyone" was experiencing the same difficulty, that the bizarre technical glitches were part of the live experience.

"I am right here with you," he proclaimed, emphasizing the presence so essential to the theatrical experience and positioning himself sincerely as a performer with no control over the vicissitudes of the theatrical encounter.

As the oxymoron suggests, the "live rebroadcast" clumsily wed past and present, artifact and performance, even as it starkly dichotomized its actors and audience, representation and spectation. Dispersed across the globe, the present audience watched a literal object, a two-dimensional image of Phaedra that lacked even the acknowledging stare of Guérin's painting. This Phaedra was a past Phaedra, Helen Mirren being no longer Phaedra but safely elsewhere and safely someone else; she couldn't convey her dissolution. In Racine's play, when Phaedra attempts to seduce Hippolytus in act 2, she begs him—or his hand, or his arm, or even his sword—to serve as a supplement for her subjectival deficiencies, her failures of body and volition. "Here is my heart," she declares:

> here your hand must strike.
> Already impatient to atone for its offence,
> I feel it advance toward your arm.
> Strike. Or if you believe it unworthy of your blows,
> If your hatred would deny me such a mild death,
> Or if my too vile blood would stain your hand,
> If not your arm, lend me your sword.
> Give![3]

Offering him her heart and longing to be penetrated by his sword, Phaedra has literalized her desire for bodily integration with him, but by doing so she has also betrayed how penetrated by him she already is. The scene represents Phaedra's full collapse under her yoke to her stepson, under the burden of her guilt, and under her sanguinary inheritance from her family. Left physiologically incapacitated by these weights, she has neither reason nor capacity for action. *Phèdre* thus thematizes the importance of the subject's boundaries. But the boundaries in place at the "live rebroadcast" were insurmountable; the likelihood of emotional exchange, slim. Phaedra's body became an image for ocular apprehension rather than coterminous with a subject for encounter.

Too often, philosophy and theater mimic the view of *Phèdre*'s 2010 spectators, sitting aloof in the amphitheater and objectifying a foreign (and at times frozen) image. Philosophers take such a view of Descartes when they see him as disembodied, two-dimensional, cut to fit the frame. Seeing mind severed from body, they thus miss corporal evidence like that of Corneille's heroic Nicomède, standing on the stage of the Comédie-Française as recently at 1989: a Cartesian notion brought to life. Such material can teach us a great deal not only about Descartes's reception—how his contemporaries and successors understood him—but also about his theory in practice. If we heed the traces as Theramenes does as he searches for Hippolytus's body along the shore, we may likewise arrive at startling conclusions. Theater historians, meanwhile, adopt a too-limited viewpoint when they focus only on artifacts and thus miss the immaterial agency—call it mind—that inhabits a text and brings it to performed life in the present. If we instead leverage the epistemological benefits of performance, we become more attuned to the immaterial and dare to consider what playwrights or actors or designers were thinking when they did what they did. Imagining (for example) Molière onstage in *Nicomède*, imagining an evanesced past, we may lose perspective and risk intentional fallacies or ahistoricity. But good sight lines, we have seen, sometimes come at the cost of an unhelpful objectification. Better that theater and philosophy risk some lost perspective in favor of seeing Descartes differently—and seeing one another not as distant objects but as subjects for encounter.

The sometimes uncomfortable thrills of *Phèdre* inhere precisely in such encounters, which is why the "live rebroadcast" so disappointed. On September 23, 2010, whatever divine or at least meteorological impediment was jeopardizing the satellite transmission and widening the chasm between subjects was surmounted, and Helen Mirren's Phaedra and Dominic Cooper's Hippolytus could get on with coming apart at the seams, with enacting the grim Racinian dismemberments that the camera angles achieved with such brutal, soulless efficiency. Finally, borrowing a climactic trick from Euripides's *Bacchae*, Hytner had Hippolytus's demolished body dragged onto the stage by Ruth Negga's Aricia. Theramenes's description of the mess caused by Neptune—his sea monster "vomits in the eyes" of the bystanders, in Racine's wonderful formulation[4]—was rendered visible: both Negga and John Shrapnel were drenched in blood. Racine's distinction between ocular apprehension and sanguinary contamination was duly collapsed. But even with this literal *sanglante image* projected in front of me, I felt that Racine's dangers were less acute than ever. The power of *Phèdre*, after all, resides in its malignant flirtation with the audience. With live actors, blood rushing through their veins and arteries, the play's characters can represent the (sometimes sinister) effects of emotion while bombarding the spectators with emotional stimuli and daring them to consider their own physiological perturbations. This emotional exchange—constituted by animal spirits moving through spectators and actors, as audience and cast react to one another—links one set of bodies to another, breaching the proscenium and blurring the boundary between stage and house. This is Descartes's explanation for the *frisson*, and any other physiological consequences, of the theatrical encounter. To avoid it, as the Jansenists demanded, would be to stunt one's experiential knowledge of the world.

Descartes frequently pressed the epistemological benefits of such encounters, of an experiential knowledge that is registered and retained in the body. Let his posthumously published *The Search for Truth by Means of the Natural Light* serve as a final example. The work—a critical dialogue like Dryden's *Of Dramatick Poesie*—was found among Descartes's papers in Stockholm after his death, only a short time after *The Birth of Peace* had celebrated the Peace of Westphalia and a new understanding of mind-body union. Many mysteries cling to the text. The discovered manuscript was apparently in French and obviously unfinished—the inventory describes only "thirteen sheets" (*treize feuillets*)[5]—and this text was lost sometime after 1701, when the work appeared in print in a Latin translation.[6] At the turn of the twentieth century a putatively faithful copy of one section of the French text was found among Leibniz's papers (apparently having been obtained by him in 1676), so that we have two incomplete versions, neither guaranteed to be the original.[7] Descartes's reasons for writing the dialogue are unknown. Does it express his early promise, quoted in my prologue, to take to the stage?[8] Does it recast key ideas from the *Discourse on Method* or *Meditations* in a less solipsistic key? Does it realize the interest in philosophical dialogue revealed in his letters to Elisabeth? The date of composition, too, is unknown and the source of much debate, with guesses ranging from very early to very late in the philosopher's career.[9]

Descartes's 1644 *Principles of Philosophy* adumbrated the distinction between artifact and performance that I have deployed throughout this book: in dedicating his work to Princess Elisabeth of Bohemia,

Descartes privileged the *expérience* (in the sense of both "experience" and "experiment") that intersubjective encounter in the world could provide. Similarly, *The Search for Truth* counters book knowledge with the epistemological benefits of performing "good actions."[10] And these two ways of knowing are set against one another in the dialogue's primary agon, which opposes Epistemon (a man knowledgeable about anything that can be learned from reading) to Eudoxus (his Cartesian foil, whose modest intellect is uncorrupted by false beliefs). Their conflicting worldviews are staged for the benefit of Poliander, whose everyman resonances are captured in his name. In the end, or at least by the time the text breaks off, Eudoxus has prevailed, and Poliander pledges to be governed by his own experience—tempered by the Cartesian skepticism that has been instilled in him, since (Eudoxus, like Descartes, teaches) the various perceptions that initiate experience can mislead.

I am mindful of Eudoxus's warnings about too many books, and, in writing *The Mind-Body Stage*, I have wished to do more than simply add another to the large corpus that now glosses Descartes's writing. Rather, I have sought to demonstrate how theatrical performance might bring experiential and epistemological benefits to our search for keener understanding. In the preface to *The Search for Truth* Descartes notes that his discoveries might have been found by anyone who might "cast his eyes in the best direction," and this image, too, stresses the importance of a new perspective.[11] My method has been to animate two bodies of literature by imagining the performances that generated and enacted them, and then to bring these bodies into dialogue in order to illuminate the benefits of the encounter. I have put theater and philosophy into contact by braiding a philosophical reading of mind-body union to a theatrical reading of the embodied history that manifested this union and tested, revised, and sometimes corrupted Descartes's ideas. His notion of mind-body dualism declares that we are constituted of a union between two different natures and that we neglect one of them at our peril. Philosophy and theater, too, may be well understood as distinct from one another, but their union is essential, at least if we are to understand the stage after Descartes.

A telling detail from *The Search for Truth*: Eudoxus leverages Poliander's life experience by recalling him to his time in the theater, to those plays where characters question whether they are asleep or awake (and thus self-reflexively highlight the ontological ambiguity of their onstage existence).[12] The analogy does not compare theater to the false perceptions that dreams bring or otherwise trivialize the theatrical endeavor any more than Descartes did when he celebrated the contentment Elisabeth might feel when "seeing some pitiable or disastrous action represented on the stage" or when he bemoaned the "fatal conclusion of England's tragedies" after Elisabeth's uncle Charles I was executed.[13] Rather, as in the familiar *theatrum mundi* trope, Eudoxus likens reality *to* theater—one kind of performance to another—and calls theatrical pretense forth as an epistemological aid in navigating the search for truth. He reveals to Poliander the natural light that we find, perhaps paradoxically, in contemplating actors on a stage pretending to be other than they really are. And thus he thrusts Poliander into the spotlight of his own experiential journey. "The time has now come," he instructs.[14]

The Search for Truth by Means of the Natural Light may be more illuminating, then, for being only a partial text in Latin (and further truncated in its French version)—pages of it lost even to the archive—and for being, so far, unstaged. Epistemon and Poliander and even Eudoxus remain characters whose contours are delimited only by dramatic dialogue in an unfinished play, not yet inhabited by the human actors that could bring it to life. As the final line of the original 1701 printing puts it, "*Catera [sic] desunt.*"[15] Other things are missing. Their philosophy lacks the necessary theatrical supplement. In the text's preface Descartes announces that "the items of knowledge that lie within reach of the human mind are all linked together" by a "marvelous" bond—one we can liken to André Félibien's *je ne sais quoi*, that ineluctable agency and performative extra that inextricably ties mind to body and, I have suggested, might wed theater to philosophy.[16] The discovery of this knowledge, Descartes advises, will be gained by moving "stage by stage."[17] But it merits restating that the work is unfinished.

Notes

PROLOGUE

1. The literature on Descartes and theater history is severely limited. Jean Émelina, "Corneille et la catharsis," *Littératures classiques* 32 (Jan. 1998): 105–20, at 106, does usefully define Cornelian stage emotion by reference to Descartes. And Henry Phillips, "Descartes and the Dramatic Experience," *French Studies* 39, no. 4 (1985): 408–22, at 408, attempts to "reconstruct the degree to which Descartes's views may or may not have constituted a good defense of drama against those who condemned it as immoral." More recently, Kara Reilly's *Automata and Mimesis on the Stage of Theatre History* (Basingstoke: Palgrave Macmillan, 2011) connects Descartes to the history of theater in a radically different way than I do here.

2. Plato, *Republic*, trans. Desmond Lee (London: Penguin, 2007), 242.

3. David Hume, *A Treatise of Human Nature: Being an Attempt to Introduce the Experimental Method of Reasoning into Moral Subjects* (London: John Noon, 1739), 1:439.

4. Daniel C. Dennett, *Consciousness Explained* (Boston: Little, Brown, 1991), 39.

5. Ibid., 113; Hume, *Treatise*, 1:439; Plato, *Republic*, 241.

6. "Ie demeurois tout le iour enfermé seul dans vn poësle, ou i'auois tout loysir de m'entretenir de mes pensées." René Descartes, *Discours de la méthode pour bien conduire sa raison, & chercher la verité dans les sciences, plus la Dioptrique, les Météores et la Géométrie qui sont des essais de cette méthode* (Leiden: Jan Maire, 1637), 12–13.

7. Stephen Sondheim, "Putting It Together," in *Look, I Made a Hat: Collected Lyrics (1981–2011) with Attendant Comments, Amplifications, Dogmas, Harangues, Digressions, Anecdotes, and Miscellany* (New York: Alfred A. Knopf, 2011), 39.

8. Ibid.

9. Ibid., 47.

10. Deborah J. Brown, *Descartes and the Passionate Mind* (Cambridge: Cambridge University Press, 2006), 8.

11. Ibid., 29.

12. Nancy Tuana, *Woman and the History of Philosophy* (New York: Paragon House, 1992), 38.

13. "On peut generalement nommer ses passions, toutes les sortes de perceptions ou connoissances qui se trouvent en nous, à cause que souvent ce n'est pas nostre ame qui les fait telles qu'elles sont, & que tousjours elle les reçoit des choses qui sont representées par elles." René Descartes, *Les passions de l'âme* (Paris: Henry Le Gras, 1649), 28–29. "All the sorts of cases of perception or knowledge to be found in us can generally be called its passions, because it is often not our soul that makes them such as they are, and because it always receives them from things that are represented by them." René Descartes, *The Passions of the Soul,* trans. Stephen H. Voss (Indianapolis: Hackett, 1989), 28.

14. Amy Morgan Schmitter, "The Passionate Intellect: Reading the (Non)-Opposition of Reason and Emotion in Descartes," in *Persons and Passions: Essays in Honor of Annette Baier*, ed. Joyce Jenkins et al. (Notre Dame, IN: University of Notre Dame Press, 2005), 48–82, at 61.

15. See Geneviève Rodis-Lewis in her introduction to Descartes, *The Passions*, xv–xxv, at xv.

16. Here I borrow the opposition made in Diana Taylor, *The Archive and the Repertoire: Performing Cultural Memory in the Americas* (Durham, NC: Duke University Press, 2003), 2–4.

17. Joseph Roach, *The Player's Passion: Studies in the Science of Acting* (Ann Arbor: University of Michigan Press, 1993), 11.

18. Both *Inquisitio veritatis per lumen naturale* (discussed in my epilogue) and the unfinished, unnamed play were found among his papers after his death. Of the latter Descartes's first biographer notes that "nous avons cette comédie Mss" (we have this play in manuscript), but it was never published and is now lost. Adrien Baillet, *La vie de Monsieur Des-Cartes,* 2 vols. (Paris: Daniel Horthemels, 1691), 2:484. Descartes is also widely credited with writing the ballet libretto *La naissance de la paix,* a key text in my first chapter.

19. René Descartes, *La naissance de la paix: Ballet dansé au chasteau royal de Stokholm, le jour de la naissance de sa Majesté* (Stockholm: Jean Janssonius, 1649), 16.

20. See Leah S. Marcus, *Unediting the Renaissance: Shakespeare, Marlowe, Milton* (London: Routledge, 1996), 5.

21. See, e.g., R. Darren Gobert, "Historicizing Emotion: The Case of Freudian 'Hysteria' and Aristotelian 'Purgation,'" in *Emotion, Place and Culture,* ed. Mick Smith et al. (Aldershot: Ashgate, 2009), 57–76; and R. Darren Gobert, "Behaviorism, Catharsis, and the History of Emotion," *Journal of Dramatic Theory and Criticism* 26, no. 2 (Spring 2012): 109–25.

22. On this point see Daniel Garber, "Does History Have a Future?" in *Descartes Embodied: Reading Cartesian Philosophy Through Cartesian Science* (Cambridge: Cambridge University Press, 2011), 13–30.

23. Erec R. Koch, *The Aesthetic Body: Passion, Sensibility, and Corporeality in Seventeenth-Century France* (Newark: University of Delaware Press, 2008), 77.

24. See Descartes's dedication to the *Principles of Philosophy*: Renati Des-Cartes [i.e., René Descartes], *Principia philosophiæ* (Amsterdam: Ludovic Elzivier, 1644), 2^r–4^v.

25. My translation is of the first French edition, René Descartes, *Les principes de la philosophie* (Paris: Henry Le Gras, 1647), aii$^{r–v}$, which reads: "Le principal fruit que j'aye receu des écrits que j'ay cy-deuant publiez a esté qu'à leur occasion j'ay eu l'honneur d'estre connu de VOSTRE ALTESSE, & de luy pouuoir quelquefois parler. Ce qui m'a donné moyen de remarquer en elle des qualitez si estimables, & si rares; que je croy que c'est rendre seruice au public de les proposer à la posterité pour exemple." The 1644 Latin original is addressed more informally to Elisabeth in the second-person singular: "Maximum fructum percepi scriptorum, quæ antehac in lucem edidi, quòd ea perlegere dignata sis; quódque eorum occasione in notitiam tuam admissus, tales dotes tuas esse cognoverim, ut è re gentis humanæ esse putem, eas seculis in exemplum proponi" (Descartes, *Principia philosophiæ*, 2^r).

26. Elisabeth and Descartes lived near enough to one another in Holland for much of their correspondence (although he also writes from Paris and Stockholm, she from Germany). Therefore, it is presumed that the two met in person, but how often remains a matter of speculation. (Some have imagined a quite improbable romantic relationship: see, e.g., Léon Petit, *Descartes et la Princesse Elisabeth: Roman d'amour vécu* [Paris: Editions A.-G. Nizet, 1969]). Gaps in the correspondence narrative are of no help, since these may indicate lost letters.

27. Elisabeth was pressed to publish her letters by Pierre Chanut, who had the unhappy task of relaying news of Descartes's death. See Chanut's two letters to Elisabeth in February 1650, in René Descartes, *Œuvres de Descartes*, ed. Charles Adam and Paul Tannery, 11 vols. (Paris: J. Vrin, 1983), 5:471–74. Thirty-one of Descartes's letters to Elisabeth were published by his literary executor, Claude Clerselier, in René Descartes, *Lettres de Monsieur Descartes, où sont traittées les plus belles questions de la morale, physique, medecine, & des mathematiques* (Paris: Henry Le Gras, 1657).

28. The letters take on a different narrative momentum in the order in which Clerselier put them (all undated); it will say something to note that Descartes's first letter to the princess appears as the twenty-fourth.

29. "La littérature philosophique pleurera toujours ce vide." Cited in Ludger Oeing-Hanhoff, "Descartes et la princesse Elisabeth," *Bulletin cartésien 11*, in *Archives de philosophie 45*, no. 4 (1982): 1–33, at 8.

30. Alexandre Foucher de Careil had begun his investigation into the mutual influence of Descartes and Elisabeth in his *Descartes et la princesse palatine; ou, De l'influence du cartésianisme sur les femmes au XVIIe siècle* (Paris: Auguste Durand,

1862). Because of his previous work on Elisabeth, and because he had searched for the letters in antiquarian circles, Foucher de Careil was contacted by Frederick Muller when the discovery was made; Muller had been tasked with cataloguing a collection found at Rosendael Castle outside Arnhem, in the Netherlands. He then published the letters for the first time in Alexandre Foucher de Careil, *Descartes, la Princesse Élisabeth, et la Reine Christine, d'après des lettres inédites* (Paris: Germer-Baillière, 1879), which explains the letters' provenance in its preface. On the revised dating of the letters in light of his discovery, see ibid., iv: "au moyen des lettres d'Élisabeth qui on date certaine, rectifier et compléter la chronologie des lettres mêmes de Descartes."

31. "Sum enim vnus ex illis qui negant hominem corpore intelligere" (Descartes, *Œuvres* 3:374–75).

32. For example, Richard A. Watson, *Descartes's Ballet: His Doctrine of the Will and His Political Philosophy* (South Bend, IN: St. Augustine's Press, 2007), devotes ten pages (75–85) to the question "Did Descartes Read Corneille?" (His conclusion: "two elephants dancing in the same ring cannot avoid bumping into one another" [85]). And Charles Adam, *Descartes: Ses amitiés féminines* (Paris: Boivin, 1937), claims that Descartes must have known Corneille's work for various reasons, including their shared acquaintanceship with Constantijn Huygens (65–67). Conversely, André Stegmann, *L'héroïsme cornélien: Genèse et signification*, 2 vols. (Paris: Armand Colin, 1968), 2:262, claims that "Descartes n'a jamais manifesté, dans sa vaste correspondance, le moindre intérêt pour Corneille ni en général, pour le théâtre" (Descartes never showed, in his vast correspondence, the least interest in Corneille or the theater in general)—a fact contradicted, incidentally, in Descartes's correspondence with Elisabeth. Louis Rivaille, *Les débuts de Pierre Corneille* (Paris: Boivin, 1936), 494–95, represents one early critic determined to unearth a shared, Jesuit influence between the playwright and the philosopher, a task undertaken more recently by Amy Henshaw, "Descartes and Corneille: A Re-examination," *Neophilologus* 86 (2002): 45–56.

33. "Effets des mêmes causes, expressions indépendantes du même esprit." Gustave Lanson, "Le héros cornélien et le 'généreux' selon Descartes," *Revue d'histoire littéraire de la France* 1 (1894): 397–411, at 397.

34. See Chapter 2n5.

35. The point is made in Jennifer Montagu, *The Expression of the Passions: The Origin and Influence of Charles Le Brun's "Conférence sur l'expression générale et particulière"* (New Haven, CT: Yale University Press, 1994), 17.

36. "Ce je ne sçay quoy . . . qu'on ne peut bien exprimer, est comme le nœud secret qui assemble ces deux parties du corps & de l'esprit." André Félibien, *Entretiens sur les vies et sur les ouvrages des plus excellens peintres anciens et modernes*, 5 vols. (Paris: Pierre le Petit, 1666), 1:38.

37. This rehabilitation was slow. In France (where the trajectory mirrors that in other countries) it begins with Richelieu's 1641 declaration of the respectability of the profession, which appears at François-André Isambert et al., eds., *Recueil général des anciennes lois françaises, depuis l'an 420 jusqu'à la Révolution de 1789* (Paris: Belin-Leprieur, 1821–33), 16:536–37.

38. "Les passions n'y sont présentées aux yeux que pour montrer tout le desordre dont elles sont cause." Jean Racine, *Phèdre et Hippolyte* (Paris: Claude Barbin, 1677), aiv^v.

39. Here I cite Jacques Le Goff, *History and Memory*, trans. Steven Randall and Elizabeth Claman (New York: Columbia University Press, 1992), xvii: "Today documents include the spoken word, the image, and gestures."

40. "Il faut par fois se faire violence." Molière, *L'impromptu de Versailles*, in *Les œuvres de Monsieur de Molière*, 8 vols. (Paris: Denys Thierry, Claude Barbin, et Pierre Trabouillet, 1682), 7:87–126, at 113.

41. Luce Irigaray, "L'admiration: Lecture de Descartes, *Les passions de l'âme*, art. 53," in *L'éthique de la différence sexuelle* (Paris: Minuit, 1984), 75–84, at 75: "Il faut relire un peu Descartes." The remarks come from Irigaray's teaching, and I wish to emphasize (as she does in her preface) that the published text is an inadequate trace of an encounter: her exchange with her students during the semester she taught at the University of Rotterdam, when they read together and debated philosophers ranging from Plato and Aristotle to Emmanuel Levinas and Maurice Merleau-Ponty. The experience of that semester was one of dialogue, not traditional lecturing. See ibid., 7–8.

42. *Memoirs of Sophia, Electress of Hanover, 1630–1680*, trans. H. Forester (London: Richard Bentley and Sons, 1888), 12.

43. See Elizabeth Godfrey [i.e., Jessie Bedford], *A Sister of Prince Rupert: Elizabeth Princess Palatine and Abbess of Herford* (London: John Lane the Bodley Head, 1909), 85: "In the winter of 1640 a new interest dawned upon Elizabeth's horizon, one more consonant with her serious bent than the round of amusement, the masques, the plays, the tournaments in which her brothers and sisters took pleasure. A visitor was one day introduced at the reception of the Queen of Bohemia, M. René Descartes, not unknown to the Princess by reputation. She had already read some of his philosophical writings, and had found in them a new principle which so appealed to her that she declared she would cast aside all that she had hitherto learned and begin to build anew from the very foundation."

44. René Descartes, "Early Writings," trans. John Cottingham, in *The Philosophical Writings of Descartes* (Cambridge: Cambridge University Press, 1984), 1:2–5, at 2. The original: "hoc mundi theatrum conscensurus, in quo hactenus spectator exstiti" (Descartes, *Œuvres*, 10:213).

CHAPTER I

1. Scholars agree on very little about the ballet, starting with its date, which is given as December 7, 8, or 9 (in the Julian calendar, since Sweden had not yet converted to the Gregorian). The argument for the seventh, which presumes that the libretti were printed after the fact, is insupportable. The best argument for the eighth hinges on the fact that both the Swedish and German libretti for the ballet mention this date, Christina's birthday, although the ballet seems to have been delayed after the libretti went to print. See *Freds-Afl: Ballet danssat på Stokholms slott på hennes K. M.:s Drottning Christinæ födelse-dag den 8 decemb* (Stockholm: Henrich Keyser, 1649), Ai^r; and *Des Friedens Geburts-tag: Ballet so in dem Königlichen Schloß zu Stockholm gedanzt worden auff Ihr. Kön. Man.:t Geburts-tag den 8 Christmonats* (Stockholm: Henrich Keyser, 1649), Ai^r. I date the ballet to the ninth on the basis of two letters. First, there is Descartes's letter to the Count of Brégy on December 18 (New Style, i.e., December 8 in Old Style), in which he writes that the ballet will be danced "demain au soir" (tomorrow night); René Descartes, *Œuvres de Descartes*, ed. Charles Adam and Paul Tannery, 11 vols. (Paris: J. Vrin, 1983), 5:457. Second, there is the letter of courtier Johan Ekeblad, who wrote on December 10 (Old Style):

> Uti detta innelykta paquet öfver sänder jag min käre farkär de verser, som på den sista balleten gjorda äro, hvilken blef dansad den 9 hujus på ballet-salen, hvilket mycket vackert att se var. Hennes m:t enkedronningen var där och tillstädes, och var där ett sådant tillopp utaf folk, att dronningen näpligen själf igenom kom.
>
> [Included in this packet I send my dear father the verses made for the last ballet which was danced on the 9th in the *salle de ballet*, which was very beautiful to see. Her Majesty the Dowager Queen [Christina's mother, Maria Eleonora] was in attendance, and there was such a throng there that the queen herself could hardly get through.]

Johan Ekeblad, *Johan Ekeblads bref, 1: Från Kristinas och Cromwells hof*, ed. Nils Sjöberg (Stockholm: P. A. Norstedt & Söners, 1911), 28.

2. My understanding of the production in these paragraphs largely follows Agne Beijer, "'La naissance de la paix': Ballet de cour de René Descartes," in *Le lieu théâtral à la Renaissance*, ed. Jean Jacquot (Paris: Centre national de la recherche, 1964), 409–22, supplemented by the fuller picture of Swedish court ballets granted by F. J. Fielden, "Court Masquerades in Sweden in the Seventeenth Century: I," *Modern Language Review* 16, no. 1 (1921): 47–58; by Gunilla Dahlberg, "The Theatre Around Queen Christina," *Renaissance Studies* 23, no. 2 (2009): 161–85; and Gunilla Dahlberg, "The Ballet in Sweden," in *Spectacvlvm Evropævm*, ed. Pierre Béhar and Helen Watanabe-O'Kelly (Wiesbaden: Harrassowitz, 1999),

577–82; and by Marina Grut, *Royal Swedish Ballet: History from 1592 to 1962* (Hildesheim, Germany: Georg Olms, 2007), 6–20. The libretto was lost until the twentieth century, when it was discovered in Uppsala by Johan Nordström and published by Albert Thibaudet. See Thibaudet and Nordström's "Un ballet de Descartes," *La revue de Genève* 2 (August 1920): 163–72, which precedes Thibaudet's edition of the text at 173–85. Scholarship on the ballet is thin. The best work remains Beijer, "'La naissance de la paix,'" which corrects some of Thibaudet and Nordström's misapprehensions. See also brief discussions in F. J. Fielden's "Court Masquerades in Sweden in the Seventeenth Century: II," *Modern Language Review* 16, no. 2 (1921): 150–65, at 158; in Marvin Carlson, "Scandinavia's International Baroque Theatre," *Educational Theatre Journal* 28, no. 1 (March 1976): 5–34; in Dahlberg, "Theatre," 171; and in Grut, *Royal*, 16–18. I have worked with the same text that Nordström discovered, housed at Carolina Rediviva in Uppsala.

    3. René Descartes, *La naissance de la paix: Ballet dansé au chasteau royal de Stokholm, le jour de la naissance de sa Majesté* (Stockholm: Jean Janssonius, 1649), 11.

    4. The presumption is that of Beijer, "'La naissance de la paix,'" 418; he cites the invoice for material gifted to Beaulieu by the queen. The character's name, *Terreur Panique*, merits comment. It is impossible adequately to convey in English the resonances of *panique*, here used adjectivally (and in a way rarer in modern French than in the seventeenth century) to describe the suddenness of terror's descent.

    5. There are puzzles about these texts, starting with how liberally they depart from one another (for this ballet as for others at Christina's court). For instance, in both the Swedish and the German versions of the libretto, the nineteenth and twentieth entrées are reversed. See *Freds-Afl*, Dii^r; and *Des Friedens Geburts-tag*, Di^r. Another open question is whether these verses were recited during the performance, distributed in advance to help the audience follow, or distributed after the performance as a memento. Each of these options was employed in various courts in Europe at the time. See Fielden, "Court Masquerades: I," 53. In my view at least some text must have been integrated into the performance, since parts of the French libretto are set off as *récits chantés*: Descartes, *La naissance*, 10 (before the eleventh entrée) or ibid., 16 (before the twentieth).

    6. The verse summary of the ballet, like many others produced at Christina's court, was published anonymously. Commentators have tended to accept unquestionably the attribution of *La naissance de la paix* to Descartes made by Adrien Baillet's *La vie de Monsieur Des-Cartes* and apparently confirmed by Daniel Georg Morhof in his *Polyhistor* (see Descartes, *Œuvres*, 5:459). The case would seem to hang on the letter to Brégy on the same day the libretto was distributed, in which the philosopher (perhaps cheekily) wrote: "Affin que la grosseur de ce paquet

empesche qu'il ne soit aysé à égarer, i'y adiouste les vers d'vn balet qui sera dansé icy demain au soir" (So that the weight of this letter will prevent its going easily astray, I add to it the verses for a ballet that will be danced here tomorrow evening) (Descartes, *Œuvres*, 5:457). Fielden, "Court Masquerades: II," analyzes Stiernhielm's Swedish edition; it is unclear if Fielden had seen the original French text. In any case he does not discuss the attribution controversy but credits the ballet to Hélie Poirier (ibid., 151). More recently, Richard A. Watson makes detailed if not quite convincing arguments against Descartes's authorship in his "René Descartes n'est pas l'auteur de *La naissance de la paix*," *Archives de philosophie* 53, no. 1 (1990): 382–401; and *Descartes's Ballet: His Doctrine of the Will and His Political Philosophy* (South Bend, IN: St. Augustine's Press, 2007), which also reprints and translates the libretto. Because *La naissance de la paix* is so different from the libretti that preceded and followed it at court, I am inclined to agree with the attribution to Descartes, which has received renewed support from contemporary French critics: Geneviève Rodis-Lewis, *Le développement de la pensée de Descartes* (Paris: J. Vrin, 1997), 204–20; Geneviève Rodis-Lewis, *Descartes: Biographie* (Paris: Calmann-Lévy, 1995), 274–76; and Jean-François de Raymond, *Pierre Chanut, ami de Descartes: Un diplomate philosophe* (Paris: Beauchesne Éditeur, 1999), 103.

One fact, entirely overlooked in the attribution debate, further recommends Descartes as the libretto's author. The philosopher's rhetorical move in his letter to Brégy—drawing attention to the enclosed document while proclaiming, with false modesty, its unimportance—was one Descartes had used previously. In his January 31, 1648, letter to Elisabeth, he had enclosed his *Notae in programma quoddam* (published without his permission) but protested that "l'enuoye auec cette lettre vn liuret de peu d'importance" (I send with this letter a pamphlet of little importance). René Descartes, *Lettres de Monsieur Descartes, où sont traittées les plus belles questions de la morale, physique, medecine, & des mathematiques* (Paris: Henry Le Gras, 1657), 98.

7. "La Cour n'étoit occupée que des rejouïssances qui s'y faisoient pour la paix de Munster, & la Reine qui voulut qu'il y joüat son rôle, voyant qu'elle ne pouvoit obtenir de luy qu'il dansat des balets, sçut l'engager au moins à composer des vers françois pour le bal" (Baillet, *La vie*, 2:395). (The Court was occupied entirely with the celebrations of the Peace of Munster, and the Queen, who wanted him [i.e., Descartes] to play his part, seeing that she could not get him to dance in the ballets, knew how to involve him at least so much as to compose French verses for the dance.)

8. Timothy J. Reiss, "Denying the Body? Memory and the Dilemmas of History in Descartes," *Journal of the History of Ideas* 57, no. 4 (1996): 587–607, at 604. Reiss elaborates this idea in his *Mirages of the Selfe: Patterns of Personhood in Ancient and Early Modern Europe* (Stanford: Stanford University Press, 2003), 489–97.

9. Descartes, *La naissance*, 3.

10. Ibid., 4:

Iᴇ veux faire trembler tous les coins de la Terre,
Et monstrer aux mortels qu'aucun des autres Dieux
N'eut jamais tant que moy de pouvoir en ces lieux.
Non pas mesme celuy qui lance la tonerre.

Ses esclairs & ses feux ne font qu'un peu de peur,
Au lieu que mes canons & mes autres machines,
Mes mortiers, mes petards, mes brusleaux & mes mines
Portent partout la mort avecque la terreur.

11. An overview of the argument and recent scholarship is provided in Marjorie Grene, *Descartes Among the Scholastics* (Milwaukee: Marquette University Press, 1991).

12. Terror is gendered as female—she refers to herself as a "fille de la nuit" (daughter of the night) at Descartes, *La naissance*, 5—but was danced by a man, as was customary for grotesque female characters. See Fielden, "Court Masquerades: II," 58.

13. Descartes, *La naissance*, 5–6:

C'est a tort que Pallas & Mars
Se vantent que dans les hasars
Leur pouvoir est incomparable,
Le mien est bien plus redoutable.
Il leur faut beaucoup de travail:
Il leur faut un grand attirail:
De poudres, de chevaux & d'armes,
Et de gens qui vont aux alarmes,
Pour ne livrer qu'un seul combat

. . . .

Quand je veux donner l'espouvante,
A un milion de guerriers,
Et fouler aux pieds leurs lauriers,
Il ne me faut qu'une chimere,
Un songe, ou une ombre legere,
Qui j'envoye dans leurs cerveaux.
Et ils tremblent comme des veaux
Ils fuient, ils devienent blesmes,
Et souvent se jetent eux mesmes,
En des maux plus a redouter
Que ceux quilz pensent eviter.

14. On the evolution of the word's connotations—from militaristic to psychological—see Alain Rey et al., eds., *Dictionnaire historique de la langue française*, 4th ed. (Paris: Dictionnaires le Robert, 2012), s.v. "alarme," "arme."

15. In the second act Phaedra disingenuously tells Hippolytus that she comes to express her worries in light of Theseus's apparent death: "Je vous viens pour un Fils expliquer mes allarmes." Jean Racine, *Phèdre et Hippolyte* (Paris: Claude Barbin, 1677), 30. In the fourth act she tells Oenone that she has tried to keep her distress hidden: "sous un front serein déguisant mes allarmes" (ibid., 62).

16. "L'Action & la Passion ne laissent pas d'estre tousjours une mesme chose, qui a ces deux noms, à raison des deux divers sujets ausquels on la peut raporter." René Descartes, *Les passions de l'âme* (Paris: Henry Le Gras, 1649), 3.

17. See, e.g., Paul Hoffman, "Cartesian Passions and Cartesian Dualism," in his *Essays on Descartes* (Oxford: Oxford University Press, 2009), 105–24.

18. Deborah J. Brown, *Descartes and the Passionate Mind* (Cambridge: Cambridge University Press, 2006), 141.

19. René Descartes, *The Passions of the Soul*, trans. Stephen H. Voss (Indianapolis: Hackett, 1989), 38. Descartes, *Les passions*, 51–52, reads:

> si nous voyons quelque animal venir vers nous, la lumiere refleschie de son corps en peint deux images, une en chacun de nos yeux; & ces deux images en forment deux autres, par l'entremise des nerfs optiques, dans la superficie interieure du cerveau, qui regarde ses concavitez; puis de là, par l'entremise des esprits dont ces cavitez sont remplies, ces images rayonnent en telle sorte vers la petite glande que ces esprits environnent, que le mouvement qui compose chaque point de l'une des images, tend vers le mesme point de la glande, vers lequel tend le mouvement, qui forme le point de l'autre image, lequel represente la mesme partie de cet animal; au moyen de quoy les deux images qui sont dans le cerveau n'en composent qu'une seule sur la glande, qui agissant immediatement contre l'ame, luy fait voir la figure de cet animal.

20. Descartes, *Les passions*, 20–23. The *Dioptrique* appears in René Descartes, *Discours de la méthode pour bien conduire sa raison, & chercher la verité dans les sciences, plus la Dioptrique, les Météores et la Géométrie qui sont des essais de cette méthode* (Leiden: Jan Maire, 1637), which is not continuously paginated.

21. "Un certain air ou vent tres-subtil" (Descartes, *Les passions*, 11); "ces parties du sang tres-subtiles" (ibid., 15). In other words Descartes borrows the term *spirits* from Galenist medicine but employs it much more banally.

22. Descartes, *The Passions*, 40. Descartes, *Les passions*, 56: "vers les nerfs, qui servent à remuër les jambes pour fuïr . . . causent un autre mouvement en la mesme glande, par le moyen duquel l'ame sent & aperçoit cette fuite, laquelle peut en cette façon estre excitée dans le corps, par la seule disposition des organes, & sans que l'ame y contribuë."

23. Descartes, *Les passions*, 68: "qu'une seule ame, & cette ame n'a en soy aucune diversité de parties; la mesme qui est sensitive, est raisonnable."

24. See Stephen H. Voss's gloss at Descartes, *The Passions*, 44n47.

25. Descartes, *Les passions*, 68: "L'erreur qu'on a commise en luy faisant jouër divers personnages."

26. Ibid., 46–47.

27. A more detailed explanation of how the passions express representational content can be found at Brown, *Descartes*, 84–115.

28. The second image is a detail of the "Plan des Tuilleries du costé de la Cour achevé sous Louys le Grand" (as listed in the "Table des planches") from *Architecture française*, by Jean and Daniel Marot. I found the image while searching through seventeenth-century architectural renderings looking for an image of the *salle des machines*. The book—an undated, unpaginated set of architectural plans and renderings—has no publication information but is listed in the catalogue of the Bibliothèque nationale de France as being printed by P.-J. Mariette. The first edition of the so-called Grand Marot was published in 1670.

29. Renati Des-Cartes [i.e., René Descartes], *Meditationes de prima philosophia* (Paris: Michaelum Soli, 1641), 11.

30. Susan James, *Passion and Action: Emotions in Seventeenth-Century Philosophy* (Oxford: Oxford University Press, 1999), 107.

31. See the second and third chapters of Michel Foucault, *Les mots et les choses: Une archéologie des sciences humaines* (Paris: Gallimard, 1966); or, in translation, Michel Foucault, *The Order of Things: An Archaeology of the Human Sciences* (New York: Vintage, 1973).

32. Descartes, *Les passions*, 28–29: "on peut generalement nommer ses passions, toutes les sortes de perceptions ou connoissances qui se trouvent en nous, à cause que souvent ce n'est pas nostre ame qui fait telles qu'elles sont, & que tousjours elle les reçoit des choses qui sont representées par elles."

33. Being, for the philosopher, is of course grounded in pure thought, but it is also more complicated than that; it requires the interaction of body and mind. That is, his "ie pense, donc ie suis" in the fourth part of Descartes, *Discours* (at 33) is importantly qualified at the end of the fifth (at ibid., 59, and quoted at note 46 below).

34. Descartes, *La naissance*, 8:

Qui voit comme nous sommes faits
Et pense que la guerre est belle,
Ou qu'elle vaut mieux que la Paix,
Est estropié de cervelle.

The unusual, difficult-to-translate first clause is elaborated in the French compared with the German—"Wer uns beschawt" (*Des Friedens Geburts-tag*, B2ʳ)— or the Swedish—"See på Oss" (*Freds-Afl*, B2ʳ).

35. Descartes, *La naissance*, 8.

36. *Le monde reiovi, balet, dansé pour la regence de sa Maiesté, à Stockholm le premier de janvier de l'année 1645* (Stockholm: Henrich Keyser, 1645), Civ^r. "Cette Princesse . . . / Aime autant les Soldats comme faisoit sonpere" (ibid., Civ^v).

37. "Quelques fuyarts que la Terreur Panique a fait sortir de l'Armée avant le combat" (Descartes, *La naissance*, 6).

38. Ibid.

39. "Vous reteniez les nostres [cœurs]. . . . S'ils vous plaist nous donner les vostres" (ibid., 7). The entire dance is danced, according to the libretto, "AUX DAMES" (ibid., 6).

40. See, e.g., Andrea Nye, "Elisabeth, Princess Palatine: Letters to René Descartes," in *Presenting Women Philosophers*, ed. Cecile T. Tougas and Sara Ebenreck (Philadelphia: Temple University Press, 2000), 129–37, which notes that this consideration was "much less evident to Descartes, waiting out the war in a well-provisioned retreat in the Dutch countryside" (133). This comment ignores Descartes's personal experience of the war, which was directly implicated in his philosophy. We know from Descartes that this philosophy originated in dreams; he had these dreams in November 1619 when, as he explained, "l'étois . . . en Allemaigne où l'occasion des guerres qui n'y sont pas encore finies m'auoit appelé" (I was in Germany, where I had been called by the wars that are not yet finished there) (Descartes, *Discours*, 12).

41. Because Elisabeth's early letters so pointedly set Descartes on the path that would culminate in *The Passions of the Soul*, it is inconceivable that late Cartesian thought could have existed without her, as argued, too, by Carole Talon-Hugon, *Descartes, ou "Les passions" rêvées par la raison: Essai sur la théorie des passions de Descartes et de quelques-uns de ses contemporains* (Paris: J. Vrin, 2002), 89.

42. "Il est pourtant très-difficile à comprendre qu'une âme, comme vous l'avez décrite, après avoir eu la faculté et l'habitude de bien raisonner, peut perdre tout cela par quelques vapeurs, et que pouvant subsister sans le corps et n'ayant rien de commun avec luy, elle en soit tellement régie." Elisabeth to Descartes, June 10, 1643, in Alexandre Foucher de Careil, *Descartes, la Princesse Élisabeth, et la Reine Christine, d'après des lettres inédites* (Paris: Germer-Baillière, 1879), 50–51. On the dating of this letter see Lisa Shapiro's note in her edition of the letters, *The Correspondence Between Princess Elisabeth of Bohemia and René Descartes* (Chicago: University of Chicago Press, 2007), 58–59.

43. "Ie la [her Highness] suplie de vouloir librement atribuër cette matiere & cette extension à l'ame, car cela n'est autre chose que la conceuoir vnie au cors" (Descartes to Elisabeth, June 28, 1643, in Descartes, *Lettres de Monsieur Descartes*, 118).

44. "Car conceuoir l'vnion qui est entre deux choses, c'est les conceuoir comme vne seule" (ibid., 116).

45. Descartes to Elisabeth, June 1645: "j'y remarque tou jours des pensées si nettes, & des raisonnemens si fermes, qu'il ne m'est pas possible de me persuader qu'vn esprit capable de les conceuoir soit loge dans vn corps foible & malade" (ibid., 94).

46. "Il ne suffit pas, quelle soit logée dans le cors humain ainsi qu'vn pilote en son nauire, sinon peutestre pour mouuoir ses membres, Mais qu'il est besoin quelle soit iointe, & vnie plus estroitement auec luy, pour auoir outre cela des sentimens, & des appetits semblables aux nostres, & ainsi composer vn vray homme" (Descartes, *Discours*, 59).

47. René Descartes, *Meditations on First Philosophy*, in *"Discourse on Method" and "Meditations on First Philosophy,"* trans. Donald A. Cress, 3rd ed. (Indianapolis: Hackett, 1993), 45–105, at 99. The original reads: "Me non tantùm adesse meo corpori vt nauta adest nauigio, sed illi arctissimè esse coniunctum & quasi permixtum, adeò vt vnum quid cum illo componam" (Descartes, *Meditationes*, 102).

48. Descartes, *La naissance*, 5:

Aussy est elle en nostre corps
Le chef sans quoy il ne peut vivre;
Et nous faisons tous nos efforts
Pour avoir l'honneur de la suivre.
Sans elle ce cors divisé
Seroit d'un chascun mesprisé.

49. Descartes, *Meditationes*, 109–10.

50. Descartes, *The Passions*, 35. Descartes, *Les passions*, 43–44: "l'ame est veritablement jointe à tout le corps, & . . . on ne peut pas proprement dire qu'elle soit en quelcune de ses parties, à l'exclusion des autres, à cause qu'il est un, & en quelque façon indivisible."

51. Descartes explains this function in depth in *Les passions*, 181–83.

52. Descartes, *The Passions*, 92. Descartes, *Les passions*, 182: "leur usage naturel est d'inciter l'ame, à consentir & contribuer aux actions qui peuvent servir à conserver le corps."

53. On the close relationship between joy and love see Descartes, *Les passions*, 186: "Amour . . . ne manque jamais de produire la Ioye."

54. Descartes, *La naissance*, 16: "nous vivons dans un corps, / Dont nous sommes les bras, vous la divine flamme / Qui seule conduit tout, & qu'on appele l'ame."

55. Lilli Alanen, *Descartes's Concept of Mind* (Cambridge, MA: Harvard University Press, 2003), 165. See also Amy Morgan Schmitter, "Representation, Self-Representation, and the Passions in Descartes," *Review of Metaphysics* 48, no. 2 (Dec. 1994): 33–57, 342: "the perceptions that most clearly show the connection between body and soul . . . are passions in the strict sense of the term."

56. Descartes, *La naissance*, 16.

57. Ibid.

58. Descartes distinguishes the passion of joy (an "agreable emotion de l'ame") from the "joye purement intellectuelle, qui vient en l'ame par la seule action de l'ame" (Descartes, *Les passions*, 123–24).

59. These complexities are handled well, and in considerable detail, in Schmitter, "Representation," 344–48.

60. "Pendant que l'ame est jointe au corps, cette joye intellectuelle ne peut gueres manquer d'estre accompagnée de celle qui est une passion" (Descartes, *Les passions*, 124). Schmitter presses the same point: "so intermingled can the two sorts of emotions become that we may be hard-pressed to tell what we are experiencing, or which came first." Amy Morgan Schmitter, "The Passionate Intellect: Reading the (Non)-Opposition of Reason and Emotion in Descartes," in *Persons and Passions: Essays in Honor of Annette Baier*, ed. Joyce Jenkins et al. (Notre Dame, IN: University of Notre Dame Press, 2005), 48–82, at 55.

61. Descartes, *The Passions*, 73, 80. Descartes, *Les passions*, 134, 153:

> Le poulx est égal & plus vite qu'à l'ordinaire. . . . On sent une chaleur agreable, qui n'est pas seulement en la poitrine, mais qui se répand aussi en toutes les parties exterieures du corps, avec le sang qu'on voit y venir en abondance. . . .
>
> Ainsi la joye rend la couleur plus vive & plus vermeille, pource qu'en ouvrant les escluses du cœur, elle fait que le sang coule plus viste en toutes les veines; & que devenant plus chaud & plus subtil, il enfle mediocrement toutes les passages du visage, ce qui en rend l'air plus riant & plus gay.

62. Descartes, *La naissance*, 16.

63. Erec R. Koch, *The Aesthetic Body: Passion, Sensibility, and Corporeality in Seventeenth-Century France* (Newark: University of Delaware Press, 2008), 77.

64. Jacques Bénigne Bossuet, *Maximes et réflexions sur la comédie* (Paris: Jean Anisson, 1694), 59–60 (his emphasis): "En imitant . . . on devenoit esclave avec un esclave; vicieux avec un homme vicieux; & sur tout, en representant les passions, il falloit former au-dedans celles dont on vouloit porter au dehors l'expression & le caractere. Le spectateur entroit aussi dans le mesme esprit: il louoit & admiroit un comedien qui luy causoit ces émotions. . . . Ainsi tout l'appareil du theatre ne tend qu'à faire des hommes passionnez, & à fortifier *cette partie brute & déraisonnable*, qui est la source de toutes nos foiblesses." Note that Bossuet's adjective *passionné*, viewed in the theological and historical context in which it was written, is far more pejorative than it seems to us today.

65. "Ie m'abstiens, le plus qu'il m'est possible, des questions de Theologie" (Descartes, *Œuvres*, 4:119).

66. Descartes's explanation is somewhat complicated. Since a passion is seldom experienced unalloyed to some other passion, a body is typically moved in multiple directions by the emotional cocktails that constitute experience. For example, fear of an object might send the limbs flying while stubborn pride might prevent them from retreating. Without mental judgment sorting through these various reactions, the will is turned against itself. See Descartes, *Les passions*, 72: "Mais il y en a qui ne peuvent esprouver leur force. . . . Les ames les plus foibles de toutes, sont celles dont la volonté ne se determine point ainsi à suivre certains jugemens, mais se laisse continuellement emporter aux passions presentes." ("However, there are some who cannot test their strength. . . . The weakest souls of all are those whose will does not decide in this way to follow certain judgments, but continually allows itself to be carried away by present passions" [Descartes, *The Passions*, 46].)

67. See Descartes, *Les passions*, 73: "La volonté . . . s'oppose continuellement à soy mesme, & ainsi rend l'ame esclave & malheureuse." ("The will . . . is in continual opposition to itself, and so renders the soul enslaved and unhappy" [Descartes, *The Passions*, 47].)

68. Descartes, *Les passions*, 73: "Ceux mesme qui ont les plus foibles ames, pourroient acquerir un empire tres-absolu sur toutes leurs passions." ("Even those who have the weakest souls could acquire a quite absolute dominion over all their passions" [Descartes, *The Passions*, 49].)

69. "Repousser les choses qui nuisent & peuvent destruire" (Descartes, *Les passions*, 183).

70. See Racine, *Phèdre et Hippolyte*, aiv^v. Such a position on the theater obviously represented a break with Racine's antitheatrical Jansenist educators.

71. "Generalement elle se plaist de sentir émouuoir en soy des passions, de quelle nature qu'elles soient, pourvû qu'elle en demeure maistresse" (Descartes, *Lettres de Monsieur Descartes*, 37).

72. Tad M. Schmaltz, "What Has Cartesianism to Do with Jansenism?" *Journal of the History of Ideas* 60, no. 1 (Jan. 1999): 37–56, notes that in the second half of the seventeenth century there existed "a fairly widespread belief in France of an intimate link between the two movements that the work of Descartes and Jansen inspired" (37), making reference to Francisque Bouillier's influential generalization, published in 1868, that there is a "natural alliance between the doctrines of Jansenius and those of Descartes" (41). While the two movements are interrelated insofar as each emerged from the intellectual battles of seventeenth-century France, more explicit connections are hard to draw, especially in light of Descartes's avoidance of theological debates.

73. Nicholas Malebranche, *De la recherche de la verité*, 2 vols. (Amsterdam: Henry Desbordes, 1688), 1:244: "Car le cerveau de ceux qui ont l'imagination forte recevant . . . des traces profondes des sujets qu'ils imaginent, ces traces sont

naturellement suivies d'une grande émotion d'esprits, qui dispose d'une maniére prompte & vive tout leur corps pour exprimer leurs pensées. Ainsi l'air de leur visage, le ton de leur voix, & le tour de leurs paroles animant leurs expressions, préparent ceux qui les écoutent & qui les regardent à se rendre attentifs, & à recevoir machinalement l'impression de l'image qui les agite."

74. "Car enfin un homme qui est pénétré de ce qu'il dit en pénétre ordinairement les autres" (ibid.).

75. See, e.g., Erwin Panofsky, *Perspective as Symbolic Form*, trans. Christopher S. Wood (New York: Zone, 1997), 66.

76. On the popularization of Vitruvian architecture, starting in Italy, see T. E. Lawrenson, *The French Stage and Playhouse in the XVIIth Century: A Study in the Advent of the Italian Order*, 2nd ed. (New York: AMS, 1986), 21–39.

77. As Alberto Pérez-Gómez and Louise Pelletier explain in *Architectural Representation and the Perspective Hinge* (Cambridge, MA: MIT Press, 2000), 45–46, Vitruvius's remarks on optics (*prospettiva*) have been read as a view of stagecraft because of a confusion between *sciographia* and *scenographia*. See also ibid., 97–101, 105–17.

78. See Dahlberg, "Ballet," 581; and Grut, *Royal*, 13.

79. The arch is confirmed by the ballet's libretto (*Le monde reiovi*, Aiᵛ), which notes: "Dessus l'Arc de Triomfe qui Paroist a l'ouuerture du Theatre est grauée cette Inscription: CHRISTINÆ REGINÆ SUECIÆ." (Engraved above the triumphal arch, which appears at the opening of the stage is this inscription: CHRISTINA, QUEEN OF SWEDEN.)

80. Sources differ, some putting Beaulieu in Sweden later than seems likely: I follow Dahlberg, "Ballet," 578.

81. Frederick J. Marker and Lise-Lone Marker, *A History of Scandinavian Theatre* (Cambridge: Cambridge University Press, 1996), 35; Carlson, "Scandinavia's," 13. More details of the space are provided in Agne Beijer, "Une maquette de décor récemment retrouvée pour le 'Ballet de la prosperité des armes de France' dansé à Paris, le 7 février 1641," in *Le lieu théâtral à la Renaissance*, ed. Jean Jacquot (Paris: Centre national de la recherche, 1964), 377–403.

82. The presumption is in Dahlberg, "Theatre," 170.

83. "La premiere ouverture estoit representée par vne merveilleuse perspective ou le mont Parnasse & les nœuf belles sœurs estoient de peintes si naifvement & avec tant d'Art que le jugement en estoit Trompé par la Veve." *Le Parnasse triumphant, divisé en trois ouvertures differentes* (Stockholm: Jean Janssonius, 1651), *1ʳ.

84. See Susan Bordo, *The Flight to Objectivity* (Albany: State University of New York Press, 1987), esp. 59–73 and 100–118.

85. Ibid., 68, 78.

86. Descartes, *Meditations*, 72. The original is in Descartes, *Meditationes*, 36–37: "Præcipuus autem error & frequentissimus qui possit in illis reperiri,

consistit in eo quòd ideas, quæ in me sunt, iudicem rebus quibusdam extra me positis similes esse, siue conformes."

87. Descartes, *Meditations*, 72; Descartes, *Meditationes*, 36: "Nam siue capram, siue chimæram imaginer, non minùs verum est me vnam imaginari quàm alteram."

88. The surviving libretto—*Les passions victorievses et vaincves: Ballet dancé en presence de leurs Majestez à Stokholm le 4 d'avril* (Stockholm: Jean Janssonius, 1649)—is also published anonymously. It is so remarkably different in style from *La naissance de la paix* that it is hard to imagine, as Richard A. Watson does, that they were written by the same person.

89. "Des ignorans ont tâché de la défigurer & de la corrompre" (ignoramuses have tried to disfigure and corrupt [the dance]), *Lettres patentes dv roy povr l'établissement de l'Academie royale de danse en la ville de Paris* (Paris: Pierre le Petit, 1663), 5; "Il s'est pendant les desordres & la confusion des dernieres guerres, introduit dans le dit Art, comme en tous les autres, vn si grand nombre d'abus" (during the disorders and the confusion of the late wars, there were a great number of abuses introduced into the said Art, as in all the others) (ibid., 4).

90. Ibid., 8.

91. See Maureen Needham, "Louis XIV and the Académie royale de danse, 1661—A Commentary and Translation," *Dance Chronicle* 20, no. 2 (1997): 173–90, at 175.

92. See, e.g., A. C. Grayling, *Descartes: The Life and Times of a Genius* (New York: Walker, 2005), 229.

93. Genevieve Lloyd, *The Man of Reason: "Male" and "Female" in Western Philosophy* (Minneapolis: University of Minnesota Press, 1984), 39–50. Lloyd writes: "We owe to Descartes an influential and pervasive theory of mind, which provides support for a powerful version of the sexual division of labour. Women have been assigned responsibility for that realm of the sensuous which the Cartesian Man of Reason must transcend, if he is to have true knowledge of things. . . . Woman's task is to preserve the sphere of the intermingling of mind and body, to which the Man of Reason will repair for solace, warmth and relaxation. If he is to exercise the most exalted form of Reason, he must leave soft emotions and sensuousness behind; woman will keep them intact for him" (50). She does concede that this development happened "in some ways despite Descartes's explicit intentions" (39). While Lloyd's formulation is the most cited, others go further. See, for example, the remarks of Nancy Tuana, who declares that a woman following Descartes's teachings "must renounce all those things that define her as female" and "become male." Nancy Tuana, *Woman and the History of Philosophy* (New York: Paragon House, 1992), 42, 41. In only two sentences—reliant on a passive-voice sleight of hand that Schmitter rightly condemns (see Schmitter, "Passionate," 72)—Tuana manages to connect Descartes's views with

Notes

those of Jacob Sprenger and Henry Kramer, authors of the notoriously misogynist screed *Malleus Maleficarium* (see Tuana, *Woman*, 39).

94. Poullain de la Barre anonymously published three texts that used the Cartesian method to argue for the equality of women: *De l'égalité des deux sexes, discours physique et moral où l'on voit l'importance de se défaire des préjugez* (Paris: Jean du Puis, 1673); *De l'education des dames pour la conduite de l'esprit dans les sciences et dans les moeurs* (Paris: Jean du Puis, 1674); and the sardonically titled *De l'excellence des hommes, contre l'égalité des sexes* (Paris: Jean du Puis, 1675). All three have been edited and translated in an English-language volume: François Poullain de la Barre, *Three Cartesian Feminist Treatises*, ed. Marcelle Maistre Welch, trans. Vivien Bosley (Chicago: University of Chicago Press, 2002).

95. See Erica Harth, "Cartesian Women," in *Feminist Interpretations of René Descartes*, ed. Susan Bordo (University Park: Penn State University Press, 1999), 213–31, at 213–14: "Conceptual and linguistic imprecision that blurred the lines between the salon and the academy persisted into the seventeenth century, but by Louis XIII's reign, informal, all-male academies specializing in scientific and erudite pursuits were distinguished from the female-led salon. The academy cultivated those aspects of Descartes's philosophy that were to have the greatest impact on the development of modern rational discourse: his dualism, mechanism, and objectivity." These informal salons would be formalized, and entry to them even more carefully policed, under Louis XIV.

96. Schmitter, "Passionate," 73.

97. Luce Irigaray, "L'admiration: Lecture de Descartes, *Les passions de l'âme*, art. 53," in *L'éthique de la différence sexuelle* (Paris: Minuit, 1984), 75–84, at 75: "Il faut relire un peu Descartes et se souvenir ou apprendre ce qu'il en est de mouvement dans les passions."

98. But this gendering is, of course, complicated, and the gendering of Athena in all versions of her origin myths is fraught. In her most celebrated appearance in theater history, in Aeschylus's *Eumenides*—in *Oresteia*, trans. Richard Lattimore (Chicago: University of Chicago Press, 1953), 133–71, at 161—Athena famously extols her own patriarchal mind-set, noting, "There is no mother anywhere who gave me birth / and, but for marriage, I am always for the male, / with all my heart, and strongly on my father's side." Surely the mixed gender messages in Athena's myths delighted Queen Christina, famous even in her day for a disavowal of her femininity, for her love of her father (who encouraged her boyishness), for her fraught relationship with her mother, and for her repudiation of marriage. See Veronica Buckley, *Christina, Queen of Sweden: The Restless Life of a European Eccentric* (London: HarperCollins, 2004).

99. Descartes, *La naissance*, 16:

PEuples que pensez vous voyant tant de merueilles,
Qui vous eblouissent les yeux?

On n'en a jamais vû sur terre des pareilles.
Pensez que vostre esprit est ravi dans les cieux.

. . . .

Ne jugerez vous pas, en regardant leurs faces,
Que tout, ce qui est beau dans le ciel, est icy?

100. Quoted in note 1 above.

101. Descartes, *The Passions*, 52. Descartes, *Les passions*, 82–83:

> Lors que la premiere rencontre de quelque objet nous surprent, & que nous le jugeons estre nouveau, ou fort different de ce que nous connoissions auparavant, ou bien de ce que nous supposions qu'il devoit estre, cela fait que nous l'admirons & en sommes estonnez. Et pour ce que cela peut arriver avant que nous connoissions aucunement si cet objet nous est convenable, ou s'il ne l'est pas, il me semble que l'Admiration est la premiere de toutes les passions. Et elle n'a point de contraire, à cause que si l'objet qui se presente n'a rien en soy qui nous surprene, nous n'en sommes aucunement émeus, & nous le considerons sans passion.

102. The spirits work to "fortifier & conserver" the impression of the object as "rare, & par consequent digne d'estre fort consideré" (ibid., 95).

103. Ibid., 96.

104. A differently formulated consideration of wonder's salutary effects on reason is provided in Schmitter, "Passionate," 61–62.

105. "Ceux qui n'ont aucune inclination naturelle à cette passion, sont ordinairement fort ignorans" (Descartes, *Les passions*, 102).

106. "Et on peut dire en particulier de l'Admiration, qu'elle est utile, en ce qu'elle fait que nous apprenons & retenons en nostre mémoire les choses que nous avons auparavant ignorées" (ibid., 101).

107. See René Descartes, *L'homme* (Paris: Charles Angot, 1664), 75.

108. See Descartes's letters to Mersenne dated June 11, 1640 (Descartes, *Œuvres*, 10:72–88) and August 6, 1640 (ibid., 10:142–49), where he describes the *pli de mémoire*.

109. Descartes, *The Passions*, 41. Descartes, *Les passions*, 60, reads: "Ainsi lors que l'ame veut se souvenir de quelque chose, cette volonté fait que la glande se penchant successivement vers divers costez, pousse les esprits vers divers endroits du cerveau, jusques à ce qu'ils rencontrent celuy où sont les traces que l'objet dont on veut se souvenir y a laissées. Car ces traces ne sont autre chose sinon que les pores du cerveau, par où les esprits ont auparavant pris leur cours, à cause de la presence de cet objet, ont acquis par cela une plus grande facilité que les autres, à estre ouverts derechef en mesme façon, par les esprits qui viennent vers eux."

110. In the summary of one critic they are "not *stored* faithfully. . . . They are just retained 'in such a way that' they play a part in the (re-)creation of the idea

on the surface of the gland. This is representation without resemblance." John Sutton, *Philosophy and Memory Traces: Descartes to Connectionism* (Cambridge: Cambridge University Press, 1998), 58.

111. Descartes to Marin Mersenne, April 1, 1640: "vn ioüeur de luth a vne partie de sa memoire en ses mains; car la facilité de plier & de disposer ses doigts en diuerses façons, qu'il a acquise par habitude, aide à le faire souuenir des passages pour l'execution desquels il les doit ainsi disposer" (Descartes, *Œuvres*, 3:48).

112. Descartes to Mersenne, March 18, 1630: "la mesme chose qui fait enuie de danser à quelques-vns, peut donner enuie de pleurer aux autres" (ibid., 1:133).

113. See Martine Clermont, "L'acteur et son jeu au XVIIe siècle: Ses rapports avec le personnage qu'il représente," *Revue d'histoire du théâtre* 33, no. 4 (1981): 379–88, at 380–81.

114. I will return to Le Brun, chancellor of the Académie royale de peinture et de sculpture, in Chapter 3. Le Brun's work codifying the passions was intended for painters, to help them represent emotions more intelligibly to their audiences. But this work was quickly taken up in acting theory.

115. Joseph Roach, *Cities of the Dead: Circum-Atlantic Performance* (New York: Columbia University Press, 1996), 5.

116. Descartes, *La naissance*, 12.

117. See Reiss, "Denying," 604–5.

CHAPTER 2

1. Best known to us for his fairy tales, Perrault was secretary of the Pétite Académie (later the Académie des inscriptions et belles-lettres), where among other tasks he edited works written in honor of Louis XIV before they were printed. As influential assistant to Jean-Baptiste Colbert, Perrault served as his representative in the Académie de l'architecture, helped found the Académie des sciences, and helped reestablish the Académie de peinture et de sculpture after internecine battles threatened it. The extent of his role in the design of several influential buildings conceived by his brother Claude is a matter of dispute (as is the veracity of his claim, made in his *Mémoires*, that he personally quashed Bernini's plan for the Louvre). Perrault was elected to the Académie française in 1671. For an overview of these and other events of Perrault's fascinating life, see Antoine Picon's "Un moderne paradoxal," in Charles Perrault, *Mémoires de ma vie*, ed. Paul Bonnefon (Paris: Macula, 1993), 1–101.

2. He writes: "Ses yeux elevés au ciel et le petit souris qu'on void sur son visage montrent la joie que lui donne une idée agreable qu'elle entrevoit, qu'elle poursuit et dont elle est sur le point de se saisir." Charles Perrault, *Le cabinet des beaux arts, ou Recueil d'estampes gravées d'après les tableaux d'un plafond où les beaux-arts sont représentés* (Paris: Gérard Edelinck, 1690), 15.

3. "Le laurier qui la couronne ne marque pas seulement la gloire qu'elle dispense aux Héros . . . mais encore celle qui lui revient de ses propres ouvrages; en un mot, l'Immortalité glorieu" (ibid., 15–16). He notes that he has not written names on the spines of the books behind Poetry, since it is "la Posterité qui s'en acquitera mieux que nous . . . a mesure que la Mort enlevera les Auteurs" (posterity which will settle it better than we . . . as death takes authors from us) (ibid., 16–17).

4. Perrault describes the instrument-playing children and their associations with specific genres at ibid., 16. The Molière collection opened toward the viewer lists six plays: *L'école des femmes*, *L'école des maris*, *Les précieuses [ridicules]*, *Le misanthrope*, *L'avare*, and *Les fâcheux*.

5. "Ce masque represente les fictions ingenieuses dont elle couvre les vérités, ou de la Nature, ou de la morale, qu'elle a toûjoûrs regardées comme la plus belle et la plus noble partie de ses productions" (ibid.).

6. Poetry "est celui de tous ses ouvrages, qui . . . lui fait le plus d'honneur et lui acquiert le plus de reputation par les applaudissements du theatre" (ibid., 17).

7. "C'est aussi le genre de Poesie ou les François surpassent davantage les Poetes des autres nations, et de tous les siecles precedens" (ibid.).

8. The play "a toujours passé pour un chef d'œuvre" (ibid.).

9. The poem, written in alexandrines, favorably compares the century of Louis XIV with that of Augustus: "Et l'on peut comparer sans craindre d'estre injuste, / Le Siecle de LOUIS au beau Siecle d'Auguste." Charles Perrault, *Le siecle de Louis le Grand* (Paris: Jean Baptiste Coignard, 1687), 3. One example of his couplets satirizing the ancients: "Platon qui fut divin du temps de nos ayeux, / Commence à devenir quelquefois ennuyeux" (Plato, who was a god in the days of our ancestors, / Is starting to get occasionally boring) (ibid., 4).

10. Absent from these classical taxonomies, wonder is in this regard unlike Descartes's other "primitive passions": love, hatred, desire, joy, and sadness. See Anthony Levi, *French Moralists: The Theory of the Passions, 1585–1649* (Oxford: Clarendon, 1964), 275, which notes that wonder "depends for its place among the passions on Cartesian physics."

11. Descartes, *Les passions de l'âme* (Paris: Henry Le Gras, 1649), 83: "L'admiration est la premiere de toutes les passions." A detailed discussion of wonder in Descartes, with an emphasis quite different from mine, appears in chapter 6 of Deborah J. Brown, *Descartes and the Passionate Mind* (Cambridge: Cambridge University Press, 2006).

12. Perrault, *Le cabinet*, 16.

13. *Mélite* may have been composed as early as 1625—see Henry Carrington Lancaster, *A History of French Dramatic Literature in the Seventeenth Century, Part 1: 1610–1634*, 2 vols. (New York: Gordian, 1966), 2:573–76—but its Paris success began at the Berthaud *jeu de paume* theater shortly after it was rented by

Montdory in December 1629. Montdory's troupe would eventually settle in the space that theater history knows as the Théâtre du Marais. See W. L. Wiley, *The Hôtel de Bourgogne: Another Look at France's First Public Theatre, Studies in Philology* 70, no. 5 (Dec. 1973): 1–113, at 12.

14. The dating of *Médée* is uncontroversial. Elisabeth's participation in a production is confirmed by Charles Adam, *Descartes: Ses amitiés féminines* (Paris: Boivin, 1937), 101, which dates the performance to the summer of 1642 (when Elisabeth was twenty-three years old), and by Elisabeth's sister Sophia, in *Memoirs of Sophia, Electress of Hanover, 1630–1680*, trans. H. Forester (London: Richard Bentley and Sons, 1888), 12. The play remained unpublished until 1639.

15. The play's premiere is sometimes dated to December 1636. I follow Georges Couton, the editor of Corneille, *Œuvres complètes*, 3 vols. (Paris: Gallimard, 1980–87); and André Le Gall, *Corneille* (Paris: Flammarion, 1997), 128. The play's success is legendary. A historian writing only fifteen years after its premiere describes it this way:

> Il est malaisé de s'imaginer avec quelle approbation cette piece fut receuë de la Cour & du public. On ne se pouvoit lasser de la voir, on n'entendoit autre chose dans les compagnies, châcun en savoit quelque partie par cœur, on la faisoit apprendre aux enfans, & en plusieurs endroits de la France, il estoit passé en proverbe, de dire, *Cela est beau comme le Cid.*

> [It is hard to imagine how well received this play was at court and by the public. One could not tire of seeing it, one heard of nothing else in society, everyone knew some part by heart, one taught it to children, and in many places in France it became proverbial to say: *This is as beautiful as Le Cid.*]

Paul Pellisson-Fontanier, *Relation contenant l'histoire de l'Académie françoise* (Paris: Augustin Courbé, 1653), 186–87.

16. Barbara G. Mittman, *Spectators on the Paris Stage in the Seventeenth and Eighteenth Centuries* (Ann Arbor: UMI Research Press, 1984), 3.

17. As is widely documented, *Le Cid* set off a flurry of pamphlets, including Georges de Scudéry's famous *Observations sur le Cid* (Paris: au despens de l'auteur [at the author's expense], 1637). The so-called quarrel of *Le Cid* led to the imposition of the rules outlined in *Les sentiments de l'Académie française sur la tragicomédie du Cid* (Paris: J. Camusat, 1638), written principally by Jean Chapelain, and later by François Hédelin, abbé d'Aubignac, in *La pratique du théâtre* (Paris: Antoine de Sommaville, 1657), both written at Richelieu's command.

18. René Descartes, *Discours de la méthode pour bien conduire sa raison, & chercher la verité dans les sciences, plus la Dioptrique, les Météores et la Géométrie qui sont des essais de cette méthode* (Leiden: Jan Maire, 1637), 33.

19. "Je suis maistre de moy comme de l'Vniuers." Pierre Corneille, *Cinna, ou La clémence d'Auguste* (Rouen: Toussainct Quinet, 1643), 106.

20. See, e.g., Gustave Lanson, "L'influence de la philosophie cartésienne sur la littérature française," *Revue de métaphysique* (1896): 517–50; Paul Bénichou, *Morales du grand siècle* (Paris: Gallimard, 1948), whose critique of Lanson leads him to a modified thesis concerning Corneille's Cartesian inflections; and Ernst Cassirer, *Descartes: Lehre—Persönlichkeit—Wirkung* (Hamburg: Felix Meiner, 1995), which, at 116–17, briefly suggests the key connection—emotional wonder (*Bewunderung*)—that I take up here. More recently, see the short but forceful article by Jean-Marie Beyssade, "Descartes et Corneille ou les démesures de l'égo," *Laval théologique et philosophique* 47, no. 1 (1991): 63–82. There are, of course, dissenters: see, e.g., Levi, *French Moralists*, 28; and Robert Champigny, "Corneille et le *Traité des passions*," *French Review* 26 (1952): 112–20, which finds the comparisons between Corneille and Descartes forced and declares that in any case "la philosophie et le théâtre sont ennemis" (philosophy and theater are enemies) (120).

21. "La pitié d'un malheur où nous voyons tomber nos semblables, nous porte à la crainte d'un pareil pour nous; cette crainte au desir de l'éviter; & ce desir à purger, modérer, rectifier, & mesme déraciner en nous la passion, qui plonge à nos yeux dans ce malheur les personnes que nous plaignons: par cette raison commune, mais naturelle & indubitable, que pour éviter l'effet il faut retrancher la cause." Pierre Corneille, "Discovrs de la tragedie, et des moyens de la traiter; selon le vray-semblable ou le necessaire," in *Le theatre de P. Corneille, reveu & corrigé par l'autheur*, 3 vols. (Paris: Guillaume de Luyne, 1660), 2:v–lxiv, at vi–vii. Spectators, Corneille divines, are meant to pity the hero who, yielding to a specific passion, brings misfortune on himself—and thus they moderate their own passions out of fear of a similar fate. In its lucidity and specificity his paraphrase undoubtedly misrepresents Aristotle: pity and fear are separated and then causally related, and specific vices other than pity and fear are said to be moderated.

22. Corneille notes that Rodrigue and Chimène in *Le Cid*

> tombent dans l'infélicité par cette foiblesse humaine dont nous sommes capables comme eux: leur malheur fait pitié, cela est constant, & il en a coûté assez de larmes aux Spectateurs pour ne le point contester. Cette pitié nous doit donner une crainte de tomber dans un pareil malheur, & purger en nous ce trop d'amour qui cause leur infortune, & nous les fait plaindre; mais je ne sçay si elle nous la donne, ny si elle le purge. (Ibid., xii–xiii)

> [fall into unhappiness through human frailty of which we are also capable; their misfortune invariably causes pity, and it has cost enough spectators' tears that we need not argue the point at all. This pity ought to instill in us a fear of falling into similar misfortune and ought to purge in us the excess of love that caused their misfortune and made us pity them; but I do not know if it instills fear in us, nor if it purges it.]

23. "Si la purgation des passions se fait dans la Tragédie, je tiens qu'elle se doit faire de la manière que je l'explique; mais je doute si elle s'y fait iamais, & dans celles-là mesme qui ont les conditions que demande Aristote" (ibid., xii).

24. "Une belle idée, qui n'ait iamais son effet dans la vérité" (ibid., xiii).

25. "Je ne comprens point sa pensée" (ibid., xv).

26. "Pour nous faciliter les moyens de faire naistre cette pitié & cette crainte, où Aristote semble nous obliger, il nous aide à choisir les personnes & les événemens, qui peuvent exciter l'une & l'autre" (ibid., ix).

27. This resemblance has been described in Bénichou, *Morales*, 102–9; and in Georges Couton, *Corneille et la Fronde* (Clermont-Ferrand: Publications de la Faculté des lettres de l'Université de Clermont, 1951), 67–77.

28. "Esclaue ... Qui tremble à voir vn Aigle." Pierre Corneille, *Nicomede* (Rouen: Laurens Maurry, 1651), 4.

29. Ibid., 19:

Ie veux bien mettre à part, auec le nom d'aisné,
Le rang de vostre maistre où ie suis destiné,
Et nous verrons ainsi qui fait mieux vn braue homme,
Des leçons d'Annibal, ou celles de Rome.

30. Corneille's play was inspired by the Latin historian Justin's brief account of Nicomedes II in book 34 of his *Epitome historiarum philippicarum*, augmented by other classical sources including Appian and Plutarch; Jean de Rotrou's 1649 play *Cosroès* likely suggested Corneille's treatment. See Lawrence Riddle, *The Genesis and Sources of Pierre Corneille's Tragedies from "Médéé" to "Pertharite"* (Baltimore: Johns Hopkins [University] Press, 1926), 153–54.

31. "Adieu, pensez-y bien, ie vous laisse y réuer" (Corneille, *Nicomede*, 19). On the meditative denotations of *rêver* in the period in general and Corneille in particular, see Alain Rey et al., eds., *Dictionnaire historique de la langue française*, 4th ed. (Paris: Dictionnaires le Robert, 2012), s.v. "rêver."

32. "Ce Heros de ma façon sort vn peu des regles de la Tragedie. ... Il est bon de hazarder vn peu, et ne s'attacher pas tousiours si seruilement à ses Preceptes" (Corneille, "Au lecteur," in *Nicomede*, bii^v).

33. He writes: "L'exclusion des personnes tout à fait vertüeuses qui tombent dans le malheur, bannit les Martyrs de nostre Théatre" (The exclusion of completely virtuous characters who fall into misfortune banned martyrs from our theater) (Corneille, "Discovrs de la tragedie," xiv). Corneille presumably has in mind Aristotle's stipulation in chapter 13 of the *Poetics* that the tragic hero should not be outstanding.

34. "Corneille a fait vivre le *généreux* de Descartes." V. L. Saulnier, *La littérature française du siècle classique* (Paris: Presses universitaires de France, 1970), 53. More fully fledged readings of Cornelian *générosité* are provided by Gustave Lanson, "Le

héros cornélien et le 'généreux' selon Descartes," *Revue d'histoire littéraire de la France* 1 (1894): 397–411; Pierre-Henri Simon, *Le domaine héroïque des lettres françaises* (Paris: Armand Colin, 1963), 141–44; and André Stegmann, *L'héroïsme cornélien: Genèse et signification*, 2 vols. (Paris: Armand Colin, 1968), 2:467–71.

35. Descartes, *The Passions of the Soul*, trans. Stephen H. Voss (Indianapolis: Hackett, 1989), 104; but note that I have made a minor amendment to Voss's English translation: his pronoun (*it*) refers to the antecedent *free control*; Descartes's (*en*) stresses the antecedent *volitions*. See Descartes, *Les passions*, 210: "partie en ce qu'il connoist qu'il n'y a rien qui veritablement luy appartiene, que cette libre disposition de ses volontez, ny pourquoy il doive estre loüé ou blasmé, sinon pource qu'il en use bien ou mal; & partie en ce qu'il sent en soy mesme une ferme & constante resolution d'en bien user, c'est à dire de ne manquer jamais de volonté, pour entreprendre & executer toutes les choses qu'il jugera estre les meilleures. Ce qui est suivre parfaitement la vertu."

36. Descartes, *The Passions*, 105. Descartes, *Les passions*, 214: "n'estimant que fort peu toutes les choses qui dependent d'autruy." On the signal importance of *générosité* see also Amy Morgan Schmitter, "How to Engineer a Human Being: Passions and Functional Explanation in Descartes," in *A Companion to Descartes*, ed. Janet Broughton and John Carriero (Oxford: Blackwell, 2008), 426–44, at 440.

37. Dalia Judovitz, *Subjectivity and Representation in Descartes: The Origins of Modernity* (Cambridge: Cambridge University Press, 1988).

38. Descartes, *The Passions*, 105. Descartes, *Les passions*, 213–14: "pource qu'ils n'estiment rien de plus grand que de faire du bien aux autres hommes, & de mespriser son propre interest pour ce sujet, ils font tousjours parfaitement courtois, affables, & officieux envers un chacun."

39. See Descartes's "Response to the Second Letter," prefatory to Descartes, *Les passions*, at ***7ᵛ–***8ʳ: "mon dessein n'a pas esté d'expliquer les Passions . . . en Philosophe moral, mais seulement en Physicien."

40. In private discussion with Laodice, Nicomède worries that "ma generosité céde enfin à sa [i.e., Arsinoé's] haine" (Corneille, *Nicomede*, 62). He worries unnecessarily.

41. Laodice notes that Prusias "ne voit pas que par ses yeux," an effect of Arsinoé's pretentiously parading before him, as Nicomède alleges: "auec tant de pompe à vos yeux elle étale" (ibid., 2, 80).

42. See ibid., 86:

NICOMÈDE. Seigneur, voulez-vous bien vous en fier à moy?
Ne soyez l'vn ny l'autre. [i.e., neither father nor husband]
PRUSIAS. Et que dois-ie estre?
NICOMÈDE. Roy.

43. "L'admiration de tant d'hommes parfaits . . . / N'est pas grande vertu si l'on ne les imite" (ibid., 42).

44. For his emphasis of Nicomède's filial role see Corneille, "Discovrs de la tragedie," xxvii or xxi, where the playwright refers to "la générosité de ce fils" (generosity of the son) and calls him a "fils genereux" (generous son).

45. Corneille, *Nicomede*, 123:

Ce n'est plus des Romains l'esclaue ambitieux,
C'est la liberateur d'vn sang si precieux.
Mon frere, auec mes fers vous en brisez bien d'autres,
Ceux du Roy, de la Reyne, . . . & les vostres.

46. The letter appears in Alexandre Foucher de Careil, *Descartes, la Princesse Élisabeth, et la Reine Christine, d'après des lettres inédites* (Paris: Germer-Baillière, 1879), 76–78.

47. Descartes to Elisabeth, Oct. 6, 1645: "si nous ne pensions qu'à nous seuls, nous ne pourions jouïr que des biens qui nous sont particuliers; au lieu que si nous nous considerons comme parties de quelque autre Cors, nous participons aussi aux biens qui luy sont communs, sans estre priué pour cela d'aucun de ceux qui nous sont propres." René Descartes, *Lettres de Monsieur Descartes, où sont traittées les plus belles questions de la morale, physique, medecine, & des mathematiques* (Paris: Henry Le Gras, 1657), 36.

48. See Article 203, "Que la Generosité sert de remede contre ses [anger's] exces" (That generosity serves as a remedy against excesses) (Descartes, *Les passions*, 272–73); and Article 148, "Que l'exercice de la vertu est un souverain remede contre les Passions" (That the exercise of virtue is the prime remedy for the passions) (ibid., 203–4). Despite the latter article's misleading title, in it Descartes explains how passion can increase the soul's capacity for joy by helping it to "connoistre sa perfection" (understand its perfection) (ibid., 204).

49. Descartes's reference to "la chasse, le jeu de la paume, & autres semblables" appears in Descartes to Elisabeth, Oct. 6, 1645, in Descartes, *Lettres de Monsieur Descartes*, 37.

50. Corneille, *Nicomede*, 23–24:

I'ay creu pour le mieux
Qu'il failloit de son fort l'attirer [i.e., Nicomède] en ces lieux.
Metrobate l'a fait par des terreurs Paniques.
Feignant de luy trahir mes ordres tyranniques,
Et pour l'assassiner se disant suborné,
Il me l'a, grace aux Dieux, doucement amené.
Il vient s'en plaindre au Roy; luy demander justice,
Et sa plainte le jette au bord du précipice:

Sans prendre aucun soucy de m'en iustifier,
Je sçauray m'en seruir à me fortifier.
Tantost en le voyant i'ay fait de l'effrayée,
I'ay changé de couleur, ie me suis écriée,
Il a creu me surprendre, & l'a creu bien en vain,
Puisque son retour mesme est l'oeuure de ma main.

51. "Ce fils donc . . . a pressé la soif de sa vengeance" (ibid., 22).
52. "Entierement maistres de leurs Passions" (Descartes, *Les passions*, 214).
53. Corneille, *Nicomede*, 122:

Seigneur, faut-il si loin pousser votre victoire,
Et qu'ayant en vos mains & mes iours, & ma gloire,
La haute ambition d'vn si puissant vainqueur
Veüille encor triompher iusques dedans mon cœur?
Contre tant de vertu ie ne le puis défendre,
Il est impatient luy-mesme de se rendre.

54. "La Tragédie se propose pour son but la trāquillité de l'Ame, puisque sa fin principalle est de calmer les passions." [Hippolyte] Jules [Pilet] de La Mesnardière, *La poëtique* (Paris: Antoine de Sommaville, 1639), K^r.
55. "Que peut-estre Aristote n'a sçeu prévoir" (Corneille, "Discovrs de la trage-die," xx).
56. "N'excite que de l'admiration dans l'ame du Spectateur" (Corneille, "Au lecteur," in *Nicomede*, aiii^v).
57. "Nous aimons naturellement d'en estre emeus et d'en suivre les mouve-mens, il n'y a que les incommodités procédant de cette suite qui nous apprennent qu'elles peuvent estre nuisibles. Et c'est à mon jugement ce qui fait que les tra-gédies plaisent d'autant plus qu'elles excitent plus de tristesse, parce que nous cognoissons qu'elle ne sera point assez violente pour nous porter à des extrava-gances ni assez durable pour corrompre la santé." Elisabeth to Descartes, Oct. 28, 1645, published in Foucher de Careil, *Descartes, la Princesse*, 80.
58. Descartes to Elisabeth, Oct. 6, 1645: "la fatigue & la peine . . . augmente le plaisir" (Descartes, *Lettres de Monsieur Descartes*, 37).
59. "Le contentement qu'elle [i.e., the soul] a de pleurer en voyant represen-ter quelque action pitoyable & funeste sur vn theatre, vient principalement de ce qu'il luy semble qu'elle fait vne action vertuese ayant compassion des affligez" (ibid.).
60. "Ce plaisir de l'Ame . . . n'est pas inséparable de la gayeté & de l'ayse du Cors" (ibid.).
61. Descartes, *The Passions*, 101. Descartes, *Les passions*, 202–3, reads: "Et lors que nous lisons des avantures estranges dans un livre, ou que nous les voyons

representer sur un theatre, cela excite quelquefois en nous la Tristesse, quelquefois la Ioye, ou l'Amour, ou la Haine, & generalement toutes les Passions,
selon la diversité des objets qui s'offrent à nostre imagination; mais avec cela
nous avons du plaisir, de les sentir exciter en nous, & ce plaisir est une Ioye
intellectuelle, qui peut aussi bien naistre de la Tristesse, que de toutes les autres
Passions."

62. Corneille declares it difficult to find "cette purgation effective & sensible
des passions, par le moyen de la pitié & de la crainte" (Corneille, "Discovrs de la
tragedie," xvi).

63. Emotions "sont accompagnés effectivement de diverses réactions phy-
siques. De là est née la confusion et la dérive. Ces passions [pity and fear] peuvent
avoir un aspect dynamique et volontaire, quoique difficile à maîtriser." ([The pas-
sions] are accompanied by diverse physical reactions. Here originate confusion
and deviation. These passions [of pity and fear] can have a dynamic and volun-
tary aspect, however difficult to master.) Jean Émelina, "Corneille et la catharsis," *Littératures classiques* 32 (Jan. 1998): 105–20, at 106.

64. "Ne sont pas si sévérement retranchez dans l'éxacte vertu, qu'ils ne soient
susceptibles des passions [of pity and fear]" (Corneille, "Discovrs de la tragedie,"
ix).

65. Descartes, *The Passions*, 40. Descartes, *Les passions*, 57: "La mesme impression que la presence d'un objet effroyable fait sur la glande, & qui cause la peur
en quelques hommes, peut exciter en d'autres le courage & la hardiesse: dont la
raison est, que tous les cerveaux ne sont pas disposez en mesme façon."

66. François Hédelin, abbé d'Aubignac, begins *La Pratique du théâtre* by
arguing for the necessity of public spectacles, as evidenced by the esteem in
which they were held by the Greeks: "il est traitté de la Necessité des Spectacles,
en quelle estime ils ont esté parmy les Anciens, & en quel estat ils sont mainte-
nant parmy nous" (23).

67. Descartes to Elisabeth, May or June, 1645: "qui ne s'ocuperoit qu'à considérer des obiets de tristesse & de pitié . . . qui verroit continuellement representer
deuant soy des Tragédies"; "émouuoir son imagination, sans toucher son entendement" (Descartes, *Lettres de Monsieur Descartes*, 91).

68. See Elisabeth to Descartes, Oct. 28, 1645, in Foucher de Careil, *Descartes,
la Princesse*, 80 (quoted at note 57 above).

69. "D'assassins acheptez par sa haine" (Corneille, *Nicomede*, 6).

70. "Fuyez donc les fureurs qui saisissent mon ame. / Apres le coup fatal de
cette indignité / Je n'ay plus ny respect, ny generosité" (ibid., 115).

71. "L'amour que i'ay pour vous a commis cette offence" (ibid., 32).

72. He writes: "Je ne voy point qu'elle [i.e., fear or terror] puisse jamais estre
loüable ny utile" and explains that fear diminishes the subject's power to resist
evil (Descartes, *Les passions*, 240–41).

73. "Sans aucune faute de leur part" (Corneille, "Discovrs de la tragedie," xiv). Corneille uses the examples of Polyeucte, Héraclius, and Nicomède, who "ne nous donnent rien à craindre" (ibid.).

74. Descartes, *The Passions*, 59. Descartes, *Les passions*, 100: "L'utilité de toutes les passions ne consiste qu'en ce qu'elles fortifient & fort durer en l'ame des pensées, lesquelles il est bon qu'elle conserve. . . . Le mal qu'elles peuvent causer, consiste en ce qu'elles . . . fortifient & conservent d'autres, ausquelles il n'est pas bon de s'arrester."

75. Descartes, *The Passions*, 52. Descartes, *Les passions*, 82–83 (see Chapter 1n101).

76. The spirits work to "fortifier & conserver" the impression of the object as "rare, & par consequent digne d'estre fort consideré" (Descartes, *Les passions*, 95).

77. See ibid., 96.

78. "Ie viens en bon Sujet vous rendre le repos / Que d'autres interests troubloient mal à propos" (Corneille, *Nicomede*, 121).

79. See ibid., 120.

80. "I'ay osté de ma Scene l'horreur de [cette] Catastrophe." Pierre Corneille, "Examen de *Nicomède*," in *Le theatre de P. Corneille*, 3:lxxiv–lxxviii, at lxxiv.

81. Corneille, *Nicomede*, 121:

Pardonnez à ce peuple vn peu trop de chaleur
Qu'à sa compassion a donné mon malheur. . . .
Ie scay par quels motifs vous m'estes si contraire,
Vostres amour maternel veut voir regner mon frere.

82. Descartes explains the utility of passions in Article 74. He elaborates in Article 137, in which he explains the particular utility of sadness and joy, hatred and love. On the role of hatred and sadness in "repousser les choses qui nuisent & peuvent destruire," see Descartes, *Les passions*, 183.

83. Corneille, *Nicomede*, 122: "Ioignez cette conqueste à trois sçeptres conquis, / Et ie croiray gagner en vous vn second fils."

84. See Bruce Griffiths, "'La fourbe' and 'la générosité': Fair and Foul Play in *Nicomède*," *Forum for Modern Language Studies* 1 (1965): 339–51, at 348.

85. Erec R. Koch, *The Aesthetic Body: Passion, Sensibility, and Corporeality in Seventeenth-Century France* (Newark: University of Delaware Press, 2008), 116.

86. "Tout est calme, Seigneur, vn moment de ma veuë / A soudain appaisé la populace émeuë" (Corneille, *Nicomede*, 120).

87. "L'amour qu'elle nous donne pour cette vertu que nous admirons, nous imprime de la haine pour le vice contraire" (Corneille, "Examen," lxxvii).

88. The tragedy's one complete action "laisse l'esprit de l'Auditeur dans le calme." Pierre Corneille, "Discovrs des trois unitez, d'action, de iour, & de lieu," in *Le theatre de P. Corneille*, 3:v–xxxvii, at vii.

89. "La grandeur de courage de Nicomede nous laisse une auersion de la pusil-lanimité, & la genereuse reconnoissance d'Heraclius qui expose sa vie pour Mar-tian, à qui il est redevable de la sienne, nous jette dans l'horreur de l'ingratitude" (Corneille, "Examen," lxxvii).

90. "Les passions n'y sont présentées aux yeux que pour montrer tout le desordre dont elles sont cause." Jean Racine, *Phèdre et Hippolyte* (Paris: Claude Barbin, 1677), aiv^v. Racine had annotated his personal translation of Aristotle's *Poetics* by writing that, in exciting "la pitié et la terreur," tragic representation "purge (et tempère) ces sortes des passions. (C'est-à-dire qu'en émouvant ces pas-sions, elle leur ôte ce qu'elles ont d'excessif et de vicieux, et les ramène à un état modéré et conforme à la raison.)" (By exciting pity and fear, tragic representa-tion purges and moderates these kinds of emotions. That is, by exciting these emotions, tragedy removes what is excessive and vicious from them, bringing them to a state that is restrained and in accordance with reason.) Jean Racine, "Extraits de la *Poétique* d'Aristote," in *Œuvres complètes*, ed. Raymond Picard, 2 vols. (Paris: Gallimard, 1950), 1:919–28, at 919.

91. See, e.g., d'Aubignac's *The Practice of Theater*, which had commanded—in a formulation foreign to Aristotle—that

> la force de la Vertu brillante au milieu méme des persecutions; elle y est souvent couronnée; & quand méme elle y succombe, elle demeure toûjours glorieuse; Elle nous découvre toutes les deformitez du vice; elle le punit souvent, & quand méme il triomphe par violence, il ne laisse pas d'estre en abomination; d'où les Spectateurs tirent d'eux-mémes & naturellement cette consequence, *Qu'il vaut mieux embrasser la Vertu au peril d'un trait-ement iniuste, que de se laisser corrompre par le vice, avec esperance méme d'impunité.* C'est ainsi principalement que le Theatre doit estre instructif au public. (Hédelin, *La pratique*, 419)
>
> [the force of brilliant virtue triumphing even in the midst of persecutions is often rewarded, and even if it succumbs to them it remains glorious. Through virtue all the deformities of vice are revealed; vice is often pun-ished, and even when it triumphs by means of violence, it does not cease to be an abomination from which Spectators naturally, and on their own, draw this conclusion: *that it is better to embrace Virtue even at the peril of unjust persecution than to be corrupted by vice even with hopes of impunity.* It is thus principally that the Stage ought to be instructive to the public.]

He himself acknowledges the novelty of his didactic poetics: "Voicy vne matiere nouvelle en l'Art Poëtique, & dont ie n'ay rien trouvé dans les Autheurs qui nous en ont fait de gros Volumes" (Here is matter new to the art of Poetics, of which I have found nothing in the Authors who have written us thick vol-umes) (411).

92. Émelina, "Corneille," 119; cf. Ferdinard Alquié, ed., *Œuvres philosophiques*, by René Descartes, 3 vols. (Paris: Classiques Garnier, 1989), 3:999. Descartes's distinction between *admiration* and *étonnement*—the latter leaving one "immobile comme une statuë"—appears at Descartes, *Les passions*, 99.

93. A perceptive article articulates precisely this distinction between a didactic lesson and one apprehended in light of emotional wonder: see Henry Phillips, "Descartes and the Dramatic Experience," *French Studies* 39, no. 4 (1985): 408–22, esp. 418, where he notes that "although the theatre may constitute in some ways a model of response . . . we do not learn from plays in any sense." Indeed, Descartes concedes that wonder is not quite universal: certain people are largely immune to its passionate workings—the physiological explanation he provides for ignorance. See Descartes, *Les passions*, 102.

94. Ibid., 95: "rares et extraordinaires."

95. See Nicolas Boileau [Despréaux], "L'art poëtique," in *Œuvres diverses du Sieur D**** (Paris: Denis Thierry, 1674), 119.

96. The remarks were published for the first time in a later edition of Boileau's *Œuvres*. See Nicolas Boileau [Despréaux], "A Monsieur Perrault de l'Academie françoise," in *Œuvres diverses du S' Boileau Despreaux*, 2 vols. (Paris: Denis Thierry, 1701), 2:126: "Corneille . . . fait inventer un nouveau genre de Tragedie inconnu à Aristote. . . . Il n'a point songé, comme les Poëtes de l'ancienne Tragedie, à émouvoir la Pitié & la Terreur; mais à exciter dans l'ame des Spectateurs, par la sublimité des pensées, & par la beauté des sentimens, une certaine admiration, dont plusieurs Personnes, & les jeunes gens sur tout, s'accommodent souvent beaucoup mieux que des veritables passions Tragiques."

97. Aristotle, *On Poetry and Style*, ed. and trans. G. M. A. Grube (Indianapolis: Hackett, 1989), 20, 53.

98. See Martin T. Herrick, "Some Neglected Sources of Admiratio," *Modern Language Notes* 62, no. 4 (1947): 222–26, at 225. Robortello, for example, writes, "Tragic actions are constructed from the pitiful, the fearful, and the marvelous (or admirable)"—presumably *admirabilem* in the original (quoted in ibid., 225).

99. Aristotle, *On Poetry*, 20.

100. "Dans l'admiration qu'on a pour sa vertu ie trouue vne maniere de purger les passions, dont n'a point parlé Aristote, & qui est peut-estre plus seure que celle qu'il prescrit à la Tragedie par le moyen de la pitié & de la crainte" (Corneille, "Examen," lxxvii).

101. See Descartes, *Météores*, 157, in Descartes, *Discours*. Note that the volume is not continuously paginated: the *Météores* follows the *Dioptrique*.

102. The treatise ends: "I'espere que ceux qui auront compris tout ce qui a esté dit en ce traité, ne verront rien dans les nuës a l'auenir, dont-ils ne puissent aysement entendre la cause, ny qui leur donne suiet d'admiration" (Descartes, *Discours*, 294).

103. Geneviève Rodis-Lewis, *Œuvres de Descartes: À la recherche de la vérité*, 2 vols. (Paris: J. Vrin, 1971), 1:190.

104. On Descartes's shift from physics to metaphysics as an appropriate object of wonder, see Donald Rung, "Images of Rainbows: The Rhetoric of Admiration in Descartes's *Les météores*," *Papers on French Seventeenth Century Literature* 21, no. 41 (1994): 453–69, at 456.

105. Epistemon alleges that we should know about wondrous stimulus only to prevent the effects of "nostrum admiratione rei cujusdam ignotæ." René Descartes, *Inquisitio veritatis per lumen naturale*, in *Opuscula posthuma, physica et mathematica* (Amsterdam: P. & J. Blaev, 1701), 67–90, at 72.

106. William Shakespeare, *Mr. William Shakespeares Comedies, Histories, & Tragedies* (London: Isaac Jaggard and Edward Blount, 1623), at 206 and 17. For these two examples I am indebted to Peter G. Platt, *Reason Diminished: Shakespeare and the Marvelous* (Lincoln: University of Nebraska Press, 1997), xi–xii, a book whose impressive consideration of Shakespearean wonder nonetheless fails to register the substantial differences between it—a superficial wonder based on appearances, such as that Descartes implicitly criticized in the *Météores*—and the emotion Descartes calls *admiration* in *Les passions de l'âme*.

107. John Dryden, *Of Dramatick Poesie, an Essay* (London: Henry Herringman, 1668), A3^r.

108. Ibid., 1. The date of the English victory over the Dutch—June 3, 1665—is known to history but identified by Dryden only as "that memorable day, in the first Summer of the late War, when our Navy ingag'd the Dutch" (ibid.). In fact, Dryden likely wrote the *Of Dramatick Poesie* during an equally unsettled time: exiled by the theater closures during the plague in 1666.

109. In his discussion of eighteenth-century poetry appended to the 1815 edition of his *Lyrical Ballads* (for which he wrote an essay supplementary to its famous preface), Wordsworth first distinguishes between "wonder" and "legitimate admiration" in the context of a withering assessment of Dryden, whose verses are deemed "forgotten." See William Wordsworth, "Essay, Supplementary to the Preface," in *Poems by William Wordsworth: Including the Lyrical Ballads and the Miscellaneous Pieces of the Author, with Additional Poems, a New Preface, and a Supplementary Essay*, 2 vols. (London: Longman, Hurst, Rees, Orme, and Brown, 1815), 2:341–75, at 358 and 359. The opposition of "genuine admiration" to "blind wonderment" follows, at 360.

110. John Dryden, *The Indian Emperour; or, The Conquest of Mexico by the Spaniards* (London: Henry Herringman, 1667), 45.

111. Ibid., A3^v. The divergent conditions in which Dryden and Corneille worked are aptly described thus: "Dryden wrote in a theatrical tradition which accented physical action and which was placing increasing stress upon physical scenery; Corneille wrote for a theater which was evolving a stage of physical austerity, a

difference which probably worked in Corneille's favor, since Dryden frequently had to compete with spectacle." Arthur C. Kirsch, "Dryden, Corneille, and the Heroic Play," *Modern Philology* 59, no. 4 (May 1962): 248–64, at 258.

112. The conclusion that the more Dryden agrees, the louder his denunciation of his source is drawn by and evidenced in Pierre Legouis, "Corneille and Dryden as Dramatic Critics," in *Seventeenth-Century Studies Presented to Sir Herbert Grierson* (New York: Octagon, 1967), 269–91, at 288.

113. A. A. Tilley, "The Essay and the Beginning of Modern English Prose," in *The Age of Dryden*, vol. 8 of *The Cambridge History of English Literature*, ed. A. W. Ward and A. R. Waller (Cambridge: Cambridge University Press, 1932), 368–90, at 374.

114. See Dryden, *Of Dramatick Poesie*, at 12, 34, and 44. Other instances appear at ibid., 13, 19, 36, and 54.

115. See ibid., at A2ᵛ, 27, 31, 35, 51, and 60. I am indebted to William T. Arnold, whose chronicle of Dryden's sources appears in his revised edition of John Dryden, *An Essay of Dramatic Poesy*, 3rd ed. (Oxford: Clarendon, 1918). As he writes at xxiv, "Perhaps the most prominent feature of my revision is the copiousness of quotation from Corneille. In no other way did it seem possible to bring home to the reader the greatness of Dryden's debt—extending not only to ideas and arguments, but even phrases—to his French contemporary."

116. Dryden, *Of Dramatick Poesie*, 19.

117. Compare Corneille, "Discovrs des trois unitez," xxiii: "Euripide dans les Suppliantes fait partir Thesée d'Athenes auec vne Armée, donner vne bataille deuant les murs de Thebes, qui en estoient esloignez de douze ou quinze lieuës, & reuenir victorieux en l'Acte suiuant; & depuis qu'il est party, jusqu'à l'arriuée du Messager qui vient faire le recit de sa victoire, Aethra & le Chœur n'ont que trente-six Vers à dire." For other examples of direct borrowings see Dryden, *Of Dramatick Poesie*, 21 (a Terence reference) and 31–32 (Dryden's lengthy discussion of "protatick persons"), both similarly borrowed from Corneille's "Discourse on the Three Unities."

118. Dryden, *Of Dramatick Poesie*, 46. Dryden has in mind early English Renaissance comedies such as *Gammer Gurton's Needle*, whose rocky hexameter might not hold its own against the alexandrines of, say, *Le Cid*.

119. Ibid., 39.

120. Ibid., 37, 45.

121. Ibid., 40.

122. Ibid., 27.

123. *Neander* is a portmanteau of *neo* plus *andros* according to Frank Livingstone Huntley, "On the Persons in Dryden's *Essay of Dramatic Poesy*," *Modern Language Notes* 63, no. 2 (1948): 88–95, at 95.

124. Indeed, this influence was greater than has sometimes been acknowledged. It is a truism that Cartesianism in England was stunted by the influence

of later British thinkers, such as Locke or Newton, but it is truer to say that Descartes's early, profound influence in England came to be eroded in the eighteenth century. An excellent overview of Descartes's reception in England—Kenelm Digby spoke glowingly of the philosopher's "most vigorous and strong braine" as early as October 1637—is provided by Marjorie Nicolson's meticulous "The Early Stage of Cartesianism in England," *Studies in Philology* 26 (1929): 356–74, in which Digby is quoted at 358.

125. Dryden, *Of Dramatick Poesie*, A2ᵛ.

126. John Dryden, *Secret-Love, or the Maiden Queen* (London: Henry Herringman, 1669), a3ʳ.

127. Thomas Shadwell, *The Tory-Poets: A Satyr* (London: R. Johnson, 1682), 6.

128. John Dryden, "A Defence of an Essay of Dramatique Poesie, Being an Answer to the Preface of *The Great Favourite, or the Duke of Lerma*," in *The Indian Emperour; or, The Conquest of Mexico by the Spaniards*, 2nd ed. (London: Henry Herringman, 1668), 3–21, at 13.

129. Ibid., 13, 15.

130. "Cela aideroit à tromper l'Auditeur" (Corneille, "Discovrs des trois unitez," xxxiv). Thus, to use Corneille's own examples, *Cinna* changes scenes without leaving Rome, or *Le Cid* changes more often but without leaving Seville (ibid., xxxiii–xxxiv).

131. Dryden, "Defence," 17.

132. Ibid., 14.

133. Elisabeth's "extravagances" appears in Foucher de Careil, *Descartes, la Princesse*, 80; Descartes's "Ioye intellectuelle" and "diversité des objets qui s'offrent à nostre imagination," in *Les passions*, 202–3.

134. Dryden, "Defence," 17.

135. René Descartes, *The Passions of the Soule in Three Books* (London: J. Martin and J. Ridley, 1650). The book appeared only a year after the first ever English translation of Descartes (his *Discourse on Method*), although French and Latin originals circulated as early as 1637. See Nicolson, "Early Stage of Cartesianism," 356–59.

136. Dryden, "Defence," 17.

137. See Mark Van Doren, *Dryden: A Study of His Poetry* (Bloomington: Indiana University Press, 1960), 8. Nicolson, "Early Stage of Cartesianism," 360–69, treats the early introduction of Descartes into the curriculum at Cambridge.

138. See H. T. Swedenburg Jr., "Challenges to Dryden's Editor," in *Stuart and Georgian Moments: Clark Library Seminar Papers on Seventeenth and Eighteenth Century English Literature*, ed. Earl Roy Miner (Berkeley: University of California Press, 1972), 93–108, at 95–96.

139. From the fawning dedication to Charles Sackville: "they who have Convers'd with you, are for ever after inviolably yours. This is a Truth so

generally acknowledg'd, that it needs no Proof: 'Tis of the Nature of a first Principle, which is receiv'd as soon as it is propos'd; and needs not the Reformation which *Descartes* us'd to to his: For we doubt not, neither can we properly say, we think we admire and love you, above all other men." John Dryden, "A Discourse Concerning the Original and Progress of Satire," in *The Satires of Decimus Junius Juvenalis Translated into English Verse* (London: Jacob Tonson, 1693), i–ii.

140. John Dryden, *The State of Innocence, and Fall of Man: An Opera Written in Heroique Verse* (London: Henry Herringman, 1677), 8.

141. Dryden, *Of Dramatick Poesie*, 28.

142. Ibid., 24.

143. Dryden, "Defence," 6. See also ibid., 11.

144. John Dryden, *Aureng-zebe, a Tragedy* (London: Henry Herringman, 1676), 87.

145. John Dryden, *The Conquest of Granada by the Spaniards: In Two Parts* (London: Henry Herringman, 1672), 9.

146. Ibid., 7.

147. John Dryden, "Of Heroique Playes, An Essay," in Dryden, *Conquest*, a2^r–b2^v, at a2^v.

148. Dryden, *Conquest*, 9.

149. Ibid., 129, 141.

150. Dryden, "Of Heroique Playes," b1^r.

151. Samuel Johnson, *Prefaces, Biographical and Critical, to the Works of the English Poets*, 10 vols. (London: John Nichols, 1779), 3:42.

152. On Dryden's turn to pity see Anne T. Barbeau, *The Intellectual Design of John Dryden's Heroic Plays* (New Haven, CT: Yale University Press, 1970), 160.

153. John Dryden, "To the Most Honourable John, Lord Marquess of Normanby, Earl of Mulgrave, &c. and Knight of the Most Noble Order of the Garter," in *The Works of Virgil: Containing His Pastorals, Georgics, and Æneis, Translated into English Verse* (London: Jacob Tonson, 1697), a1^r–f4^v [i.e., 151–98], at a2^r [i.e., 153].

154. Ibid.

155. Molière's actor La Grange (i.e., Charles Varlet) recorded in the preface to *Les œuvres de Monsieur de Molière* that "les Fameux Comediens qui faisoient alors si bien valoir l'Hostel de Bourgogne, étoient presens à cette representation." Molière, *Les œuvres de Monsieur de Molière*, 8 vols. (Paris: Denys Thierry, Claude Barbin, et Pierre Trabouillet, 1682), 1:aiiii^r.

156. "Les Representations sembloient moins estre des Comedies que la verité mesme." Charles Perrault, *Les hommes illustres qui ont parus en France pendant ce siecle: Avec leurs portraits au naturel* (Paris: Antoine Dezallier, 1697), 79.

157. "La Troupe . . . Commança au Louvre deuant S. M^{té}. Le 24me octobre 1658 par Nicomede." *Le registre de La Grange, 1659–1685, reproduit en fac-similé*, ed. Bert Edward

Young and Grace Philputt Young (Paris: Droz, 1947), 1. Even this record is retrospective: La Grange joined Molière's troupe six months after the court performance.

158. "La Trouppe ne réüssit pas cette premiere fois" (Perrault, *Les hommes*, 79).

159. "Ces nouveaux Acteurs ne déplurent point, & on fut sur tout fort satisfait de l'agrément & du jeu des Femmes" (Molière, *Les œuvres*, 1:aiiii^r).

160. The first assumption is that of Léopold Lacour, *Molière acteur* (Paris: Félix Alcan, 1928), 56; the second is that of Ramon Fernandez, *La vie de Molière* (Paris: Gallimard, 1929), 66.

161. Molière, *Les œuvres*, 1:aiiii^r: "La Piece étant achevée, Monsieur de Moliere vint sur le Theatre, & aprés avoir remercié Sa Majesté en des termes tres-modestes, de la bonté qu'elle avoit euë d'excuser ses deffauts & ceux de toute sa Troupe, qui n'avoit paru qu'en tremblant devant une Assemblée si Auguste; il luy dit que l'envie qu'ils avoient euë d'avoir l'honneur de divertir le plus grand Roy du monde, leur avoit fait oublier que Sa Majesté avoit à son service d'excellens Originaux, dont ils n'estoient que de tres-foibles copies."

162. See, e.g., Molière, *L'impromptu de Versailles*, in *Les œuvres*, 7:87–126, at 98–99.

163. On Molière's fidelity to his new acting principles see, e.g., Georges Mongrédien, *La vie privée de Molière* (Paris: Hachette, 1950), 185; or Lacour, *Molière*, 91. My tally of Molière's performances of Corneille is based on the tables provided in W. D. Howarth, *Molière: A Playwright and His Audience* (Cambridge: Cambridge University Press, 1982), 313–15.

164. "[Corneille] est allé au fond de leur ame chercher le principe de leurs actions, il est descendu dans leur cœur pour y voir former les passions; & y découvrir ce qu'il y a de plus caché dans leurs mouvemens." Saint-Évremond, "Sur les tragedies," in *Œuvres meslées*, 11 vols. (Paris: Claude Barbin, 1684), 11:1–20, at 10–11.

165. "Jamais Réputation n'a été si bien établie que la vôtre en *Angleterre* & en *Hollande*." The letter was published in the posthumous London edition—Saint-Évremond, *Œuvres meslées de Mr. de Saint-Evremond, publiées sur les manuscrits de l'auteur*, 2 vols. (London: Jacob Tonson, 1705), 1:421—and also, identically, in the Dutch edition—Saint-Évremond, *Œuvres melées [sic] de Mr. de Saint-Evremond, publiés sur les manuscrits de l'auteur*, 5 vols. (Amsterdam: Pierre Mortier, 1706), 2:349. It is absent from the contemporaneous printing in Paris.

166. Dominique Labbé, *Corneille dans l'ombre de Molière* (Paris: Impressions nouvelles, 2003).

167. Corneille, *Cinna*, 106.

CHAPTER 3

1. The date—even the year—of Le Brun's lecture is a source of scholarly controversy. I follow two detailed editions of Le Brun, both published in 1994, whose

arguments can be seen as summative. I take my date from Jennifer Montagu, *The Expression of the Passions: The Origin and Influence of Charles Le Brun's "Conférence sur l'expression générale et particulière"* (New Haven, CT: Yale University Press, 1994), which discusses the dating controversies at 141–43. Julien Philipe, ed., *L'expression des passions et autres conférences, Correspondance*, by Charles Le Brun (Maisonneuve, France: Dédale, 1994), 273, concurs about 1668 but dates the lecture to April 17.

2. "Les mouvemens du sang & des esprits." The term is Descartes's, used throughout his treatise. See, e.g., René Descartes, *Les passions de l'âme* (Paris: Henry Le Gras, 1649), 131.

3. See ibid., 82–83. On the extant drawings see the detailed inventory created in Montagu, *Expression*, 144–55.

4. Louis Hourticq, *De Poussin à Watteau, ou Des origines de l'école parisienne de peinture* (Paris: Hachette, 1921), 68.

5. Le Brun's lecture on Poussin receives a sensitive analysis in Stephanie Ross, "Painting the Passions: Charles Le Brun's *Conférence sur l'expression*," *Journal of the History of Ideas* 45, no. 1 (1984): 25–47, at 41–45. Le Brun's text on Poussin appears at Philipe, *L'expression*, 159–89.

6. David Wiles, *A Short History of Western Performance Space* (Cambridge: Cambridge University Press, 2003), 5. Many other critics explore the connection. Two of the most coruscating are Shearer West, *The Image of the Actor: Verbal and Visual Representation in the Age of Garrick and Kemble* (London: Pinter, 1991), 92–106; and Joseph Roach, "Garrick, the Ghost, and the Machine," *Theatre Journal* 34, no. 4 (1982): 431–40, later put into a fuller context in his indispensable *The Player's Passion: Studies in the Science of Acting* (Ann Arbor: University of Michigan Press, 1993).

7. For example, Stephen H. Voss's English edition of Descartes, frequently cited here, makes liberal use of Le Brun's drawings.

8. Rensselaer W. Lee, *Ut pictura poesis: The Humanistic Theory of Painting* (New York: Norton, 1967), 27–28.

9. Charles Le Brun, *Conférence de Monsieur Le Brun, premier peintre du roy de France, chancelier et directeur de l'Académie de peinture et sculpture, sur l'expression generale & particuliere* (Paris: Etienne Picart, 1698), 1–3:

Dans l'Assemblée derniere vous approuvâtes le dessein que je pris de vous entretenir de l'Expression. Il est donc necessaire avant toutes choses de sçavoir en quoi elle consiste.

L'Expression, à mon avis, est une naïve & naturelle ressemblance des choses que l'on a à representer: . . . c'est elle qui marque les veritables caracteres de chaque chose; c'est par elle que l'on distingue la nature des corps; que des figures semblent avoir du mouvement, & tout ce qui est feint paroît être vrai. . . .

C'est, MESSIEURS, ce que j'ai tâché de vous faire remarquer dans les Conférences passées; aujourd'hui j'essaierai de vous faire voir que l'Expression est aussi une partie qui marque les mouvemens de l'Ame, ce qui rend visible les effets de la passion.

The text of the lecture is even more fraught than its date—see Philipe, *L'expression*, 43–46; and Montagu, *Expression*, 108–11—because it went unpublished during Le Brun's lifetime and different, competing versions made their way into print only after his death in 1690. Montagu has cross-referenced five primary editions and many secondary sources to produce a French text that notes even minor variations; this text appears at Montagu, *Expression*, 112–24. (She translates her reconstruction into English at ibid., 26–40.) Philipe's text, which leans more heavily on the first edition published by Picart in 1698, appears in Philipe, *L'expression*, 49–109. He similarly cross-references multiple sources but wisely places less faith in nineteenth-century editions than does Montagu. Montagu's reliance on later transcripts, allegedly copies of "lost" seventeenth-century manuscripts, leads her, in the passage I have quoted, for example, to choose "mouvements du Coeur" over "mouvements de l'ame," as appears in a seventeenth-century manuscript, as well as in Picart's edition. "Movements of the soul" is much closer to the Cartesian leanings of Le Brun's physiology, even if he sometimes anachronistically lapses into a scholastic understanding of the heart's role in the emotions.

In keeping with my usual practice in this book, I have preferred the first edition in spite of some textual issues and provided my own translations, more literal than Montagu's. In the quoted passage, for example, her choice of "image" for Le Brun's *ressemblance* may more clearly convey Le Brun's sense, but it nonetheless misses something crucial: Le Brun's intention to emphasize both the phonetic consonance and conceptual dissonance between *ressemblance* and *representation* in ways that "image" cannot capture. Similarly, I have preferred "true characteristics" as the translation for Le Brun's *veritables caracteres*, since he means to emphasize *caractère* in this sense, rather than the sense of essential nature conveyed by Montagu's wording, "true character."

10. See Descartes, *Les passions*, 151.

11. Ibid., 136: "les muscles qui sont autour des intestins & de l'estomac."

12. Le Brun, *Conférence*, 19: "Mais s'il est vrai qu'il y ait une partie où l'Ame exerce plus immediatement ses fonctions, & que cette partie soit celle du cerveau, nous pouvons dire de même que le visage est la partie du corps où elle fait voir plus particulierement ce qu'elle ressent." (But if it is true that there is one part where the soul exercises its functions most immediately, and that this part is the brain, then we can also say that the face is the part of the body where it reveals its feelings most particularly.)

13. This resemblance is illuminated in Descartes, *Les passions*, 151.

14. "L'amour est toujours accompagnée de désir et de joye, ou de désir et de tristesse et à mesure qu'il se fortifie, les autres croissent aussi." Quoted in Alexandre Foucher de Careil, *Descartes, la Princesse Élisabeth, et la Reine Christine, d'après des lettres inédites* (Paris: Germer-Baillière, 1879), 91.

15. "Le mien fait que la tristresse m'emporte toujours l'appétit, quoy qu'elle ne soit mêlée d'aucune haine, me venant seulement de la mort de quelque ami" (ibid.).

16. "Ce je ne sçay quoy . . . qu'on ne peut bien exprimer, est comme le nœud secret qui assemble ces deux parties du corps & de l'esprit." André Félibien, *Entretiens sur les vies et sur les ouvrages des plus excellens peintres anciens et modernes*, 5 vols. (Paris: Pierre le Petit, 1666), 1:38. I owe the discovery of Félibien's reliance on the mind-body metaphor to Line Cottegnies, "Codifying the Passions in the Classical Age: A Few Reflections on Charles Le Brun's Scheme and Its Influence in France and in England," *Études epistémè* 1 (2002): 141–58.

17. Félibien, *Entretiens*, 1:38–39.

18. Richard Rorty, *Philosophy and the Mirror of Nature*, Thirtieth-Anniversary ed. (Princeton, NJ: Princeton University Press, 2009), 50.

19. René Descartes, *The Passions of the Soul*, trans. Stephen H. Voss (Indianapolis: Hackett, 1989), 115. Descartes, *Les passions*, 239–40: "un trouble & un estonnement de l'ame, qui luy oste le pouvoir de resister aux maux qu'elle pense estre proches."

20. Descartes, *The Passions*, 34. Descartes, *Les passions*, 41: "du nombre des perceptions que l'estroite alliance qui est entre l'ame & le corps rend confuses & obscures."

21. Lilli Alanen, *Descartes's Concept of Mind* (Cambridge, MA: Harvard University Press, 2003), 188.

22. Descartes, *The Passions*, 89. Descartes, *Les passions*, 173:

> L'Autre cause est la Tristesse, suivie d'Amour, ou de Ioye, ou generalement de quelque cause qui fait que le cœur pousse beaucoup de sang par les arteres. La Tristesse y est requise, à cause que refroidissant tout le sang, elle étrecit les pores des yeux. Mais pourcequ'à mesure qu'elle les étrecit, elle diminüe aussi la quantité des vapeurs, ausquelles ils doivent donner passage, cela ne suffit pas pour produire des larmes, si la quantité de ces vapeurs n'est à mesme temps augmentée par quelque autre cause. Et il n'y a rien qui l'augmente davantage, que le sang qui est envoyé vers le cœur en la passion de l'Amour. Aussi voyons nous que ceux qui sont tristes, ne jettent pas continuellement des larmes, mais seulement par intervalles, lors qu'ils font quelque nouvelle reflexion sur les objets qu'ils affectionent.

23. Descartes to Elisabeth, May or June 1645: "vne personne qui auroit d'ailleurs toute sorte de sujet d'estre contente"; "qui ne s'ocuperoit qu'à considérer des

objets de tristesse & de pitié"; "qui verroit continuellement representer deuant soy des Tragédies"; "qui auroit une infinité de veritables sujets de déplaisir"; "s'étudie-roit auec tant de soin à en détourner son imagination, qu'elle ne pensast iamais à eux, que lors que la necessité des affaires l'y obligeroit." René Descartes, *Lettres de Monsieur Descartes, où sont traittées les plus belles questions de la morale, physique, medecine, & des mathematiques* (Paris: Henry Le Gras, 1657), 91–92.

24. "Acoutumer son cœur à se resserrer, & à jetter des soupirs" (ibid., 91).

25. "Déliurer l'esprit de toutes sortes de pensées tristes"; "imiter ceux, qui en regardant la verdeur d'vn bois, les couleurs d'vne fleur, le vol d'un oyseau . . . se persuadent qu'ils ne pensent à rien" (ibid., 92).

26. Ibid., 91.

27. Descartes, *Les passions*, 73.

28. Descartes, *The Passions*, 79. Descartes, *Les passions*, 151–52: "generalement toutes les actions, tant du visage que des yeux, peuvent estre changées par l'ame, lors que voulant cacher sa passion, elle en imagine fortement une contraire: en sorte qu'on s'en peut aussi bien servir à dissimuler ses passions, qu'à les declarer."

29. "Sans toucher son entendement" (Descartes, *Lettres de Monsieur Descartes*, 91).

30. This subject is elaborated in the first chapter of Erec R. Koch, *The Aesthetic Body: Passion, Sensibility, and Corporeality in Seventeenth-Century France* (Newark: University of Delaware Press, 2008).

31. Descartes to Elisabeth, Oct. 6, 1645: "generalement elle [i.e., the soul] se plaist de sentir émouuoir en soy des passions, de quelque nature qu'elles soient, pourvû qu'elle en demeure maistresse" (Descartes, *Lettres de Monsieur Descartes*, 37).

32. "L'Action & la Passion ne laissent pas d'estre tousjours une mesme chose, qui a ces deux noms, à raison des deux divers sujets ausquels on la peut raporter" (Descartes, *Les passions*, 3).

33. Descartes to Elisabeth, Sept. 15, 1645: "imprimée en nostre esprit, qu'elle soit tournée en habitude" (Descartes, *Lettres de Monsieur Descartes*, 32).

34. See Chapter 1niii.

35. John Genest, *Some Account of the English Stage, from the Restoration in 1660 to 1830*, 10 vols. (Bath: H. E. Carrington, 1832), 4:14.

36. Roach, *Player's Passion*, 30. My own assessment mirrors that of West, who notes in *Image* that "although modern historians have tried to puncture these stereotypes [of "classical" or "natural" acting], the evidence itself continually leads them back to the same conclusions" (58).

37. John Bulwer, *Chirologia: or the Naturall Language of the Hand. Composed of the speaking motions, and discoursing gestures thereof. Whereto is added, Chironomia: or, the Art of manuall rhetoricke*, 2 vols. (London: Henry Twyford, 1644).

38. Roach, *Player's Passion*, 34.

39. The anonymous report, dating from after Molière's death, describes the playwright's widow, Armande [Béjart] Molière, and La Grange in *Le malade imaginaire*. It is recorded in François Parfaict, *Histoire du théâtre françois depuis son origine jusqu'à présent*, 15 vols. (Paris: P. G. Le Mercier et Saillant, 1747), 11:324: "Leur jeu se cache si bien dans la nature, que l'on ne pense pas à distinguer la vérité de la seule apparence."

40. "Caracteres si bien marquez, que les Representations sembloient moins estre des Comedies que la verité mesme." Charles Perrault, *Les hommes illustres qui ont parus en France pendant ce siecle* (Paris: Antoine Dezallier, 1697), 79.

41. Le Brun, *Conférence*, 2: "tout ce qui est feint paroît être vrai."

42. This piece plays a key role in Molière's canon, suggesting the playwright's thought on the practice and philosophical implications of dramatic expression. For example, see Patrick Dandrey, *Molière ou l'esthétique du ridicule* (Paris: Klincksieck, 1992), 87. But the *Impromptu*'s importance to theater studies has been inadequately recognized outside French-language scholarship, even if the play is no longer as "determinedly neglected" as Francis Lawrence found it to be in his "Artist, Audience and Structure in *L'impromptu de Versailles*," *Œuvres et critiques* 6, no. 1 (1981): 125–32, at 125. See, more recently, Cecile Lindsay, "Molière in the Post-Structuralist Age: *L'impromptu de Versailles*," *Theatre Journal* 34, no. 3 (1982): 373–83; Abby Zanger, "Acting as Counteracting in Molière's *The Impromptu of Versailles*," *Theatre Journal* 38, no. 2 (1986): 180–95; and Vincent Desroches, "Représentation et métatexte dans *L'impromptu de Versailles* et la querelle de *L'école des femmes*," *Romance Notes* 38, no. 3 (1998): 321–31.

43. The *querelle* begins with Molière's *L'école des femmes*, which premiered on December 26, 1662. The play, its uneasy resonances with Molière's marriage to Armande Béjart, and (no doubt) its success elicited various attacks on Molière, who was accused scurrilously of having married his lover's daughter. Molière answered the attacks in *La critique de L'école des femmes*, which premiered on June 1, 1663. *Le portrait du peintre*, subtitled to the point as *La contre-critique de L'école des femmes*, premiered at the Hôtel de Bourgogne in October 1663. Although the *Impromptu* was Molière's final word in the feud, it did not yet end: the Bourguignons would respond with *La réponse à L'impromptu de Versailles ou La vengeance de marquis* and *L'impromptu de l'Hôtel de Condé*. The Bourguignon plays are united in Georges Mongrédien, ed., *La querelle de L'école des femmes*, 2 vols. (Paris: Didier, 1971).

44. Molière, *L'impromptu de Versailles*, in *Les œuvres de Monsieur de Molière*, 8 vols. (Paris: Denys Thierry, Claude Barbin, et Pierre Trabouillet, 1682), 7:87–126, at 126.

45. Molière, *The Rehearsal at Versailles*, in *One-Act Comedies of Molière*, trans. Albert Bermel (New York: Frederick Ungar, 1962), 95–118.

46. Albert Bermel, *Molière's Theatrical Bounty: A New View of the Plays* (Carbondale: Southern Illinois University Press, 1990), 107.

47. For example, see Gougenot, *La comédie des comédiens* (Paris: Pierre David, 1633); Georges de Scudéry, *La comédie des comédiens* (Paris: Augustin Courbé, 1635); Philippe Quinault, *La comédie sans comédie* (Paris: Guillaume de Luyne, 1657); or Dorimond, *La comédie de la comédie et les amours de Trapolin* (Paris: Gabriel Quinet, 1661).

48. La Grange's handwritten register notes that "Le Jeudy 11ᵐᵉ Octobre La Troupe Est partie par ordre du Roy pour Versailles" and that among the plays the troupe performed was "*l'Impromptu* dit, a Cause de La nouveauté et du Lieu, de Versailles." *Le Registre de La Grange, 1659–1685, reproduit en fac-similé*, ed. Bert Edward Young and Grace Philputt Young (Paris: Droz, 1947), 60–61.

49. Alain Rey et al., eds., *Dictionnaire historique de la langue française*, 4th ed. (Paris: Dictionnaires le Robert, 2012), s.v. "impromptu." Although such attributions are notoriously unreliable, it is telling that the dictionary attributes both the noun (denoting the genre) and the adjective (meaning "improvised") to Molière himself.

50. "Je suis diablement fort sur les Impromptus." Molière, *Les précieuses ridicules* (Paris: Guillaume de Luyne, 1660), 64.

51. The scholarship gives at least five dates for the premiere. The first publication in 1682 records October 14—see Molière, *Les œuvres*, 7:89—but this date has been doubted for various reasons.

52. "La double énonciation inhérente à tout discours théâtral se trouve réduite à une énonciation unique." Georges Forestier, *Le théâtre dans le théâtre* (Geneva: Droz, 1981), 154.

53. Molière, *L'impromptu*, 106–7:

MOLIÈRE.   Souvenez-vous bien, vous de venir, comme je vous ay dit, là avec cet air qu'on nomme le bel air, peignant vostre Perruque, & grondant une petite chanson entre vos dents. La, la, la, la, la, la. Rangez-vous donc vous autres, car il faut du terrein à deux Marquis, & ils ne sont pas gens à tenir leur personne dans un petit espace, allons parlez.
LA GRANGE.   Bon jour Marquis.
MOLIÈRE.   Mon Dieu, ce n'est point là le ton d'un Marquis, il faut le prendre un peu plus haut, & la pluspart de ces Messieurs affectent une maniere de parler particuliere pour se distinguer du commun. Bon jour Marquis, recommencez-donc.
LA GRANGE.   Bon jour Marquis.
MOLIÈRE.   Ah! Marquis, ton serviteur.

54. See, e.g., the Pléiade edition—Molière, *Œuvres complètes*, ed. Georges Couton, 2 vols. (Paris: Gallimard, 1971), 1:675–98, at 685.

55. "Souffrir leurs manieres de campagne" (La Grange's preface to Molière, *Les œuvres*, 1:aiiii^r).

56. "Trois ou quatre fois depuis que nous sommes à Paris"; "je n'ay attrappé de leur maniere de reciter" (Molière, *L'impromptu*, 97).

57. The others were Louis Béjart, Mlle (i.e., Madeleine) Béjart, Mlle Hervé (i.e., Geneviève Béjart), and, of course, Molière. See *Le Registre de La Grange*, 2.

58. "Le plus naturellement qui luy auroit esté possible" (Molière, *L'impromptu*, 98).

59. "Te le diray-je Araspe, il m'a trop bien servy, / Augmentant mon pouvoir" (ibid.). See also (and identically except for punctuation) Pierre Corneille, *Nicomede* (Rouen: Laurens Maurry, 1651), 29.

60. "Il faut dire les choses avec emphase. Ecoutez-moy. Te le diray-je, Araspe. . . . &c. *Imitant Monfleury excellent Acteur de l'Hostel de Bourgogne.* Voyez-vous cette posture? remarquez bien cela. là [*sic*] appuyer comme il faut le dernier Vers. Voilà ce qui attire l'approbation, & fait faire le brouhaha" (Molière, *L'impromptu*, 98–99).

61. "Il me semble qu'un Roy qui s'entretient tout seul avec son Capitaine des Gardes, parle un peu plus humainement, & ne prend gueres ce ton de demoniaque" (ibid., 99).

62. On this point see Bermel, *Molière's Theatrical Bounty*, 107.

63. "Faire ronfler les Vers, & s'arrester au bel endroit" (Molière, *Les précieuses ridicules*, 78).

64. "Les autres sont des Ignorans, qui recitent comme l'on parle" (ibid.).

65. Forestier, *Théâtre*, 220, notes that, however difficult it is to imagine in hindsight, the *jeu emphatique* was privileged in tragedy; André Villiers, "Le comédien Molière et l'expression du tragique," *Revue d'histoire du théâtre* 26, no. 1 (1974): 27–52, at 49, notes that the Hôtel de Bourgogne was in effect the most esteemed acting school for the tragic performer. See also Mongrédien, *La vie privée de Molière* (Paris: Hachette, 1950), 185.

66. "Contrefaire un Comedien dans un rôle Comique, ce n'est pas le peindre luy-mesme, c'est peindre d'aprés luy les Personnages qu'il represente. . . . Mais contrefaire un Comedien dans des rôles serieux, c'est le peindre par des défauts qui sont entierement de luy, puisque ces sortes de Personnages ne veulent, ny les gestes, ny les tons de voix ridicules, dans lesquels on le reconnoist" (Molière, *L'impromptu*, 97).

67. "Une doctrine d'art alors révolutionnaire." Léopold Lacour, *Molière acteur* (Paris: Félix Alcan, 1928), 87.

68. "Tâchez-donc de bien prendre tous le caractere de vos rôles, & de vous figurer que vous estes ce que vous representez" (Molière, *L'impromptu*, 101).

69. Rey, *Dictionnaire*, s.v. "caractère," describes how the meaning of *caractère* as sign or printed mark underwent a "grande expansion" in the seventeenth century, when the word came to designate "abstraitement le caractère distinctif d'une chose (1662, d'un sentiment)" and "l'ensemble de traits dominants de

la physiognomie morale d'un homme (av. 1662, Pascal)." Compare the *OED*, whose earliest usages in English are in the sense of a "distinctive mark impressed, engraved, or otherwise formed; a brand, stamp." The first listed instance of the word in the sense of "sum of the moral and mental qualities which distinguish an individual . . . viewed as a homogeneous whole" is 1647.

70. "Entrez bien dans ce caractere" (Molière, *L'impromptu*, 102).

71. William Shakespeare, *Mr. William Shakespeares Comedies, Histories, & Tragedies* (London: Isaac Jaggard and Edward Blount, 1623), 256.

72. "Vous deviez faire une Comedie où vous auriez joüé tout seul" (Molière, *L'impromptu*, 96).

73. "Je ne sçaurois aller joüer mon rôle si je ne le repete tout entier" (ibid., 123).

74. To Molière's demand that they "employons ce temps [the rehearsal] . . . , & voir la maniere dont il faut jouer les choses," La Grange responds: "Le moyen de joüer ce qu'on ne sçait pas?" (ibid., 93).

75. See Robert J. Nelson, "*L'impromptu de Versailles* Reconsidered," *French Studies* 11 (1957): 305–14, at 306.

76. A year before Molière's return to Paris, for example, Vincent de Paul had reported that some actors had changed their delivery and were now speaking familiarly to the spectators: "Croiriez-vous, Monsieur, que les comédiens . . . ont changé leur manière de parler et ne récitent plus leurs vers avec un ton élevé, commes ils faisaient autrefois? Mais il le font avec une voix médiocre et comme parlant familièrement à ceux qui les écoutent." Saint Vincent de Paul, *Correspondance, entretiens, documents*, ed. Pierre Coste (Paris: Lecoffre, 1922), 6:378–79. For his discovery of this letter I am indebted to Jacques Truchet, *La tragédie classique en France* (Paris: Presses universitaires de France, 1975).

77. "Il faut peindre d'aprés Nature." Molière, *La critique de L'escole des femmes* (Paris: Gabriel Quinet, 1663), 83.

78. "Comment pretendez-vous que nous fassions, si nous ne sçavons pas nos rôles?" (Molière, *L'impromptu*, 95).

79. "Vous les sçaurez, vous dy-je" (ibid.).

80. Dorante lauds a "bon sens naturel" (Molière, *La critique*, 86). He is concerned not with the actor but the spectator, whose judgment is deemed a superior guide to the classical *règles*. See ibid., 50, 97.

81. René Descartes, *Discours de la méthode pour bien conduire sa raison, & chercher la verité dans les sciences, plus la Dioptrique, les Météores et la Géométrie qui sont des essais de cette méthode* (Leiden: Jan Maire, 1637), 11:

> Sitost que l'aage me permit de sortir de la suietion de mes Precepteurs, ie quittay entierement l'estude des lettres. Et me resoluant de ne chercher plus d'autre science, que celle qui se pourroit trouuer en moymesme, oubien dans le grand liure du monde, l'employay le reste de ma ieunesse . . . à faire

telle reflexion sur les choses qui se presentoient que i'en pusse tirer quelque profit.

[As soon as age permitted me to leave the constraints of my teachers, I completely abandoned the study of letters. And resolving to search for no science other than what could be found within myself, or else in the great book of the world, I spent the rest of my youth . . . doing such reflection upon the things that presented themselves to me that I could derive some profit from them.]

82. Renati Des-Cartes [i.e., René Descartes], *Meditationes de prima philosophia* (Paris: Michaelum Soli, 1641), 7–8: "Animaduerti iam ante aliquot annos quàm multa ineunte ætate falsa pro veris admiserim, & quàm dubia sint quæcunque istis postea superextruxi, ac proinde funditùs omnia semel in vita esse euertenda, atque à primis fundamentis denuò inchoandum, si quid aliquando firmum, & mansurum cupiam in scientiis stabilire." René Descartes, *Meditations on First Philosophy*, in *"Discourse on Method" and "Meditations on First Philosophy,"* trans. Donald A. Cress, 3rd ed. (Indianapolis: Hackett, 1993), 45–105, at 59: "Several years have now passed since I first realized how numerous were the false opinions that in my youth I had taken to be true, and thus how doubtful were all those that I had subsequently built upon them. And thus I realized that once in my life I had to raze everything to the ground and begin again from the original foundations, if I wanted to establish anything firm and lasting in the sciences."

83. To Du Croisy: "Vous devez vous remplir de ce personnage"; to Mlle Béjart: "Ayez toûjours ce caractere devant les yeux"; to Mlle De Brie: "Entrez bien dans ce caractere" (Molière, *L'impromptu*, 101–2).

84. He ends his directions by noting: "Je vous dis tous vos caracteres, afin que vous vous les imprimiez fortement dans l'esprit" (ibid., 103).

85. Dandrey, *Molière*, 109, reads *caractère* as an "abstraction en voie d'incarnation, phase transitoire entre les personnes et les personnages, fantôme par lequel le comédien doit se laisser envahir, fasciner et hanter . . . pour à son tour en féconder un rôle pour l'instant tout verbal et à peine visuel" (abstraction in the process of incarnation; a transitory phase between people and characters; a phantom which the actor must let invade, fascinate and haunt him . . . in order to fertilize a role, which for the moment is verbal and barely visual). Although Dandrey's image is rather phantasmatic, it usefully suggests the *caractère*'s function in the actor's process, that is, the mental representation that will precede and guide the physical representation ultimately performed.

86. "Je vous dis tous vos caracteres" (Molière, *L'impromptu*, 103). In French, *caractère* does not typically mean "role" or "part": Molière's unusual usage is noted in Rey, *Dictionnaire*, s.v. "caractère." In English, the usage of *character* in

the sense of "role assumed by a stage actor" dates from 1664, according to the *OED*.

87. See Nelson, "*L'impromptu de Versailles* Reconsidered," 305–6.

88. See René Bray, *Molière: Homme de théâtre* (Paris: Mercure de France, 1954), 149.

89. "Cela est vray" (Molière, *L'impromptu*, 101).

90. She and her husband had joined the Théâtre du Marais. See *Le registre de La Grange*, 3.

91. Henry Lyonnet, *Dictionnaire des comédiens français (ceux d'hier)*, 2 vols. (Geneva: Slatkine Reprints, 1969), 1:616.

92. On the troupe's changing composition and its relationship to Molière's increasingly naturalistic writing, see Roger Herzel, "Le jeu 'naturel' de Molière et de sa troupe," *Dix-septième siècle* 132 (1981): 279–83, at 281–82.

93. "Il a . . . entendu admirablement les habits des Acteurs en leur donnant leur veritable caractere, & il a eu encore le don de distribuer si bien les Personnages & de les instruire ensuite si parfaitement, qu'ils sembloient moins des Acteurs de Comedie que les vrayes Personnes qu'ils representoient" (Perrault, *Hommes*, 80).

94. Robert Garapon notes that Molière had abandoned monologues almost entirely by 1663. See "Les monologues, acteurs et le public en France," in *Dramaturgie et société: Rapports entre l'œuvre théâtrale, son interprétation et son public aux XVIe et XVIIe siècles*, ed. Jean Jacquot, 2 vols. (Paris: Centre national de la recherche scientifique, 1968), 1:254.

95. See Molière, *L'impromptu*, 95.

96. For example, within a single volume of a single edition, we have both: in volume 8 of the 1682 *Les œuvres*, *Le malade imaginaire* lists its "Acteurs" at 134, and *Les aman[t]s magnifiques* lists its "Personnages" at 6. The same phenomenon is seen in other volumes.

97. See Martine Clermont, "L'acteur et son jeu au XVIIe siècle: Ses rapports avec le personnage qu'il représente," *Revue d'histoire du théâtre* 33, no. 4 (1981): 379–88, at 380–81.

98. See also four such usages of *acteur* by Éraste in Molière, *Les fascheux* (Paris: Guillaume de Luyne, 1662), 8, 8, 9, 9; one by Sbrigani in Molière, *Monsieur de Pourceaugnac* (Paris: Jean Ribou, 1670), 8; one by Covielle in Molière, *Le bourgeois gentilhomme* (Paris: Pierre Le Monnier, 1671), 111; and one by the countess in *La Comtesse d'Escarbagnas*, in *Les œuvres de Monsieur de Molière*, 8:114.

99. Clermont, "L'acteur," 380.

100. Nicoll writes: "It has been said again and again . . . that the eighteenth century was an age, not of the author, but of the actor." Allardyce Nicoll, *A History of Early Eighteenth Century Drama, 1700–1750* (Cambridge: Cambridge University Press, 1952), 39.

101. Molière, *L'impromptu*, 90.

102. Jacques Truchet makes this point in *"L'impromptu de Versailles*: 'Comédie des comédiens,'" in *Langue, littérature du XVIIe et du XVIIIe siècle*, ed. Roger Lathuillère (Paris: Sedes, 1990): 153–61, at 154. By contrast, *L'école des femmes* had used eight of the troupe; *La critique de L'école des femmes*, six.

103. Molière, *L'impromptu*, 93.

104. Felicity Nussbaum, *Rival Queens: Actresses, Performance, and the Eighteenth-Century British Theater* (Philadelphia: University of Pennsylvania Press, 2010), 18.

105. On the birth of celebrity as a concept in England, see Mary Luckhurst and Jane Moody, eds., *Theatre and Celebrity in Britain, 1660–2000* (Basingstoke: Palgrave Macmillan, 2005), 3; and Nussbaum, *Rival*, 7 (both of which relate the rise of celebrity to the media apparatuses, especially print, that facilitated it). See also Roach on the ultimate *je ne sais quoi*, the factor known as "it," which "intensifies the craving for greater intimacy" with actors who are, of course, "ultimately unavailable": Joseph Roach, *It* (Ann Arbor: University of Michigan Press, 2007), 44.

106. Molière, *L'impromptu*, 113: "Il faut par fois se faire violence." Du Parc's real name was Marquise-Thérèse de Gorla.

107. See Dane Farnsworth Smith, *Plays About the Theatre in England from "The Rehearsal" in 1671 to the Licensing Act in 1737; or, The Self-Conscious Stage and Its Burlesque and Satirical Reflections in the Age of Criticism* (London: Oxford University Press, 1936). Smith itemizes Molière's bequests to *The Rehearsal* and explores the vogue for rehearsal burlesques unleashed by *The Rehearsal* after its 1671 premiere (245–46). See also Peter Lewis, *Fielding's Burlesque Drama: Its Place in the Tradition* (Edinburgh: Edinburgh University Press, 1987). Lewis notes: "*The Rehearsal* undoubtedly made a highly original contribution to English drama, its structure and methods being derived from Molière's *L'impromptu de Versailles* (1663) rather than from any previous English play" (11).

108. Note that the thinness of the third player's role derives from its emotional inconsistency or inscrutability. [George Villiers], *The Rehearsal, as It Was Acted at the Theatre-Royal* (London: Thomas Dring, 1672), 5. The play was published anonymously, although Villiers's authorship is now generally accepted.

109. Bayes is a composite of various playwrights, including William Davenant, William Killigrew, Robert Stapylton, and Henry Howard (see Smith, *Plays About the Theatre*, 12), but Lacy's performance impersonated Dryden in particular. One critic notes: "Dryden's voice, his mode of dressing, his gait and manners, were all carefully imitated, so that in representation there must have been a thousand touches now lost to us." Montague Summers, ed. *The Rehearsal*, by George Villiers, Duke of Buckingham (Stratford-upon-Avon: Shakespeare Head, 1914), xi.

110. See Villiers, *The Rehearsal*: "THUN: I am bold *Thunder*. / BAYES: Mr. *Cartwright*, pr'ythee speak a little louder, and with a hoarser voice" (10); and: "BAYES: You did that very well, Mr. *Cartwright*" (45).

111. See ibid., when the First Player notes that "Sir, Mr. *Ivory* is not come yet" (11); and when Bayes addresses the actor by his real name: "Hark you, Mr. *Ivory*" (51).

112. See ibid.: "Mr. *Wintershull* has inform'd me of this Play before" (13).

113. Anton Chekhov, *The Seagull*, in *Four Plays*, trans. Stephen Mulrine (London: Nick Hern, 2005), 1–66: "Oh yes, she'll tend the sick like a ministering angel, but you just let her hear you praising Eleanora Duse. Oh, no. You must worship her alone, she's the only one you can write or shout about—you've got to go into ecstasies over her wonderful acting in *The Lady of the Camellias* or *The Fumes of Life*" (6).

114. Villiers, *The Rehearsal*, 18.

115. The First Player: "But, before we go, let's see *Haynes* and *Shirley* practice the last Dance; for that may serve for another Play" (ibid., 54).

116. See Marvin Carlson, *The Haunted Stage: The Theatre as Memory Machine* (Ann Arbor: University of Michigan Press, 2001), esp. chap. 3, "The Haunted Body." Shirley's career is sketched at Philip H. Highfill Jr. et al., eds., *A Biographical Dictionary of Actors, Actresses, Musicians, Dancers, Managers and Other Stage Personnel in London, 1660–1800* (Carbondale: Southern Illinois University Press, 1987), 13:364.

117. A consideration of corpsing appears in Nicholas Ridout, *Stage Fright, Animals, and Other Theatrical Problems* (Cambridge: Cambridge University Press, 2006), 130–46.

118. The precise premiere date of *The Female Wits* is unknown. But the play capitalizes on the recent success of *The Royal Mischief* (toward the end of the 1695–96 season); therefore, a date early in the 1696–97 season seems certain. On the other evidence for a September or October 1696 premiere, see *The London Stage, 1660–1800, Part 1: 1660–1700*, ed. William Van Lennep (Carbondale: Southern Illinois University Press, 1965), 467. The play's publication would have to wait until 1704: *The Female Wits; or, The Triumvirate of Poets at Rehearsal* (London: William Turner, 1704). Unless otherwise noted, all quotations herein are taken from this 1704 edition, which describes the author only as "Mr. W. M."

119. Even among otherwise careful critics, the playwright is more often known as Mary de la Rivière Manley or some other variant starting with "Mary" because of a spurious nineteenth-century error, blindly followed. See Patricia Koster, "Delariviere Manley and the *DNB*: A Cautionary Tale About Following Black Sheep," *Eighteenth Century Life* 3 (1977): 106–11. The minor question of "Delarivier" vs. "Delariviere" remains unsettled.

120. Lucyle Hook, introduction to *The Female Wits* (Los Angeles: Augustan Reprint Society, 1967; repr. New York: AMS, 1993), iv.

121. The Actors' Rebellion of 1694–95, which saw the division of Rich's United Company and the establishment of what would become known as Thomas Betterton's company is treated definitively in Judith Milhous, *Thomas Betterton and the Management of Lincoln's Inn Fields, 1695–1708* (Carbondale: Southern Illinois University Press, 1979), 51–79. On *The Royal Mischief* see Milhous, *Thomas Betterton*, 98.

122. Milhous, *Thomas Betterton*, 98; Hook, introduction, iv. On *The Royal Mischief*'s uncertain premiere dates see *The London Stage, 1660–1800*, pt. 1, 461.

123. The argument for Haines's authorship is given at Hook, introduction, xii. Haines knew Manley well, having acted—along with *Female Wits* cast members Benjamin Johnson, Frances Maria Knight, William Pinkethman, George Powell, and Susanna Verbruggen—in Manley's previous play, *The Lost Lover*. See the dramatis personae page of Delarivier Manley, *The Lost Lover; or, The Jealous Husband* (London: R. Bently, 1696), B2^{r-v}.

124. Elkanah Settle, *The World in the Moon*, 2nd ed. (London: Abel Roper, 1697). Haines is not listed on the dramatis personae page but appears, in the second act, after three characters go to the theater: "Joe Hayns *meets 'em*," as the stage direction reads at 13. Haines thereafter assumes a pivotal role in the play, never playing anyone other than himself.

125. *Female Wits*, A1^{v}.

126. The assessment is that of Hook, introduction, i.

127. Lucas's coffee drinking is a recurrent joke: see, e.g., *Female Wits*, 17.

128. Ibid., 14.

129. When Cross expresses surprise—"At the Tavern in a Morning?"—Johnson upbraids her for not being in on the joke, as the audience presumably is: "Why, how long have you been a Member of this Congregation, pretty *Miss*, and not known honest *George* regards neither Times nor Seasons in Drinking?" (ibid., 13). Powell was a notorious drunk, a fact that dominates biographical speculation about him from the time of his contemporaries (like Colley Cibber) to the present (see Highfill, *Biographical Dictionary*, 12:107–14).

130. The initial run is confirmed in *Female Wits*, A1^{r}; that of *The Royal Mischief*, in the introduction to Delarivier Manley, *The Early Modern Englishwoman: A Facsimile Library of Essential Works, Series II: Printed Writings, 1641–1700: Part III*, ed. Stephanie Hodgson-Wright (Aldershot: Ashgate, 2006), xi.

131. The play's satire of "female wits" has been overemphasized. Despite its title, the parody of Pix (here, mocking her legendary girth, called Mrs. Wellfed but identified in the prologue as Mrs. P---x [at *Female Wits*, A2^{r}]) and Trotter (called Calista and identified as Mrs. T----r [ibid.]) is peripheral to the play's satire of Manley and the Lincoln's Inn Fields actors. One fact completely ignored in

the criticism seems significant: both Wellfed and Calista are as unkind toward Marsilia (or Mrs. *M---y* [ibid.]) as the troupe is. See, e.g., their remarks at ibid., 15; or Calista's pointed aside at ibid., 33: "I never heard such stuff in my Life," she says of Marsilia's play.

132. Ibid., 51.

133. My understanding of *Female Wits* in performance here is indebted to Hook, introduction, ix.

134. James Peck, "Albion's 'Chaste Lucrece': Chastity, Resistance, and the Glorious Revolution in the Career of Anne Bracegirdle," *Theatre Survey* 45, no. 1 (2004): 89–113, at 89. Bracegirdle's facility with a certain type—the imperiled maiden—went hand in hand with her celebrated pathetic style, in which Marsilia schools Cross: "Your pardon, Mrs. give me leave to instruct you in a moving Cry. Oh! there's a great deal of art in crying: Hold your Handkerchief thus; let it meet your Eyes, thus; your Head declin'd, thus; now, in a perfect whine, crying out these words, *By these Tears, which never cease to Flow*" (*Female Wits*, 50).

135. *Female Wits*, 32. Statira is a role in Nathaniel Lee's heroic tragedy *The Rival Queens*, renowned (and pilloried even in the period) for the unbridled passion of its titular roles. In her career Barry actually played the other queen, Roxana. See also ibid., 30: "Good Mrs. *Knight* speak that as passionately as you can, because you are going to Swoon, you know; and I hate Women shou'd go into a Swoon, as some of our Authors make 'em, without so much as altering their Face, or Voice." When Knight, acting as Lady Loveall in Marsilia's play, lands her Barry impersonation—"I am a Libertine, and being so, I love my Husband's Son, and will enjoy him"—Marsilia praises her: "There's a Rant for you!" (ibid., 31).

136. Ibid., 65–66.

137. In his day Macklin was praised by Aaron Hill, author of the Le Brun–inspired *The Art of Acting*; Hill's praise of Macklin is recorded in James Thomas Kirkman, *Memoirs of the Life of Charles Macklin, Esq., Principally Compiled from His Own Papers and Memorandums*, 2 vols. (London: Lackington, Allen, 1799), 1:293–95. The twentieth century would see Macklin as the paradigmatic naturalistic actor because of the iconic article of Alan S. Downer, "Nature to Advantage Dressed: Eighteenth-Century Acting," *PMLA* 58 (1943): 1002–37.

138. Macklin's biographer quotes Hill; see Kirkman, *Memoirs*, 1:293–94:

We are at present getting more into nature, in playing, and if the violence of gesture be not quite suppressed, we have nothing of the recitative of the old tragedy.

It is to the honour of Mr. Macklin that he began this great improvement. There was a time he was excluded [from] the Theatres and supported himself by a company, whom he taught to play, and some of whom afterwards made no inconsiderable figure. It was his manner to check all the cant and cadence of tragedy: he would bid his pupil first speak the passage as he would in common life, if he had occasion to pronounce the same words; and then giving them more force, but preserving the same accent, to deliver them on the Stage.

That Macklin's instruction focused on tragic acting is confirmed by his students' first public performance: *Othello*.

139. The shows satirized the era's best-known actors (and other public figures) with Molière-like impersonations; versions were played in various forms under various titles over many years. The play's reliance on the rehearsal burlesque is noted at Simon Trefman, *Sam. Foote, Comedian, 1720–1777* (New York: New York University Press, 1971), 27. Even his onetime teacher Macklin eventually was ridiculed: an extant record of one of Foote's later diversions lampoons Macklin for falling into the same tendency toward codification that he had fought against. See Samuel Foote, *The Second Act of Diversions of the Morning*, in vol. 4 of Tate Wilkinson, *The Wandering Patentee; or, A History of the Yorkshire Theatres, from 1770 to the Present Time* (York: Wilson, Spence, and Mawman, 1795), 237–50, at 243–44.

140. Samuel Foote, *Treatise on the Passions, so Far as They Regard the Stage* (London: C. Corbet, [1747]), 8.

141. Ibid., 12.

142. Ibid., 10.

143. His views are made clear at Molière, *L'impromptu*, 95.

144. Not incidentally, this conceit allowed Foote to evade the Licensing Act of 1737, too. The advertisement—from London's *Daily Advertiser*, Friday, April 24, 1747, at 1—is also quoted (with some errors) in *The London Stage, 1660–1800, Part 3: 1729–1747*, ed. Arthur H. Scouten, 2 vols. (Carbondale: Southern Illinois University Press, 1961), 2:1307.

145. *The Trial of Samuel Foote, Esq., for a Libel on Peter Paragraph* was first performed on May 11, 1763, and published in vol. 4 of Wilkinson, *Wandering*.

146. On Foote's use of his leglessness see Jane Moody, "Stolen Identities: Character, Mimicry and the Invention of Samuel Foote," in Luckhurst and Moody, *Theatre and Celebrity*, 68. He required an amputation in 1766 (see Trefman, *Sam.*, 149).

147. Foote, *Treatise*, 4. Foote also aligns his work—specifically, his play *The Minor*—with Molière's in his *A Letter from Mr. Foote, to the Reverend Author of the Remarks, Critical and Christian, on the Minor* (London: T. Davies, T. Becket, and J. Coote, 1760), 18, where he praises *Tartuffe* and notes of its author that "there is scarce a single Play of his, but has a real living Character."

148. Foote, *Treatise*, 13.

149. Descartes, *The Passions*, 79. Descartes, *Les passions*, 151: "Elles sont si peu differentes, qu'il y a des hommes qui font presque la mesme mine lors qu'ils

pleurent, que les autres lors qu'ils rient. Il est vray qu'il y en a quelques unes qui sont assez remarquables, comme sont les rides du front en la colere, & certains mouvemens du nez & des levres en l'indignation, & en la moquerie; mais elles ne semblent pas tant estres naturelles que volontaires."

150. Hill's attempt is recounted in Thomas Davies, *Memoirs of the Life of David Garrick, Esq.* (London: [Thomas Davies], 1780), 1:143–45. The influential treatise was published as Aaron Hill, *The Art of Acting, Deriving Rules from a New Principle for Touching the Passions in a Natural Manner* (London: John Osborn, 1746).

151. Whatever his differences from Le Brun, Parsons was clearly his "intellectual descendant" in the assessment of West, *Image*, 93; her treatment of Parsons's "Human Physiology Explained" and its influence appears at ibid., 92–100. See the similar assessment in Montagu, *Expression*, 101.

152. Genest, *Some Account*, 4:14–15.

153. "Car la construction de nostre cors est telle, que certains mouuemens suiuent en luy naturellement de certaines pensées; comme on voit que la rougeur du visage suit de la honte, les larmes de la compassion, & le ris de la ioye" (Descartes, *Lettres de Monsieur Descartes*, 85–86). On the problematic dating of this letter see Lisa Shapiro, ed. *The Correspondence Between Princess Elisabeth of Bohemia and René Descartes* (Chicago: University of Chicago Press, 2007), 81.

154. "Ayant vne maladie, on peut aysément se remettre par la seule force de la nature, principalement lors qu'on est encore jeune. Cette persuasion est sans doute beaucoup plus vraye & plus raisonnable, que celle de certaines gens, qui sur le raport d'vn Astrologue ou d'vn Médecin se font acroire qu'il doiuent mourir en certain tems, & par cela seul deuiennent malades, & mesme en meurent assez souuent" (Descartes, *Lettres de Monsieur Descartes*, 86).

155. "N'a t-il point quelque danger à contrefaire le mort?" Molière, *Le malade imaginaire*, in *Les œuvres de Monsieur de Molière*, 8:123–261, at 244.

156. Molière's death was frequently attributed to his portrayal of Argan: see, for example, the epitaph cited in J. D. Hubert, *Molière and the Comedy of Intellect* (Berkeley: University of California Press, 1962), 266; or the report of Bishop Bossuet quoted in Roger Duchêne, *Molière* (Paris: Arthème Fayard, 1998), 660. Lyonnet, *Dictionnaire*, 2:445, addresses the rumor that Molière died while onstage playing Argan. The legend was exaggerated, of course, and Molière was already ill before he took to the stage that evening. The earliest source, *La registre de La Grange*, 142, reports that

> apres la comedie sur les 10 heures du soir Monsieur de Moliere mourust dans sa maison Rue de Richelieu, ayant joué le rosle dud[it]. malade Imaginaire fort Incommode d'un Rhume de fluction sur la poitrine qui luy causoit une grande toux de sorte que dans les grans efforts qu'il fist pour

cracher il se rompit une veyne dans le corps et ne vescut pas demye heure ou trois quarts d'heure depuis ladite veyne rompue.

[after the play at ten in the evening Monsieur de Molière died at his home [in the] rue de Richelieu, having played the part of the titular hypochondriac very unwell with a cold and chest inflammation which caused him to cough very much so that in the great efforts he made to expectorate he burst a vein in his body and lived no more than half or three-quarters of an hour after this vein had burst.]

157. The details of Montfleury's death are provided in Lyonnet, *Dictionnaire*, 2:466. Attributing his death to overacting is common: see, e.g., W. L. Wiley, *The Hôtel de Bourgogne: Another Look at France's First Public Theatre, Studies in Philology* 70, no. 5 (Dec. 1973): 1–113, at 14.

CHAPTER 4

1. See, e.g., Walter Friedlaender, *David to Delacroix*, trans. Robert Goldwater (Cambridge, MA: Harvard University Press, 1952), 45, which calls the painting a "direct imitation" of the production. Of course, this particular constellation of characters is never onstage at once in Racine's play, so if the painting owes anything to early nineteenth-century stage representations, it must represent a composite. By contrast, James Henry Rubin, "Guérin's Painting of *Phèdre* and the Post-Revolutionary Revival of Racine," *Art Bulletin* 59, no. 4 (1977): 601–18, argues forcefully that Guérin borrowed nothing from actual productions of *Phèdre*.

2. Jean Racine, *Phèdre et Hippolyte* (Paris: Claude Barbin, 1677), 8.

3. Ibid., 46.

4. Phaedra demands: "Au defaut de ton bras preste-moy ton épée"; Theramenes then enters and describes Hippolytus as "sans épée, interdit, sans couleur" (ibid., 35).

5. "Vous aimez, vous brûlez. / Vous perissez d'un mal que vous dissimulez" (ibid., 6).

6. Details can be found in Étienne Gilson, "'Le traité des passions' de Descartes inspira-t-il 'Phèdre' de Racine?" *Nouvelles littéraires artistiques et scientifiques* 861 (April 15, 1939): 1. As his title suggests, Gilson asserts a more literal connection between the playwright and the philosopher than I do here.

7. "On doit toutes-fois penser qu'on ne sçauroit subsister seul, & qu'on est en effet l'vne des parties de l'Vniuers, & plus particulierement encore l'vne des parties de cette Terre, l'vne des parties de cet état, de cette societé, de cette famille, à laquelle on est joint par sa demeure, par son serment, par sa naissance; & il faut tou-jours préférer les interests du tout dont on est partie, à ceux de sa personne

en particulier." René Descartes, *Lettres de Monsieur Descartes, où sont traittées les plus belles questions de la morale, physique, medecine, & des mathematiques* (Paris: Henry Le Gras, 1657), 29–30.

8. René Descartes, *Discours de la méthode pour bien conduire sa raison, & chercher la verité dans les sciences, plus la Dioptrique, les Météores et la Géométrie qui sont des essais de cette méthode* (Leiden: Jan Maire, 1637), 11.

9. Descartes to Elisabeth, Sept. 15, 1645: "chacun de nous soit vne personne séparée des autres" (Descartes, *Lettres de Monsieur Descartes*, 29).

10. Today, a plaque commemorating the defunct theater stands near the corner of rues Étienne Marcel and Française.

11. Augmented by the corrections that subsequent scholars have made, the best history of the Hôtel de Bourgogne remains S. Wilma Deierkauf-Holsboer's two volumes *Le théâtre de l'Hôtel de Bourgogne I: 1548–1635* (Paris: A.-G. Nizet, 1968) and *Le théâtre de l'Hôtel de Bourgogne II: Le théâtre de la troupe royale, 1635–1680* (Paris: A.-G. Nizet, 1970). See, too, the summative work of W. L. Wiley, *The Hôtel de Bourgogne: Another Look at France's First Public Theatre, Studies in Philology* 70, no. 5 (Dec. 1973): 1–113.

12. David Wiles, *A Short History of Western Performance Space* (Cambridge: Cambridge University Press, 2003), 7. See also the indispensable Barbara G. Mittman, *Spectators on the Paris Stage in the Seventeenth and Eighteenth Centuries* (Ann Arbor: UMI Research Press, 1984), which notes at 1: "historically, there was not a formalized separation between performers and the public. As theatre troupes began performing in unused indoor tennis courts . . . there was doubtless a continuation of the informal relationship between audience and actors characteristic of medieval theatre."

13. Here I follow Wiley, who reviews the controversies over the theater's size estimates in general, and Deierkauf-Holsboer's revision of her original estimate in particular, at Wiley, *Hôtel*, 26–28. My diagram is based on that in D. H. Roy, "La scène de l'Hôtel de Bourgogne," *Revue d'histoire du théâtre* 14 (1962): 227–35, at 231.

My discussion of the theater concerns its post-1647 renovations; an even more fascinatingly chaotic design preceded this one, with a larger parterre. There has been considerable controversy about the physical layout of the loges after 1647, presumably because modern scholars—anachronistically conceiving that the main point of theatergoing is to see the play—cannot conceive of loges with such terrible sight lines. I concur with the conclusions of Wiley, Roy, and, most recently, Christa Williford, "Computer Modelling Classical French Theatre Spaces: Three Reconstructions," in *French "Classical" Theatre Today: Teaching, Research, Performance*, ed. Philip Tomlinson (Amsterdam: Rodopi, 2001), 155–64: even after the 1647 improvements, the theater retained the square-cut emplacement of the loges.

14. The loges were also sites of intersubjective contact, and the socialization that took place within them was a large part of the experience; see, e.g., Jeffrey S. Ravel, *The Contested Parterre: Public Theater and French Political Culture, 1680–1791* (Ithaca, NY: Cornell University Press, 1999), 72–73. John Lough, *Paris Theatre Audiences in the Seventeenth and Eighteenth Centuries* (London: Oxford University Press, 1957), reminds us, at 107 and at 114–15, that, while theater historians have associated female spectators with the loges, less well-off women might have sat in the amphitheater.

The space under the amphitheater was reserved for stalls selling concessions, as it had been since earlier in the century when these stalls were run by the Widow Dellin, who sold "macquarons, pain, vin et autre choses parmy le dict parterre" (macaroons, bread, wine and other things through the said parterre). Alan Howe, ed. *Le théâtre professionnel à Paris, 1600–1649* (Paris: Centre historique des Archives nationales, 2000), 263. Mittman, *Spectators*, 3, mentions concessionaires in the parterre itself.

15. See Eugène Rigal, *Le théâtre français avant la période classique* (Paris: Hachette, 1901), 208–11; and Eugène Despois, *Le théâtre français sous Louis XIV* (Paris: Hachette, 1874), 154–63. The law prohibiting "épées, dagues . . . pistolets" is quoted at ibid., 154.

16. T. E. Lawrenson, *The French Stage and Playhouse in the XVIIth Century: A Study in the Advent of the Italian Order*, 2nd ed. (New York: AMS, 1986), 231.

17. See Mittman, *Spectators*, 3–7. The frontispiece, discovered by Mittman and reproduced by her at ibid., 6, appears in Raymond Poisson, *Le Baron de la Crasse, comédie représentée sur le théâtre royal de l'Hostel de Bourgogne* (Paris: Gabriel Quinet, 1667). The play premiered at the Hôtel de Bourgogne in 1662, the date of its first publication (without this accompanying frontispiece).

18. "Les Acteurs ont souuent de la peine à se ranger sur le Théâtre, tant les aîles sont remplies de gens de qualité, que n'en peuuent faire qu'vn riche ornement." Samuel Chappuzeau, *Le théâtre françois* (Lyon: Michel Mayer, 1674), 153.

19. Molière, *Les fascheux* (Paris: Guillaume de Luyne, 1662), 10:

Lors que d'vn air bruyant, & plein d'extrauagance,
Vn homme à grans canons est entré brusquement
En criant, hola-ho, vn siege promptement;
Et de son grand fracas surprenant l'assemblée,
Dans le plus bel endroit la piece troublée.

.   .   .   .

Les Acteurs ont voulu continuer leurs Rôles:
Mais l'homme, pour s'asseoir, a fait nouueau fracas,
Et trauersant encor le Theatre à grans pas,

Bien que dans les costez il pust estre à son aise,
Au milieu du deuant il a planté sa chaise,
Et de son large dos morguant les spectateurs,
Aux trois quarts du parterre a caché les Acteurs.

Cannions, per *OED*, are "in *pl.* Ornamental rolls, sometimes indented, sometimes plain or straight, laid like sausages round the ends of the legs of breeches."

20. Contrary to popular belief, "unity of place" originates in Renaissance interpreters, not Aristotle himself. See Stephen Halliwell, *"Poetics* and Its Interpreters," in *Essays on Aristotle's "Poetics,"* ed. Amélie Oksenberg Rorty (Princeton, NJ: Princeton University Press, 1992), 409–24, at 415.

21. George R. Kernodle, *From Art to Theatre: Form and Convention in the Renaissance* (Chicago: University of Chicago Press, 1944), 207–9.

22. Lawrenson, *French Stage*, 9.

23. "Reünir les temps & les lieux." François Hédelin, abbé d'Aubignac, *La pratique du théâtre* (Paris: Antoine de Sommaville, 1657), 23.

24. The vogue for stage seating among the nobility began with *Le Cid*, whose premiere production intensified the demand for stage seating. See Mittman, *Spectators*, 3.

25. "Pourriez-vous n'estre plus ce superbe Hippolyte, / Implacable ennemy des amoureuses lois, / Et d'un joug que Thesée a suby tant de fois?" (Racine, *Phèdre et Hippolyte*, 4).

26. Ibid., 38.

27. After confessing his love to Aricia, Hippolytus remarks: "Quel étrange Captif pour un si beau lien!" (How strange a prisoner for so beautiful a bond!) (ibid., 27). Aricia: "J'aime, je l'avoûray, cet orgueil genereux / Qui jamais n'a fléchi sous le joug amoureux" (I love, I will confess, this noble pride / That has never bent under love's yoke) (ibid., 23). And a few lines later: "D'enchaisner un Captif de ses fers étonné, / Contre un joug qui luy plaist vainement mutiné" (To bind a prisoner stupefied by his irons / Who rebels in vain against a yoke he desires) (ibid.).

28. He commands her at ibid., 66: "Sortez de l'esclavage où vous estes reduite. / Osez me suivre. Osez accompagnez ma fuite" (Leave the enslavement to which you are reduced. / Dare to follow me. Dare to accompany my flight).

29. "Vous vous plaignez d'un joug imposé dés long-temps" (ibid., 63).

30. "D'un sang . . . De toutes ces horreurs plus rempli que le mien" (ibid., 57).

31. The word and its derivative *sanglant* (bloody) appear forty times in the play, which is only 1,654 lines long. Here and elsewhere in this chapter, I have used the *table de fréquences* in Xavier Darcos's edition of *Phèdre*, although I have verified his results and made corrections as necessary. The table appears in Jean Racine, *Phèdre*, ed. Xavier Darcos (Paris: Hachette, 2005), 189.

32. "Le sang de Pallante" (Racine, *Phèdre et Hippolyte*, 17); "Reste d'un sang fatal conjuré contre nous," as Hippolytus puts it (ibid., 3).

33. Oenone describes him to Phaedra as a "fier Ennemy de vous, de vostre sang" (ibid., 10).

34. Theseus asks rhetorically: "Tous les liens du sang n'ont pû le retenir?" (ibid., 50).

35. "Vers mon cœur tout mon sang se retire" (ibid., 30).

36. "Ces Dieux . . . / Ont allumé le feu fatal à tout mon sang" (ibid., 34); "sang de Minos" (ibid., 38).

37. René Descartes, *The Passions of the Soul*, trans. Stephen H. Voss (Indianapolis: Hackett, 1989), 91. René Descartes, *Les passions de l'âme* (Paris: Henry Le Gras, 1649), 180–81, reads:

> Et, pour exemple, il est aysé de penser, que les estranges aversions de quelques uns, qui les empeschent de souffrir l'odeur des roses, ou la presence d'un chat, ou choses semblables, ne vienent que de ce qu'au commencement de leur vie ils ont esté forts offensez par quelques pareils objets, ou bien qu'ils ont compati au sentiment de leur mere qui en a esté offensée estant grosse. Car il est certain qu'il y a du rapport entre tous les mouvemens de la mere, & ceux de l'enfant qui est en son ventre, en sorte que ce qui est contraire à l'un nuit à l'autre. . . . L'idée de l'Aversion qu'il avoit alors pour ces roses, ou pour ce chat, demeure imprimée en son cerveau jusques à la fin de sa vie.

38. Descartes to Elisabeth, May or June 1645: "estant né d'vne mere qui mourut peu de jours aprés ma naissance d'vn mal de poumon, causé par quelques déplaisirs, j'auois herité d'elle vne toux seiche, & vne couleur pasle, que j'ay gardéc jusques à l'âge de plus de vingt ans" (Descartes, *Lettres de Monsieur Descartes*, 93). Descartes is fibbing about his mother's death "several days" after his birth: as Adam and Tannery note at René Descartes, *Œuvres de Descartes*, ed. Charles Adam and Paul Tannery, 11 vols. (Paris: J. Vrin, 1983), 4:220n*a*, his mother died when he was almost fourteen months old.

39. "L'essieu crie & se romp" (Racine, *Phèdre et Hippolyte*, 74).

40. "De son genereux sang la trace nous conduit" (ibid., 75).

41. "Je ne me soûtiens plus" (ibid., 8).

42. Ibid., 38:

> Moy regner! Moy ranger un Estat sous ma loy!
> Quand ma foible raison ne regne plus sur moy,
> Lors que j'ay de mes sens abandonné l'empire,
> Quand sous un joug honteux à-peine je respire,
> Quand je me meurs.

43. Phaedra describes herself as "d'un sang qu'elle [Venus] poursuit" (ibid., 15).

44. "Contre tout vostre sang" (ibid., 13).

45. Oenone reports this refusal at ibid., 10.

46. See Descartes, *Les passions*, 72 (quoted above at Chapter 1n66).

47. Racine, *Phèdre et Hippolyte*, 61.

48. Descartes, *Les passions*, 9–10: "Tous ceux que l'authorité des Anciens n'a point entierement aveuglez, & qui ont voulu ouvrir les yeux pour examiner l'opinion d'Herveus touchant la circulation du sang, ne doutent point que toutes les venes & les arteres du corps, ne soient comme des ruisseaux, par où le sang coule sans cesse fort promptement." Descartes, *The Passions*, 22, reads: "All those whom the authority of the Ancients has not entirely blinded, and who have been willing to open their eyes enough to examine Harvey's opinion concerning the circulation of the blood, do not doubt that all the body's veins and arteries are like streams through which the blood ceaselessly flows with great rapidity."

49. Ravel, *Contested*, 73. Despite its title Ravel's remarkable book also treats earlier theatrical spaces, as in the passage cited.

50. Roger Herzel, "Racine, Laurent, and the *Palais à volonté*," *PMLA* 108, no. 5 (1993): 1064–82, at 1070.

51. "Vous n'avez jamais esté si belle! Si je n'estois pas amoureux, je le deviendrois aujourd'huy." The anecdote is recorded by Mme Boudin in 1688 in her *La fameuse comédienne, ou Histoire de la Guérin, auparavant femme et veuve de Molière*, ed. Jules Bonnassies (Paris: Barraud, 1870), 49.

52. The job's duties included those of a designer, technical director, and stage manager; see Herzel, "Racine," 1066.

53. See Racine, *Phèdre et Hippolyte*, 43: "Il me semble déja que ces murs, que ces voutes / Vont prendre la parole, & prests à m'accuser / Attendent mon Epoux, pour le desabuser" (I feel already that these walls, these vaults / Will acquire speech and, ready to accuse me, / Await my husband to disabuse him). The requirement of a "palais vouté" is recorded in Henry Carrington Lancaster, ed., *Le mémoire de Mahelot, Laurent, et d'autres décorateurs de l'Hôtel de Bourgogne et de la Comédie-Française au XVIIe siècle* (Paris: Librairie Ancienne Honoré Champion, 1920), 114.

54. Herzel, "Racine," 1073.

55. "Les passions n'y sont présentées aux yeux que pour montrer tout le desordre dont elles sont cause" (Racine, *Phèdre et Hippolyte*, aiv^v).

56. Alain Rey et al., eds., *Dictionnaire historique de la langue française*, 4th ed. (Paris: Dictionnaires le Robert, 2012), s.v. "objet," notes that the meaning of *objet* as "spectacle" predates its meaning as "object"; concerning the latter meaning, the editors cite Descartes's usages circa 1650.

57. Martin Heidegger, "The Age of the World Picture," in *The Question Concerning Technology and Other Essays*, trans. William Lovitt (New York: Harper Perennial, 1977), 115–54, at 127. The original appears at "Die Zeit des Weltbildes," *Holzwege* (Frankfurt am Main: Vittorio Klostermann, 1957), 69–104, at

80. Note that Heidegger interposes an estranging hyphen into the word *Vor-stellen* (to represent) in order to emphasize the separation between the representation and the person who regards it but also makes it (*Stellen*). In thinking through Heidegger's views of Descartes, I am indebted to the entry for "representation and idea" in Michael Inwood, *A Heidegger Dictionary* (London: Blackwell, 1999), 184–86.

58. "Tres-incommodes, la pluspart des loges estant trop éloignées & mal situées, & le Parterre n'ayant aucune élevation, ny aucun siege" (Hédelin, *La pratique*, 509).

59. These details are found in Henri Lagrave, *Le théâtre et le public à Paris de 1715 à 1750* (Paris: Klincksiek, 1972), 73–74.

60. Wiley, *Hôtel*, 15.

61. "Firmum & immobile"; "certum . . . & inconcussum." Renati Des-Cartes [i.e., René Descartes], *Meditationes de prima philosophia* (Paris: Michaelum Soli, 1641), 17.

62. Karsten Harries, "Descartes, Perspective, and the Angelic Eye," *Yale French Studies* 49 (1973): 28–42, at 32; Jean-Joseph Goux, "Descartes et la perspective," *L'esprit créateur* 25 (Spring 1985): 10–20, at 13.

63. Claudio Guillén, *Literature as System: Essays Toward the Theory of Literary History* (Princeton, NJ: Princeton University Press, 1971), 284.

64. The notion of an "ideal viewpoint," based on the position of the king, is elaborated in Timothy C. Murray, "Richelieu's Theater: The Mirror of the Prince," *Renaissance Drama* 8 (1977): 275–98, in which he discusses a precursor to the 1662 *salle des machines*: Richelieu's Palais Cardinal theater, whose revolutionary proscenium arch I discussed in the first chapter. On this difference between the Comédie-Française and the Italian theaters where perspective was perfected, see Louise Pelletier, *Architecture in Words: Theatre, Language and the Sensuous Space of Architecture* (New York: Routledge, 2006), 81.

65. "Trace et établi sur des formes optiques . . . relative à la meilleure manière de voir"; the plan is listed in *La Comédie-Française, 1680–1980* (Paris: Bibliothèque nationale, 1980), a catalogue of the archives of the Comédie-Française published in honor of its three hundredth anniversary, at 7.

66. Herzel, "Racine," 1077–78.

67. See Heidegger, "Age," 130: "The world picture [*Weltbild*] does not change from an earlier medieval one into a modern one, but rather the fact that the world becomes [a] picture at all is what distinguishes the essence of the modern age [*der Neuzeit*]." The original is in Heidegger, "Zeit," 83.

68. The little staircase facilitated communication between the stage and the orchestra pit; see Mittman, *Spectators*, 66.

69. John Spitzer and Neal Zaslaw, *The Birth of the Orchestra: History of an Institution, 1650–1815* (New York: Oxford University Press, 2005), 54.

70. Guillén, *Literature*, 292–93.

71. The thesis is articulated at Lawrenson, *French Stage*, 172; in the prelapsarian time prior to 1689, he asserts, "the theater [was] kept pure" (ibid., 11).

72. Thus was the meaning of the *hypokeimenon* (subject) transformed by Descartes, as Heidegger explains in "The Question Concerning Technology" and "The Age of the World Picture." The Cartesian subject transforms that which is in front of him into an object, an objectification, a picture: "What it is to be is for the first time defined as the objectiveness of representing, and truth is first defined as the certainty of representing, in the metaphysics of Descartes" (Heidegger, "Age," 127). The original is in Heidegger, "Zeit," 80.

73. Mittman, *Spectators*, 39–54.

74. For her discovery of the frontispiece I am grateful to Mittman, who also reproduces it in ibid., 14. The balustrade is discussed in ibid., 66, and in *La Comédie-Française*, 8. Finding that the "mingling" between actors and spectators creates "confusion" and "obliterates all its [i.e., the play's] beauty," the actors went further in a 1698 renovation, enlarging the balustrade and extending it as shown in Blondel's plan. Details are provided by Mittman, who located a *feuille d'assemblée* dated January 20, 1698, in the archives of the Comédie-Française; see Barbara G. Mittman, "Keeping Order on the Stage in Paris in the Seventeenth and Eighteenth Centuries," *Theatre Research International* 5, no. 2 (Spring 1980): 99–107, at 106. She provides the document's original French at ibid., 101: "pour empescher la confusion des personnes qui se meslent sur le theatre avec les acteurs qui jouent la comedie ce qui en efface toute la beauté."

75. In Paris the Opéra was the first Paris theater to have stage spectators banned, first (apparently ineffectively) in 1697 and later in 1732; at the Comédie-Française the theater was redesigned without stage seating thanks to the financial intervention of the Comte de Lauranguais in 1759; see Mittman, *Spectators*, 77–78 and 85–86. The parterre at d'Orbay's theater would finally get benches on April 9, 1782 (Ravel, *Contested*, 220). In London the practice was not common during the early years of the Restoration but became so in some theaters by the turn of the century. It was banned, famously and finally, by David Garrick in 1762. Joseph Donohue, ed. *The Cambridge History of British Theatre*, vol. 2, *1660–1895* (Cambridge: Cambridge University Press, 2004), 161.

76. Herzel, "Racine," 1078.

77. Ismene tells Aricia of Hippolytus that "ses yeux . . . ne pouvoient vous quitter" (Racine, *Phèdre et Hippolyte*, 22). Oenone tells Phaedra that she is horrified "de vous voir expirer à mes yeux" (ibid., 12) and that Theseus "va paroistre à vos yeux" (ibid., 41).

78. "Que vois-je?" (ibid., 47).

79. Oenone, in discussing Phaedra's grim condition with her, notes that it has been three nights that "le sommeil n'est entré dans vos yeux" (ibid., 10). Phaedra reports that "J'ay declaré ma honte aux yeux de ma Vainqueur" (ibid., 39).

80. Phaedra: "Mes yeux ne voyoient plus" (ibid., 15). Panope: "Son œil tout égaré ne nous reconnoist plus" (ibid., 72).

81. Hippolytus tells Aricia that "absente je vous trouve" (absent, I find you) and "Tout retrace à mes yeux les charmes que j'évite" (Everything calls to my eyes the charms that I flee) (ibid., 27). Attempting to placate Venus and to wriggle free from her curse, Phaedra recounts: "J'adorois Hippolyte, & le voyant sans cesse, / Mesme aux pié des Autels que je faisois fumer" (I adored Hippolytus, and seeing him endlessly, / Even at the feet of the altars where I burned offerings) (ibid., 15).

82. Descartes, *Meditationes*, 17.

83. Aricia: "Faut-il qu'à vos yeux seuls un nüage odieux / Dérobe sa vertu qui brille à tous les yeux?" (Must an odious cloud from your eyes alone / Conceal his virtue, which shines in all other eyes?) (Racine, *Phèdre et Hippolyte*, 69). Theseus: "Vostre amour vous aveugle" (ibid., 70). Oenone: "Que Phedre . . . n'avoit-elle mes yeux?" (ibid., 39). Phaedra: "Je le voy comme un Monstre effroyable à mes yeux" (ibid., 44).

84. Theseus: "Quel œil ne seroit pas trompé comme le mien?" (ibid., 52). He makes this comment when accusing Hippolytus; in other words his judgment is wrong. Recanting his denunciation of his son, he will later complain again that his eyes had been deceived (*abusez*) (ibid., 76). Compare Phaedra at ibid., 61: "Par quel charme ont-ils tropé [*sic*] mes yeux?" (By what magic have my eyes been deceived?).

85. Lawrenson's claim (at *French Stage*, 231) that "the simple fact that a standing audience can turn in any direction has been too much neglected" in studies of audience reception of the period remains true decades after his book's publication.

86. Racine, *Phèdre et Hippolyte*, 77. Theramenes says of Hippolytus's destroyed body, the "triste objet," that it "méconnoistroit l'œil mesme de son Pere" (ibid., 75).

87. Ibid., 73–75.

88. "Mes yeux sont éblouïs du jour" (ibid., 8). "Quand pourray-je au travers d'un noble poussiere / Suivre de l'œil un char fuyant dans la carriere!" (When may I watch, through a cloud of noble dust, / A chariot racing down the track!) (ibid., 9).

89. "Voilà ce que postule la perspective, comme le cogito: la subjectivité absolue ne contredit pas mais rend possible l'objectivité parfaite" (Goux, "Descartes," 19).

90. "Le Parterre doit estre élevé en Talut, & remply de sieges immobiles" (the parterre must be raised and raked, and filled with fixed seats) (Hédelin, *La pratique*, 513).

91. See, e.g., Graham Barlow, "Vanbrugh's Queen's Theatre in the Haymarket, 1703–1709," *Early Music* 17, no. 4 (Nov. 1989): 515–21, at 516. The circumstances of the prologue's speaking are not clear. The theater had opened, barely finished, in April 1705 with a production of a pastoral opera, Jakob Greber's *The Loves of Ergasto*: see Curtis A. Price, *Music in the Restoration Theater* (Ann Arbor: UMI Research Press, 1979), 115. Almost two years later, this prologue was printed—Samuel Garth, "Prologue Spoken at the Opening of the Queen's Theatre in the *Hay-Market*," *Muses Mercury for the Month of February, 1707* (i.e., vol. 2), 35–36—with a note that its previous printed copies were "surreptitious and false" and that this printing "is genuine, and what the worthy Author has approv'd of" (36).

92. John Vanbrugh, *The Relapse; or, Virtue in Danger* (London: Samuel Briscoe, 1697), 1.

93. Garth, "Prologue," 35–36.

94. Ibid., 36.

95. Barlow, "Vanbrugh's," 518.

96. The poor acoustics of the Tuileries *salle des machines* is confirmed by William D. Howarth, ed., *French Theatre in the Neo-Classical Era, 1550–1789* (Cambridge: Cambridge University Press, 1997), 157. The Cibber quote appears at Colley Cibber, *An Apology for the Life of Mr. Colley Cibber, Comedian, and Late Patentee of the Theatre-Royal with a Historical View of the Stage During His Own Time* (London: John Watts, 1740), 183.

Because of the theater's acoustic problems, it would undergo renovations—including the lowering of its ceiling—in the 1708–9 season. See, e.g., Barlow, "Vanbrugh's," 516; and Simon Trussler, *The Cambridge Illustrated History of British Theatre* (Cambridge: Cambridge University Press, 1994), 149.

97. Edmund Smith, *Phædra and Hippolitus: A Tragedy, as It Is Acted in the Queen's Theatre in the Hay-Market, by Her Majesty's Sworn Servants* (London: Bernard Lintott, [1707]), 31, 20, 12.

98. Ibid., 55.

99. Of course, in theory a spectator might be permitted to sit on the stage, as was still the practice, at Vanbrugh's theater, on a chair or bench added ad hoc. But the design of the theater makes clear what an aesthetic violation such a spectator would be, and, unlike other theaters, the Queen's Theatre at the Haymarket would seldom have needed the extra seating—especially for a tepidly received play like *Phædra and Hippolitus*, which had only four performances in its debut season and was not revived until some time later. For her clarifications about onstage seating at the theater, I am indebted to Judith Milhous.

100. For his discovery of the image I am grateful to Jeffrey S. Ravel, who also reproduces it in his "Seating the Public: Spheres and Loathing in the Paris Theaters, 1777–1788," *French Historical Studies* 18, no. 1 (Spring 1993): 173–210, at 178.

101. "Si les personnages ne s'étreignent ni ne se frappent sur la scène, en revanche, ils se voient. Les scènes, chez Racine, sont des *entrevues*." Jean Starobinski, *L'œil vivant* (Paris: Gallimard, 1961), 74.

102. "Voir est un acte pathétique"; "ils [les regards] troublent les âmes" (ibid., 73, 74).

103. "Le plateau du théâtre, presque nu"; "portiques, colonnades, lambris" (ibid., 74).

104. "Le mot voir, lui-même presque invisible dans sa brièveté monosyllabique, conduit l'œil du lecteur au cœur de la relation essentielle des personnages qu'unit . . . le seul échange des regards" (ibid., 76).

105. Theseus once declares her "the Daughter of [his] hated Foe" (Smith, *Phædra*, 49), but the plot point interests Smith so little that it is not otherwise mentioned, and Ismena is not even a prisoner but, bizarrely, Phaedra's nurse.

106. Ibid., 10.

107. On Betterton's position in the company during the 1707 season, see David Roberts, *Thomas Betterton: The Greatest Actor of the Restoration Stage* (Cambridge: Cambridge University Press, 2010), 170.

108. Smith, *Phædra*, 14.

109. Ibid., 2.

110. Ibid., 17.

111. "Ah! Je vois Hippolyte . . . Fay ce que tu voudras, je m'abandonne à toy . . . je ne puis rien pour moy" (Racine, *Phèdre et Hippolyte*, 45).

112. "Vous auroit peri le Monstre de la Crete. . . . C'est moy, Prince, c'est moy dont l'utile secours / Vous eust du Labyrinthe enseigné les détours" (ibid., 32–33).

113. "Cette noble pudeur coloroit son visage" (ibid., 32).

114. "Il avoit vostre port, vos yeux, vostre langage" (ibid.); "poison" (ibid., 34); "Peutestre il voudra bien lui tenir lieu de Pere" (Perhaps he will be like a father to him [i.e., Phaedra's son]) (ibid., 40).

115. Smith, *Phædra*, 6.

116. Ibid., 59.

117. "Pourriez-vous n'estre plus . . . Hippolyte?" (Racine, *Phèdre et Hippolyte*, 4).

118. Smith, *Phædra*, 30.

119. Ibid.

120. Ibid., 37.

121. Ibid., 64.

122. Ibid., 63.

123. Heidegger, "Age," 134. The original appears at Heidegger, "Zeit," 87: "das Gebild des vorstellenden Herstellens." This translation into English folds in the masculine emphasis of the immediately following sentence, whose subject is "der Mensch."

124. *The Muses Mercury for the Month of May, 1707* (i.e., vol. 5), 123.

125. This gendering is succinctly described, for example, in Susan Bordo, *The Flight to Objectivity* (Albany: State University of New York Press, 1987), 97–118.

126. Theseus accuses Hippolitus:

> Ev'n at the time you heard your Father's Death, . . .
> When thou shoud'st rend the Skies with clam'rous Grief,
> Beat thy sad Breast, and tear thy starting Hair;
> Then to my Bed to force your impious way,
> With horrid Lust t'insult my yet warm Urn;
> Make me the Scorn of Hell, and Sport for Fiends.
> These are the Fun'ral Honours paid to *Theseus*. (Smith, *Phædra*, 49)

127. Henri Lefebvre, *The Production of Space*, trans. Donald Nicholson-Smith (London: Blackwell, 1991), 406–7. The original appears at Henri Lefebvre, *La production de l'espace* (Paris: Anthropos, 1974), 467.

128. "Lors que j'ay de mes sens abandonné l'empire, . . . / Quand je me meurs" (Racine, *Phèdre et Hippolyte*, 38).

129. "Ma force m'abandonne. / Mes yeux sont ébloüis du jour que je revoy, / Et mes genoux tremblans se dérobent sous moy" (ibid., 8). Ibid., 15:

> Je le vis, je rougis, je palis à sa veuë.
> Un trouble s'éleva dans mon ame esperduë.
> Mes yeux ne voyoient plus, je ne pouvois parler,
> Je sentis tout mon corps & transir, & brûler.

130. "Ce sang deplorable" (ibid., 13).

131. Edward converted in order to marry Anne Gonzaga, the princess of Mantua. The letter appears in Alexandre Foucher de Careil, *Descartes, la Princesse Élisabeth, et la Reine Christine, d'après des lettres inédites* (Paris: Germer-Baillière, 1879), 87:

> Je croyois qu'une forte résolution de ne chercher la béatitude qu'aux choses qui dépendent de ma volonté, me rendroit moins sensible à celles qui me viennent d'ailleurs, avant que la folie d'un de mes frères m'ait fait connoître ma faiblesse. Car elle m'a plus troublée la santé du corps et la tranquillité de l'âme que tous les malheurs qui me sont encore arrivés. Si vous prenez la peine de lire la gazette, vous ne sauriez ignorer qu'il est tombé entre les mains d'une certaine sorte de gens qui ont plus de haîne pour nostre maison que d'affection pour leur culte, et s'est laissé prendre en leurs piéges jusqu'à changer de religion pour se rendre catholique romain.

132. Descartes to Elisabeth, Jan. 1646: "ceux de la Religion dont ie suis (qui sont sans doute, le plus grand nombre dans l'Europe) sont obligez de l'approuuer" (Descartes, *Lettres de Monsieur Descartes*, 49).

133. Lisa Shapiro, ed., *The Correspondence Between Princess Elisabeth of Bohemia and René Descartes* (Chicago: University of Chicago Press, 2007), 13. A letter written by Elisabeth around this time has been lost (ibid., 176n198), but his response survives: see Descartes, *Lettres de Monsieur Descartes*, 101–5. In it he refers to the execution with a theatrical metaphor, noting that it represents the "funeste conclusion des Tragédies d'Angleterre" (fatal conclusion of England's Tragedies) (ibid., 102).

134. See Shapiro, *Correspondence*, 9.

135. Elisabeth to Descartes, Sept. 13, 1645: "l'expérience . . . me montroit qu'il y en [i.e., passions] a qui nous portent aux actions raisonnables" (Foucher de Careil, *Descartes, la Princesse*, 75).

136. Descartes to Elisabeth, May 18, 1645: "La cause la plus ordinaire de la fievre lente est la tristesse; & l'opiniastreté de la Fortune à persecuter vostre maison vous donne continuellement des sujets de fascherie, qui sont si publics & si éclatans, qu'il n'est pas besoin d'vser beaucoup de conjectures, ny estre fort dans les affaires, pour juger que c'est en cela que consiste la principale cause de vostre indisposition" (Descartes, *Lettres de Monsieur Descartes*, 107).

137. Descartes to Elisabeth, Sept. 15, 1645, quoted at note 7 above.

138. Marc Fumaroli, *Héros et orateurs: Rhétorique et dramaturgie cornéliennes* (Geneva: Droz, 1966), 493–518.

139. "Un poëte de théatre est un empoisonneur public, non des corps, mais des ames des fidelles, qui se doit croire coupable d'une infinité d'homicides spirituels." Pierre Nicole, in the eleventh of his eighteen-letter suite *L'hérésie imaginaire*, published between 1664 and 1666. (The copy at the Bibliothèque nationale de France is missing its first pages and therefore lacks additional publication information.)

140. Racine, *Phèdre et Hippolyte*, 78:

J'ay fait couler dans mes brulantes veines
Un poison que Medée apporta dans Athenes.
Déjà jusqu'à mon cœur le venin parvenu
Dans ce cœur expirant jette un froid inconnu.

141. Or so the cultural myth goes: see, e.g., Jonas Barish, *The Antitheatrical Prejudice* (Berkeley: University of California Press, 1981), 191–92, where he describes Racine's "conversion" followed by an abandonment of the stage. For a less tidy account of Racine's retirement as a playwright—which was connected to his coappointment (with Nicolas Boileau) as Historiographer Royal—and of his reconciliation with his Jansenist teachers at Port-Royal, see Geoffrey Brereton, *Life of Racine: A Critical Biography* (London: Methuen, 1973), 234–37, 253–54, and 305–11.

142. The contracts for these renovations, which give us a surprising amount of detail, are still extant; they are reprinted as appendices in Deierkauf-Holsboer,

Théâtre de l'Hôtel de Bourgogne II, 182–86. For the dimensions I follow Wiley, *Hôtel*, 57.

143. In print the play preserved the title *Phèdre et Hippolyte* through several editions and in Jean Racine, *Œuvres* (Paris: Claude Barbin, 1680), first taking the name *Phèdre* in 1687, in Jean Racine, *Œuvres* (Paris: Pierre Trabouillet, 1687).

144. Jean-François Marmontel, *Supplément à l'encyclopédie, ou Dictionnaire raisonné des sciences, des arts et des metiers* (Amsterdam: Marc-Michel Rey, 1777), 4:241.

145. In the autobiographical opening to that book, one of the first thoughts that Descartes has in his stove-heated room is that "souuent il n'y a pas tant de perfection dans les ouurages composez de plusieurs pieces, & faits de la main de diuers maistres, qu'en ceux auxquels vn seul a trauaillé" (often there is less perfection in works created from several pieces, and made by various masters' hands, than in those on which one person has worked alone) (Descartes, *Discours*, 13).

146. Peggy Phelan, *Unmarked: The Politics of Performance* (London: Routledge, 1993), 147.

147. "Il suffit de tes yeux pour t'en persuader, / Si tes yeux un moment pouvoient me regarder" (Racine, *Phèdre et Hippolyte*, 34). Racine here contrasts Phaedra with Aricia, who notes that it was not her eyes alone that were bewitched by Hippolytus: "Non que par les yeux seuls laschement enchantée" (ibid., 23).

148. Ibid., 37.

149. Foucher de Careil, *Descartes, la Princesse*, 22–23. He begins by citing two of Phaedra's anguished speeches before declaring, "Eh bien! si le style est autre, et surtout si la cause est différente, c'est l'accent de cette douleur insondable qui marque ces lettres d'Élisabeth d'une empreinte bien particulière" (Well! if the style is different, and especially if the cause is different, it is the accent of this unfathomable pain that marks the letters of Elisabeth with a very particular impression).

150. Elisabeth to Descartes: "définir les passions pour les bien connoitre" (ibid., 75). In the remarkable exchange of letters from which this quotation is taken, Descartes and Elisabeth discuss Seneca's *De vita beata* and, specifically, what it means to live happily. (Elisabeth in particular is not taken with Seneca's Stoic leanings.) On August 16, 1645, Elisabeth notes that her letter writing—and her analysis of Seneca—has been delayed: "Il y a huit jours que la mauvaise humeur d'un frère malade m'empêche de vous faire cette requeste en me retenant toujours auprès de luy" (It has been eight days since the bad mood of an ill brother has prevented me from making this request [for clarification] of you, since I have had to stay near him always) (ibid., 69). Almost a month later, on September 13, 1645, they are still discussing Seneca—although increasingly steering toward the emotions more generally—when Elisabeth makes her famous request, which would lead to *Les passions de l'âme*, that Descartes define the passions.

151. Descartes to Elisabeth, Nov. 29, 1643: "I'ay esté . . . rauy de ioye" (Descartes, *Œuvres*, 4:46). The letter is one of several omitted from editions of Descartes's letters until the nineteenth century.

1. "Vostre flâme devient une flâme ordinaire." Jean Racine, *Phèdre et Hippolyte* (Paris: Claude Barbin, 1677), 18.

2. "Les flots pour jamais l'ont ravie à nos yeux" (ibid., 71).

3. Ibid., 34–35:

Voilà mon cœur. C'est là que ta main doit fraper.

Impatient déja d'expier son offense

Au devant de ton bras je le sens qui s'avance.

Frappe. Ou si tu le crois indigne de tes coups,

Si ta haine m'envie un supplice si doux,

Ou si d'un sang trop vil ta main seroit trempée,

Au defaut de ton bras preste-moy ton épée.

Donne!

4. Theramenes (who was there as we are not) reports that the monster "vomit à nos yeux" (ibid., 73).

5. René Descartes, *Œuvres de Descartes*, ed. Charles Adam and Paul Tannery, 11 vols. (Paris: J. Vrin, 1983), 10:11.

6. René Descartes, *Inquisitio veritatis per lumen naturale*, in *Opuscula posthuma, physica et mathematica* (Amsterdam: P. & J. Blaev, 1701), 67–90. But note that the *Opuscula* is not continuously paginated: the *Inquisitio*'s pages are numbered along with the *Regulæ ad directionem ingenii*, which it directly follows.

7. This text was then published as *La recherche de la verité par la lumière naturelle* in Descartes, *Œuvres*, 10:495–514. The complicated story of the text's genesis is described at ibid., 10:491–94. I have here cross-referenced the Latin with the French text where it exists.

8. See Prologue, n44.

9. One hint that has not been pursued resides in the text's invocations of wonder. As I described in Chapter 2, Descartes's view of wonder evolved from one of ambivalence (expressed, for example, in his 1637 *Meteorology*) to that in *The Passions of the Soul*, where wonder is privileged as the first of all passions and that which facilitates knowledge of both physical marvels and metaphysical truths. *The Search for Truth* suggests the earlier view on several occasions, as when Eudoxus claims that he will make Poliander wonder at machines, automatons, and visions but then leave him with "no reason to wonder." René Descartes, *The Search for Truth by Means of the Natural Light*, trans. Dugald Murdoch and Robert Stoothoff, in

The Philosophical Writings of Descartes (Cambridge: Cambridge University Press, 1984), 2:400–420, at 405. The Latin reads "machinarum," "automatûm," "visionum," "nihil amplius . . . admiremini" (Descartes, *Inquisitio*, 73); the French reads "machines," "automates," "visions," "n'admirer plus rien de tout" (Descartes, *La recherche*, 505).

10. Descartes, *Search*, 400 ("egregias actiones," Descartes, *Inquisitio*, 67; "bonnes actions," Descartes, *La recherche*, 495).

11. Descartes, *Search*, 401, translates as "right direction," but Descartes opposes better to best and not right to wrong. See Descartes, *Inquisitio*, 68 ("quod in optimam partem non conjecerit oculos") and Descartes, *La recherche*, 497 ("jetter . . . les yeux du bon costé").

12. Descartes, *Inquisitio*, 76; Descartes, *La recherche*, 511.

13. Descartes to Elisabeth, Oct. 6, 1645: "voyant representer quelque action pitoyable & funeste sur vn theatre." René Descartes, *Lettres de Monsieur Descartes, où sont traittées les plus belles questions de la morale, physique, medecine, & des mathematiques* (Paris: Henry Le Gras, 1657), 37. Descartes to Elisabeth, Feb. 22, 1649: "funeste conclusion des Tragédies d'Angleterre" (ibid., 102).

14. Descartes, *Search*, 409. "Sed nunc id tempus est" (Descartes, *Inquisitio*, 77). The French is not extant.

15. Descartes, *Inquisitio*, 90.

16. Descartes, *Search*, 400. Descartes, *Inquisitio*, 68: "cognitiones enim, quæ captum ingenii humani non superant, omnes tam mirando vinculo connexæ sunt." Descartes, *La recherche*, 496: "car les connoissances qui ne surpassent point la portée de l'esprit humain, sont toutes enchaînées avec une liaison . . . merveilleuse."

17. Descartes, *Search*, 401. We might see Murdoch and Stoothoff's translation as providing a theatrical supplement of its own; the French and Latin, less satisfying, read "degré en degré" (Descartes, *La recherche*, 497) and "per gradus" (Descartes, *Inquisitio*, 68).

Index

Page numbers in italics indicate illustrations.

Académie des inscriptions et belles-lettres, 41, 190n1
Académie française, 50–51, 53, 54, 59, 69, 74, 190n1
Académie royale de danse, 41
Académie royale de peinture et de sculpture, 41, 84, 85, 88, 190n1
acting, 13–14, 85, 89, 92–93, 109, 214n76; and celebrity, 87, 111, 113–15, 117, 217n105; by Drury Lane troupe, 114–16; emphatic, 46, 87, 98, 106, 210n36; by Hôtel de Bourgogne troupe, 80–81, 100, 103–5, 120, 213n65; and interiority, 46, 86–87, 92, 99–100, 105, 106–8, 110–13, 115–17; by Molière's troupe, 46, 80–82, 99–111; and moral training, 94–96; naturalistic, 82, 87, 94–95, 97, 98, 214n76; tragic, 80, 82, 105, 108, 116, 118, 213n65, 220n138. See also names of individual actors and troupes
action, 54, 89, 133, 202n111; and acting, 46, 109; and passion, 21, 24, 97, 119, 135, 157; and reason, 165, 168; and representation, 93–94, 96, 97, 98
admiratio, 52, 70
Aeschylus: Eumenides, 188n98
Alanen, Lilli, 5, 31, 94
animal spirits, 9, 27, 95, 180n21; and action, 32, 93; and expression, 88, 89–90; and memory, 45, 47, 90, 122; and passions, 22, 62, 89, 94, 133,

155, 167; and perception, 22, 26, 97, 160; and representation, 14, 24, 45, 93, 97; and wonder, 43, 63. See also habituation
Anne of Austria (queen regent), 53
antitheatrical prejudice, 1, 14, 33–35, 41, 46, 157–58, 171n1, 175n37
architecture. See theater architecture
Aristotle, 69, 75, 175n41, 226n20; on catharsis, 12, 50, 61, 70; and Corneille, 50, 51–52, 54, 56, 59–60, 69, 70, 77, 193n21, 194n33; peripeteia, 85; Poetics, 1, 51, 61, 70, 194n33, 200n90; Rhetoric, 50; on the soul, 22; on wonder, 70, 79
Aubignac (François Hédelin, abbé d'), 131, 138, 147; La pratique du théâtre (The practice of theater), 62, 131, 138, 147, 192n17, 198n66, 200n91

Baillet, Adrien, 18, 172n18, 177n6
Barlow, Graham, 147, 148
Barry, Elizabeth, 113, 114, 115, 220n135
Beaujoyeulx, Balthasar de: Balet comique de la Royne, 36, 37
Beaulieu, Antoine, 17, 30, 38, 40; as choreographer, 16, 19, 28, 36, 39, 41; as dancer, 17, 18, 177n4; Le monde réjoui (The delighted world), 27, 36, 186n79; Le Parnasse triumphant (Parnassus triumphant), 38–39; Les passions victorieuses et vaincues (The

victorious and vanquished passions),
40, 187n88
Béjart, Armande. *See* Molière, Mlle
Béjart, Geneviève. *See* Hervé, Mlle
Béjart, Louis, 102, 109, 213n57
Béjart, Madeleine, 81, 105, 106, 107, 109,
213n57
Bénichou, Paul, 51, 193n20
Bermel, Albert, 101, 102, 110
Betterton, Thomas, 113, 114, 115, 151,
219n121
Birth of Peace, The, 19–20, 42–44,
47, 162, 167, 176n1, 177n2, 177n5;
authorship of, 18, 177n6, 187n88;
and gender, 18, 42, 188n98; and
health, 27–29; and joy, 30–32, 44;
and memory, 18, 47; and mind-body
union, 7–8, 12, 19, 27–31, 47, 82, 89,
167; Panic Terror in, 17, 20–21, 27–28,
39, 177n4, 179n12; staging, 16, 17–18,
19, 27, 31–32, 39–41, 43, 179n12
Blondel, Jean-François, *139*, 140, 230n74
Boileau, Nicolas, 69, 235n141
Bordo, Susan, 39, 41, 234n125
Bossuet, Jacques Bénigne, 157; *Maximes
et réflexions sur la comédie* (Maxims
and reflections on the theater), 33–
34, 184n64
Boursault, Edmé: *Les fables d'Ésope*
(Aesop's fables), 142, *143*; *Le portrait
du peintre* (The painter's portrait),
100, 101, 110, 142
Bracegirdle, Anne, 113, 114, 115, 220n134
Brecht, Bertolt, 97
Brécourt (Guillaume Marcoureau), 109,
113
Brie, Mlle de (Catherine Leclerc du
Rosé or Rozay), 103, 104, 105, 107,
109
Brown, Deborah J., 5, 11, 21
Brunati, Antonio, 17, 36, 39–40; *salle de
ballet* at Stockholm's Kungliga Slott,
17, *40*
Bulwer, John: *Chirologia* and
Chironomia, 99

Carlson, Marvin, 113
Cartesian "I," 107, 140, 155; in *Cinna*,
83; in *Discourse on Method*, 51, 125; in
Meditations on First Philosophy, 10,
11, 55, 125
Cartesianism as discourse, 12, 56, 57,
121, 122, 139, 142; as distortion of
Descartes, 6–7, 41–42, 85–86, 146–
47, 155; in England, 203n124; and
Jansenism, 185n72
"Cartesian Theater," 2–3, 6, 11, 14, 79,
120, 126
Cartwright, William, 112
Cassirer, Ernst, 13, 51, 193n20
catharsis: and Aristotle, 12, 50, 61, 70;
and Corneille, 49, 51–52, 59–61, 63–
64, 193n21; and Dryden, 77, 79; and
Racine, 69, 200n90; of wonder, 13,
50, 52–53, 56, 63, 68, 69, 70–71. *See
also* tragedy
celebrity, 87, 111, 113–15, 117, 217n105
Chanut, Pierre, 173n27
Chappuzeau, Samuel, 129
"character" and interiority, 87, 99,
105, 107–8, 213n69, 215n86; in *The
Versailles Impromptu*, 105, 107–8,
109, 113, 215n86
Charles I of England (king), 156, 169
Charles II of England (king), 7, 72, 83
Charles VI of France (king), 126
Christina of Sweden (queen), 12, 17–18,
19, 40, 41, 176n1, 177n4, 188n98; as
character, 27, 31; as performer, 8, 31
Cibber, Colley, 114, 149, 219n129
Cid, Le (Corneille), 50, 52, 74, 104,
192n15, 204n130, 226n24; quarrel of,
50–51, 74, 130–31, 192n17
Clermont, Martine, 109
Clerselier, Claude, 173n27, 173n28
Comédie-Française (theater, i.e.,
Théâtre des Français), 15, 122;
design of, 16, 138, *139*, 140–42, *143*,
229n64, 230n74; onstage seating at,
141–42, 230n75; *Phèdre* at, 123, 145–
46, 159

Comédie-Française (troupe), 122, 123, 138, 142, 145, 166

Congreve, William, 147

coordinate system, 1, 35, 39, 161

Corneille, Pierre, 12–13, 44, 50–75, 77–83, 103–4, 174n32, 193n20, 202n111; and Aristotle, 50, 51–52, 54, 56, 59–60, 69, 70, 77, 193n21, 194n33; *Cinna*, 49, 51, 66, 67, 68, 78, 83, 204n130; *The Death of Pompey*, 75; "Discours de la tragédie" (Discourse on tragedy), 51–52, 54, 59–60, 193n21, 193n22, 194n33, 199n73 (see also under *Nicomède*); "Discours des trois unités" (Discourse on the three unities), 68, 75, 203n117; *Héraclius*, 68, 82; *Horace*, 104; *The Liar*, 74; *Médée*, 16, 50, 192n14; *Mélite*, 50, 191n13; *Œdipe*, 104; Perrault on, 69; *Polyeucte*, 51; *Rodogune*, 51, 82; *Sertorius*, 104; *The Theatrical Illusion*, 95; *Théodore*, 82. *See also* catharsis: of wonder; *Le Cid*; *Nicomède*

Corye, John: *The Generous Enemies*, 113

Cross, Letitia, 114, 115, 116, 219n129

Dennett, Daniel C., 2

Descartes: *Dioptrics*, 22, 23, 25, 26, 71; on dreams, 26; on *expérience*, 10, 11, 157, 168; on gender, 18–19, 42, 111, 146–47, 155, 187n93, 188n98; *Geometry*, 71; on health, 7, 12, 119; letters to Elisabeth of Bohemia, 34, 58, 95–96, 97, 119, 125, 133, 134, 178n6; *Meteorology*, 71, 82, 202n106, 237n9; *Notae in programma quoddam* (Notes on a program), 178n6; *The Principles of Philosophy*, 10–11, 167–68, 173n25; on representation, 10, 14, 24–27, 30, 86–87, 93, 119, 160; *The Search for Truth by Means of the Natural Light*, 7, 71, 72, 167–69, 172n18, 237n7, 237n9; on theater, 24, 34, 60, 62, 63, 76, 95–97, 171n1;

and Thirty Years' War, 12, 18, 19, 182n40; *Treatise on Man*, 12, 45; on wisdom, 7–8, 31, 51, 55. See also *The Birth of Peace*; *Discourse on Method*; *Meditations on First Philosophy*; *The Passions of the Soul*

Desmarets de Saint-Sorlin, Jean: *Mirame*, 38

Discourse on Method (Descartes), 51, 82, 130, 167, 181n33, 182n40; in England, 204n135; and individual subject, 3, 9, 57, 107, 125, 159, 236n145; and mind-body relationship, 27, 29, 82

D'Orbay, François, 15, 122, 138, 145, 230n75. *See also* Comédie-Française (theater)

Drury Lane. *See* Theatre Royal, Drury Lane

Dryden, John, 7, 53, 72–80, 112, 167, 202n109, 202n111, 217n109; *All for Love*, 79; *Aureng-zebe*, 77; borrowings from Corneille, 73–75, 77–78, 203n115, 203n117; *The Conquest of Granada*, 13, 77–79, 80, 112; "A Defence of an Essay of Dramatique Poesie," 75, 77; "A Discourse Concerning the Original and Progress of Satire," 76; *The Indian Emperour*, 72, 73, 75; *Of Dramatick Poesie, an Essay*, 13, 72–77, 167, 202n108, 203n115, 203n117; "Of Heroique Plays," 78; parodied in *The Rehearsal*, 112, 217n109; *Secret-Love*, 75; *The State of Innocence*, 76; *The Works of Virgil*, 79; *The Year of Wonders*, 76

Düben, Andreas, 17, 19

Duchesnois, Catherine-Joséphine, 123

Du Croisy (Philibert Gassot), 107, 109

Du Parc, Mlle (Marquise-Thérèse de Gorla), 108, 109, 111, 216n90

Du Parc (René Berthelot), 102, 106

Edward of the Palatine (prince), 156, 234n131

Elisabeth of Bohemia (princess),
11–12, 15, 16, 42, 72, 157, 169,
175n43; as actor, 16, 50, 192n14; as
correspondent of Descartes, 56, 57,
62, 161–62, 173n26, 173n27, 182n41,
236n150; on emotion, 64, 76, 92,
156–57; on health, 28, 62, 119, 156–
57, 160–61; on mind-body union,
12, 28–29, 156–57, 160–61; and *The
Passions of the Soul*, 6, 11, 182n41,
236n150; and *Principles of Philosophy*,
10, 167–68, 173n25; on subjectivity,
11, 146, 161–62; on theater, 16, 60,
62, 63, 76
Émelina, Jean, 61, 69, 171n1
emotion, 9; as disorder, 21, 58, 61, 64,
65, 66, 151, 153; and health, 12, 28;
and intersubjectivity, 57–58, 152,
155; and mind-body union, 12, 30–
31; and morality, 13, 55–56, 63, 68,
159; opposed to reason, 5, 133, 135,
155; and representation, 24–27, 76,
84–86, 87, 92, 93, 160, 185n66; and
spectatorship, 32, 33, 42–44, 60, 62–
63, 157–60, 165; subjective experience
of, 52, 61–63, 69, 79, 86–90, 92, 94,
118; universal experience of, 52, 61,
63–64, 79, 99; and visual perception,
14, 32, 43, 69, 144, 160. *See also under*
Elisabeth of Bohemia; habituation;
memory; reason
Euripides: *The Bacchae*, 166; *Hippolytus*,
152; *The Suppliants*, 73

fear, 20, 24, 93; in Descartes, 22, 63,
185n66. *See also* pity and fear
Félibien, André, 14, 92, 107, 169. *See also*
mind-body union: *je ne sais quoi*
Female Wits, The, 13, 113–16, 119,
218n118, 219n123, 219n131
Floridor (Josias de Soûlas), 104
Foote, Samuel, 116–19, 221n144,
221n146; *Diversions of the Morning*,
13, 116–17, 118, 221n139; *A Letter
from Mr. Foote*, 221n147; *The Minor*,

221n147; *Treatise on the Passions*, 14,
116–18; *The Trial of Samuel Foote*,
117, 221n145
Forestier, Georges, 102, 213n65
Foucault, Michel, 26, 86
Foucher de Careil, Alexandre, 11, 161,
173n30, 236n149
Fumaroli, Marc, 157

Garber, Daniel, 4–5, 7
Garrick, David, 98, 119, 230n75
Garth, Samuel: "Prologue Spoken
at the Opening of the Queen's
Theatre in the Hay-Market," 147–
49, 232n91
generosity (*générosité*): in Corneille, 56–
57, 58–59, 66, 70; in Descartes, 55,
58, 61; in Dryden, 72, 79
Goux, Jean-Joseph, 140, 146
Guérin, Pierre-Narcisse: *Phèdre and
Hippolyte*, 122, *123*, 124–25, 126, 144,
158, 165, 223n1
Guhrauer, Gottschalk Eduard, 11
Guillén, Claudio, 140, 141

habituation, 44–45, 60, 88, 90, 95–98;
of emotion, 30, 34, 58, 60–61, 64,
66, 94–98, 133–34
Haines, Joe, 113, 114, 219n123, 219n124
Harries, Karsten, 140
Harvey, William, 136
Heidegger, Martin, 137, 140, 141, 150,
154, 229n57, 230n72
Hervé, Mlle (Geneviève Béjart), 109,
213n57
Herzel, Roger, 137, 142
Hill, Aaron, 118, 220n137; *The Art of
Acting*, 118, 222n150
Hoffman, Paul, 5
Hôtel de Bourgogne (theater):
architecture, 14, 121–22, 126, *127*,
141, 154, 224n13; and Boursault, 100,
211n43; and Corneille, 12, 53, *65*, 68;
onstage seating, 14, *128*, 129, 137, 138;
and Poisson, 225n17; and Racine,

131–32, 135–36, 137, 138, 158–59; set design, 8, 150
Hôtel de Bourgogne (troupe), 53, 80, 81, 108, 126; acting style, 100, 120, 213n65; dissolution, 138; feud with Molière, 82, 103–5, 221n43
Hôtel de Guénégaud, 136, 138
Hume, David: *A Treatise of Human Nature*, 2
Hytner, Nicholas, 15, 163, 166

imagination, 26, 34–35, 60, 62, 75–76, 95–96, 97, 98
"impromptu," 7, 101–2, 104, 212n49. See also *The Versailles Impromptu*
improvisation, 100, 101, 108, 117
interiority, 13–14, 86, 89, 119–20; in acting, 46, 86–87, 92, 99–100, 105, 106–8, 110–13, 115–17; in dramatic characters, 87, 99, 105, 107–8, 213n69, 215n86; "interiority effect" defined, 110–12
intersubjectivity, 11, 56, 57–58, 122, 125, 155, 161, 167–68; in *The Birth of Peace*, 40, 42–43; in Guérin, 124–25; in Racine, 136, 150, 152, 157–58, 166–67; and theater architecture, 136, 154, 159–60; and theatergoing, 34–35, 36–38
Irigaray, Luce, 16, 42, 43, 155, 175n41
Ivory, Abraham, 112

James, Susan, 26
Jansenism, 34, 153, 155, 157–58, 167, 185n70, 185n72, 235n141
Johnson, Benjamin, 114, 219n123, 219n129
Johnson, Samuel, 79
Jones, Inigo, 36
Jonson, Ben, 74, 75
joy: in *The Birth of Peace*, 30–32, 44; in Descartes-Elisabeth correspondence, 60, 92, 96, 119, 162; physiology of, 32; relationship to love, 30, 64; relationship to wonder, 64; and

wisdom, 7. See also under *The Passions of the Soul*
Judovitz, Dalia, 55

Kernodle, George, 131
kissing circles, 161
Knight, Frances Maria, 114, 115, 116, 219n123, 220n135
Koch, Erec R., 10, 32, 66

Labbé, Dominique, 83
Lacour, Léopold, 105
Lacy, John, 112, 114, 217n109
La Grange (Charles Varlet), 205n155, 211n39; *Register* of, 81, 101, 206n157, 222n156; in *The Versailles Impromptu*, 102–3, 106, 109, 110, 113
La Mesnardière, Jules de: *La poëtique*, 59
Lanson, Gustave, 13, 51
La Thorillière, François Le Noir de, 109, 110
Laurent, Michel, 137, 228n52
Lawrenson, T. E., 127, 141, 231n85
Le Brun, Charles, 84–86, 87, *90, 91,* 111, 116, 118, 190n114; *Conference on General and Particular Expression,* 13–14, 46, 88, 103, 106, 109, 206n1, 207n9
Ledoux, Claude Nicolas, 149, *150*
Lee, Nathaniel: *The Rival Queens,* 220n135
Lee, Rensselaer, 86
Lefebvre, Henri, 130, 136, 155
Leibniz, Gottfried, 167
Le Pautre, Jean, 142
Lincoln's Inn Fields: theater, 72, 115; troupe, 113–15, 219n131
Lloyd, Genevieve, 42, 187n93
Longinus, 69
Louis II of Bourbon (prince of Condé), 53
Louis XIII of France (king), 127
Louis XIV of France (king), 53, 56–57, 138, 140, 149, 188n95, 190n1, 191n9; and Molière, 80, 100, 102, 103, 104, 110

Louvre *salle de la comédie*, 12, 80–82
love: in Corneille, 57, 58, 62, 66, 68; in
   Descartes-Elisabeth correspondence,
   90–92; and habituation, 30, 44,
   64, 94; and Le Brun, 89, *90*, *91*; and
   morality, 63; in Racine, 132–33, 135;
   relationship to joy, 30, 64. See also
   under *The Passions of the Soul*
Lucas, Jane, 114

machine plays, 71, 72
Macklin, Charles, 116, 119, 220n137,
   220n138, 221n139
Malebranche, Nicolas: *The Search After
   Truth*, 34–35
Manley, Delarivier, 114–16, 218n119,
   219n123, 219n131; *The Lost Lover; or,
   The Jealous Husband*, 219n123; *The
   Royal Mischief*, 113–14, 115, 218n118
Marcus, Leah, 8
Marmontel, Jean-François, 159
Mazarin, Cardinal Jules, 53
medieval theater, 121, 122, 126, 127, 130,
   159, 224n12; and mansion staging,
   36, 121, 131
Meditations on First Philosophy
   (Descartes), 167; Cartesian "I,"
   10, 11, 55, 107, 125; and mind-body
   relationship, 29, 30; on objectivity,
   139–40, 144, 161; on perception, 26,
   39
memory: corporal component, 12, 15,
   22, 45–47, 89–90, 92, 97–98, 158;
   cultural, 14, 121–22, 126, 136, 159;
   and emotion, 12, 18, 45–46, 63–64,
   90, 92, 158, 160; intellectual, 44; and
   performance, 46–47, 98; and reason,
   18; and wonder, 44–45, 63. *See also*
   habituation
Mersenne, Marin, 45, 46
mind/body dualism, 3, 5, 12, 146;
   Descartes on, 29; in Smith, 153, 155;
   in spectatorship, 141
mind-body union, 4–8, 30–31, 47, 93,
   98, 119, 168, 181n33; and acting, 92

–93, 94–96, 97–98, 99, 107–8, 115,
   116, 119; and Elisabeth of Bohemia,
   12, 28–29, 156–57, 160–61; and
   expression, 84–85, 92; and health,
   12, 27–29, 32; *je ne sais quoi* of, 14,
   92, 98, 107, 111, 117, 119, 169; and
   memory, 12, 22, 46–47, 89–90, 92,
   97–98, 122, 158; and passions, 5, 21,
   135
Minturno, Antonio, 70
Mirren, Helen, 15, 163–64, 165, 166
Molière (Jean-Baptiste Poquelin), 80–
   82, 99–112, 115, 119–20, 221n147,
   222n156; as actor, 102–3, 105, 106,
   108, 109, 110, 213n57; *Les amants
   magnifiques* (The Magnificent
   lovers), 216n96; *Le bourgeois
   gentilhomme* (The middle-class
   gentleman), 216n98; *La Comtesse
   d'Escarbagnas*, 216n98; and
   Corneille, 83; *Le docteur amoureux*
   (The doctor in love), 80; *Les fâcheux*
   (The bores), 129–30, 216n98;
   Foote on, 117, 118, 221n147; *The
   Hypochondriac*, 119, 216n96, 222n156;
   The Miser, 48, 101; *Monsieur de
   Pourceaugnac*, 216n98; parodies
   Nicomède, 103–4, 166; Perrault on,
   48, 49; quarrel of *The School for
   Wives*, 82, 100, 104, 110, 211n43; *The
   Ridiculous Young Ladies*, 48, 101,
   104; *The School for Wives Criticized*,
   106, 107, 211n43, 214n80; as troupe
   leader, 16, 46. See also *The Versailles
   Impromptu*
Molière, Mlle (Armande Béjart), 106,
   109, 110, 136, 138, 211n39, 211n43
Montdory (Guillaume Desgilberts),
   192n13
Montfleury (Zacharie Jacob), 82, 103–
   4, 120
mystery plays. *See* medieval theater

National Theatre, London, 130, 163
neoclassicism, 8–9, 51, 53, 56, 74, 80, 116

Nicole, Pierre, 158
Nicoll, Allardyce, 109
Nicomède (Corneille), 12, 51, 53–63, *65*, 76, 77, 194n30; "Au lecteur," 54, 60; "Discours de la tragédie" (Discourse on tragedy), 57, 60, 196n44, 199n73; "Examen," 68, 70; parodied by Molière, 103–4, 166; performance at Comédie-Française (1989), 166; performance at Hôtel de Bourgogne (1651), 12, 53–54, 68; performance at Louvre (1658), 12, 80–83, 99, 103, 104; and wonder, 44, 63–70, 71, 72
Nussbaum, Felicity, 110–11

objectivity, 39, 42, 140, 146–47, 161–62, 230n72; and painting, 87, 92; and perception, 56, 145; and royal academies, 41, 85; and spectatorship, 35, 126, 138, 140, 142, 145, 160
onstage seating, 130, 136, 149; abolition of, 147, 230n75; at *Cinna*, 68; at Comédie-Française, 141–42, 145; at Hôtel de Bourgogne, 14, *128*, 129, 137, 138; at *Nicomède*, *65*, 68; at Queen's Theatre in the Haymarket, 232n99; at Théâtre du Marais, 50, 131, 226n24; at Théâtre du Palais-Royal, 129–30

painting, 4, 39, 49; theory of, 84–86, 87, 88–89, 92, 106–7. *See also* Guérin, Pierre-Narcisse; Le Brun, Charles
Palais Cardinal. *See* Théâtre du Palais-Royal
Panofsky, Erwin, 35, 39
Parsons, James, 118, 222n151
parterre, 35–36, 141, 147; at Comédie-Française, 145, 230n75; in Guérin, 124; at Hôtel de Bourgogne, 126–27, 129, 136, 138, 159, 224n13, 225n14; at Queen's Theater in the Haymarket, 142
passions: anger, 58, 94; astonishment (*étonnement*), 69; compassion, 34,

60, 79, 97, 119; cowardice, 68; desire, 92; grief, 95; hatred, 34, 56, 60, 66, 68, 92, 159, 199n82; ingratitude, 68; jealousy, 135; pity, 34, 62, 63, 79, 95, 97; sadness, 34, 44, 60, 63, 64, 92, 95, 157, 199n82; shame, 119; terror, 19, 20–21, 30, 39, 43. *See also* fear; generosity; joy; love; physiology: of passions; pity and fear
Passions of the Soul, The (Descartes), 85, 97, 146, 155, 199n82; and acting, 96; and *béatitude*, 60; and Elisabeth of Bohemia, 6, 11, 182n41, 236n150; in England, 76, 204n135; and *générosité*, 55; and habituation, 34, 88, 134; and joy, 7, 12, 30–32, 64, 95, 196n48; and love, 30, 60, 66, 89, 95; and memory, 44–45; and mind-body union, 12, 21–22, 29, 30, 94; and representation, 26, 84, 185n66; and subjectivity, 61, 82–83, 118; and visual perception, 144; and wisdom, 7; and wonder, 43, 71, 237n9
performance studies, 6, 12, 15, 46–47, 89, 98–99, 113, 165–69
Perrault, Charles, 7, 50, 68, 69, 74, 190n1; *Le cabinet des beaux arts* (The cabinet of fine arts), 48–49, *49*, 191n3, 191n4; on Corneille, 13; on Molière, 81, 108; "Le siècle de Louis le Grand" (The century of Louis the Great), 50, 191n9
Phèdre (Racine), 15, 124–25; emotions in, 20–21, 155, 158, 167, 180n15; and interiority, 87; 'live rebroadcast' from National Theatre, London (2010), 163–65, 166–67; ocular vs. sanguinary readings, 14, 122, 132–35, 144–46, 150–52, 160; original title of, 124, 236n143; performance at Comédie-Française (1689), 16, 122, 137, 142, 145, 159; *Phèdre et Hippolyte* (performance at Hôtel de Bourgogne [1677]), 122, 126, 129, 131–32, 135–37, 138, 158–59; preface to, 34, 69, 137. *See also under* Smith, Edmund

Phelan, Peggy, 160
physiology: of circulation, 122, 135–36, 141; of fear, 22; in Foote, 117–18; of joy, 32; of love, 89–90; of passions generally, 14, 21, 22, 61, 62, 86, 95, 99; of perception, 22, 23, 24–26, 45, 122, 160; in Racine, 133, 158; of wonder, 43, 64, 66. *See also* animal spirits
Pinkethman, William, 114, 115, 219n123
pity and fear, 62–63; in Aristotle, 12, 52, 70, 77, 193n21; in Corneille, 12–13, 51–52, 59–60, 61, 63, 69, 70, 193n21; in Racine, 200n90. *See also* catharsis
Pix, Mary, 115, 219n131
Plato, 75; *Republic*, 1–2, 22, 50; on the soul, 22, 24
Poisson, Raymond: *Le zig-zag*, *128*, 129, 130, 225n17
Poullain de la Barre, François, 42, 188n94
Poussin, Nicolas, 84–85
Powell, George, 113, 114, 116, 219n123, 219n129
proscenium arch: as cornea, 15, 26, 140; as demarcation, 35–36, 113, 139, 141, 142, 147, 167; at Queen's Theater in the Haymarket, 148; at Théâtre du Palais-Royal, 38, *38*, 229n64

quarrel of Ancients and Moderns, 50, 69, 191n9
Queen's Theatre in the Haymarket: architecture, 142, 147, *148*, 149, 163, 232n91, 232n96; objectification in, 154, 155, 159, 160; and *Phædra and Hippolitus*, 15, 122, 151, 232n99

Racine, Jean: *Andromache*, 120; and catharsis, 69, 200n90; "Extraits de la *Poétique* d'Aristote" (Extracts from Aristotle's *Poetics*), 200n90; retirement from theater, 158, 235n141. See also *Phèdre*
Ravel, Jeffrey, 141
reason: and emotion, 27, 58, 61, 63, 153,

157; and gender, 18–19, 42, 146–47, 187n93, 188n95, 188n98; and health, 28; and imagination, 76; and memory, 18; and moral habituation, 96–97; in *Nicomède*, 56–57, 58–59, 69–70; opposed to emotion, 5, 133, 135, 155; and the soul, 22–24, 33, 62; and theater design, 146–48; and wonder, 69, 71–72
Regius, Henricus, 12
Rehearsal, The (Villiers), 13, 111–13, 114, 116, 119, 217n108; debt to Molière, 217n107; lampoon of Dryden, 80, 217n109
rehearsal burlesque, 13, 101, 111, 117, 118, 217n107, 221n139
Reiss, Timothy, 19, 47, 178n8
representation, 10, 14, 24–27, 86–87, 93, 97, 119, 160; in acting, 86–87, 92, 95, 106, 107–8, 215n85; in emotional experience, 24, 26–27, 32, 86, 93, 97, 118; Heidegger on, 137–38, 154, 229n57, 230n72; in memory, 44–45, 47, 62, 118; opposed to resemblance, 26, 39, 86, 208n9; in painting, 84, 85–86, 88, 89, 92, 208n9; in spectatorship, 14–15, 26, 60, 76; in visual perception, 22, 26, 45, 86, 160
Rich, Christopher, 113, 219n121
Richelieu, Cardinal (Armand Jean du Plessis), 50–51, 59, 62, 74, 175n37, 192n17
Roach, Joseph, 6, 46, 98–99, 100, 217n105
Robortello, Francesco, 70, 201n98
Rodis-Lewis, Geneviève, 71, 178n6
Rorty, Richard, 92
Royal Society of London, 76, 118

Saint-Évremond, Charles de, 82–83
Saulnier, V. L., 55
Schmitter, Amy Morgan, 5, 42, 183n55, 184n60, 187n93
Scholasticism, 11, 19, 22, 42, 71, 116

Seneca: *On the Happy Life*, 161, 236n150
Sentiments de l'Académie française sur la tragi-comédie du Cid, Les (The sentiments of the French Academy on the tragicomedy of *Le Cid*), 50–51, 74, 192n17
set design, 35; of *The Birth of Peace*, 17; nonperspectival staging, 36, *37*, 121, 131; *palais à volonté*, 8, 137, 140, 142, 150; perspectival staging, 35–36, 38–39, 131, 149, 159, 160
Settle, Elkanah: *The World in the Moon*, 114, 219n124
Shadwell, Thomas, 75
Shakespeare, William, 74, 202n106; *As You Like It*, 71–72; *Hamlet*, 106; *The Tempest*, 72; *Twelfth Night*, 105
Shapiro, Lisa, 5
Shirley, George, 112–13, 114, 116
Smith, Edmund, 15; *Phædra and Hippolitus* (performance at Queen's Theatre in the Haymarket [1707]), 122, 147–56, 159, 232n99; *Phædra and Hippolitus* (play), 147, 149, 150–55
Sondheim, Stephen, 3–4
spectatorship, 26, 32–36, 69, 96–97, 126–27, *128*, 129–31; in Aubignac, 200n91; in *The Birth of Peace*, 32, 36, 42–44; in Corneille, 68–70, 193n21; and intersubjectivity, 34–35, 36–38; in Molière, 214n80; and objectification, 137, 138–41, 145–47, 149, 154, 159, 160, 165; in Racine, 135–37, 145–46, 149–50, 157–60; tragic, 60–62, 63, 96–97. *See also* onstage seating; parterre; theater architecture: loges
Stanislavski, Konstantin, 97
Starobinski, Jean, 149–50
subjectivity, 1, 8, 11, 55, 69, 83, 161–62; of actor, 26–27, 41, 46, 82, 92, 98, 106–7, 115–16; and bodily experience, 89–90, 94; and catharsis, 12, 52, 61–62, 63–64, 79; Elisabeth of Bohemia on, 11, 146, 161–62; and

emotional experience, 94, 135, 152–54; and expression, 86–87, 88–90, 92, 117–19; and memory, 63, 66–68; and perception, 39, 56, 144–46, 160; and theater, 69, 160

theater architecture, 14–15, 17, 121–60; *enceintes de la balustrade*, 141–42, *143*, 230n74; loges, 129, 136, 138–39, 142, 145, 147, 224n13, 225n14; orchestra pit, 141, 229n68; seventeenth-century innovations in, 35–41, 122, 138–41, 147, 159; stage curtain, 35, 36, 38, 147; tennis court theaters, 26, 126–27, 129, 138, 139, 191n23, 224n12. *See also* onstage seating; parterre; proscenium arch; set design; visual perception: theater; *and names of individual architects and theaters*
Théâtre des Français (or François). *See* Comédie-Française (theater)
Théâtre du Marais, 50, 126, 131, 138, 139, 192n13, 216n90
Théâtre du Palais-Royal (i.e., Palais Cardinal), 38, 129–30, 138, 229n64
Theatre Royal, Drury Lane: theater, 72, 111, 113; troupe, 112, 113–16
Thirty Years' War, 12, 17, 18, 19, 28, 47, 157, 182n40
Thornhill, James, 148
Torelli, Giacomo, 44
tragedy: Aristotle on, 61, 70, 193n21, 194n33, 200n90; Aubignac on, 200n91; Boileau on, 69–70; Corneille on, 51–53, 59–60, 61–63, 69, 193n21, 194n33; Descartes and Elisabeth of Bohemia on, 60, 62–63, 95–96; Dryden on, 73–76, 77, 79–80; La Mesnardière on, 59; Racine on, 69, 200n90; Robortello on, 200n98; and wonder, 12–13, 44, 50, 57, 59–70, 72. *See also* acting: tragic; catharsis; spectatorship: tragic

Trotter, Catherine, 115, 219n131
Tuana, Nancy, 5, 187n93
Tuileries *salle des machines*, 25, 140, 141, 149, 181n28, 229n64, 232n96

unities, 35, 51, 54, 85, 226n20; in Corneille, 75, 130–31, 203n117, 204n130; in Dryden, 73, 74
universality: of expression, 88–89; in *palais à volonté* set design, 8, 140, 142

Vanbrugh, John, 7, 15, 114, 122, 147–49, 154, 155; *The Relapse*, 114, 147. *See also* Queen's Theatre in the Haymarket
Verbruggen, Susanna, 114, 115–16, 219n123
Versailles Impromptu, The (Molière), 116, 211n43, 212n48, 212n51; editorial issues, 8, 103; influence on English theater, 13, 117, 217n107; and naturalistic acting, 87, 100–110, 111, 211n42; parody of Bourguignon troupe, 82, 100, 103–5, 120
Versailles *salle de la comédie*, 16, 100, 101, 110, 113
Villiers, George (Second Duke of Buckingham). See *The Rehearsal*

visual perception, 56; and passions, 14, 32, 43, 69, 144, 160; and perspective, 35–36, 38–39, 131, 149, 159, 160; physiology of, 22, 23, 24, 25, 26, 45, 122, 160; and representation, 22, 26, 45, 86, 160; and subjectivity, 39, 56, 144–46, 160; and theater, 24–26, 122, 129–31, 137–46, 147–50, 154, 159–60
Vitruvius, 35, 186n77
volition, 30, 31, 45, 86–87, 89, 93, 97, 133; and acting, 33, 96, 119; and *générosité*, 55

Watson, Richard A., 174n32, 178n6, 187n88
Wiles, David, 85, 126
Wintershall, William, 112
wonder (*admiration*), 43–44, 70, 201n93; in Aristotle, 70, 79; in Corneille, 13, 50, 52–53, 57, 60, 63–72, 77, 193n20; in Descartes, 71–72, 191n10; in Dryden, 72–73, 77–80, 202n109, 237n9; physiology of, 43, 64, 66; in Shakespeare, 71–72, 202n106
Wordsworth, William, 73; *Lyrical Ballads*, 202n109